William Hadfield

Brazil and the River Plate, 1870-76

William Hadfield

Brazil and the River Plate, 1870-76

ISBN/EAN: 9783744793926

Printed in Europe, USA, Canada, Australia, Japan

Cover: Foto ©Andreas Hilbeck / pixelio.de

More available books at **www.hansebooks.com**

BRAZIL

AND

THE RIVER PLATE

1870-76:

BY

WILLIAM HADFIELD.

WITH SUPPLEMENT.

SUTTON, SURREY:
W. R. CHURCH, BOOKSELLER AND STATIONER.
LONDON:
EDWARD STANFORD, 55, CHARING CROSS, S.W.

1877.   [ENT. STA. HALL.

SUTTON, SURREY:
W. R. CHURCH, PRINTER, BOOKSELLER, AND STATIONER, POST OFFICE.

1877.

CONTENTS.

	Page
SOUTHAMPTON TO PERNAMBUCO	1
PERNAMBUCO TO RIO DE JANEIRO	16
RIO DE JANEIRO	25
A VISIT TO THE CANTAGALLO RAILWAY	49
RIO DE JANEIRO TO THE RIVER PLATE	79
ROSARIO TO CORDOVA	103
THE CITY OF CORDOVA	109
CORDOVA TO ROSARIO	129
MONTE VIDEO TO RIO DE JANEIRO	133
VISIT TO THE EMPEROR'S PALACE AT SANTA CRUZ	141
THE PROVINCE OF SAN PAULO AND RAILWAY COMMUNICATION	164
COMPARISON BETWEEN BRAZIL AND THE RIVER PLATE	185
FROM 1870 TO 1876	199
THE ARGENTINE REPUBLIC AT THE PHILADELPHIA EXHIBITION	229
BRAZIL	232
BRAZILIAN DEBT AND FINANCES	233
BRAZIL AND THE VATICAN	236
BANKING INSTITUTIONS IN THE RIVER PLATE	248
THE REPUBLIC OF URUGUAY	253
THE AMAZON VALLEY AND ITS COMMERCIAL FUTURE	257
TELEGRAPHIC COMMUNICATION	273
MINERAL RESOURCES OF BRAZIL AND THE ARGENTINE REPUBLIC	283
DIPLOMATIC AND CONSULAR RELATIONS	287
ARGENTINE REPRESENTATION ABROAD	290
SUPPLEMENT	296

PREFACE.

THE publication of another volume relating to "Brazil and the River Plate" may appear almost superfluous, after the previous one issued in 1868, with only two years' interval occurring between that and the date of the present narrative, which is indeed more or less supplementary. Events, however, in those countries follow each other in such rapid succession as to yield every year a record of public interest. The following pages, therefore, will speak for themselves, and supply deficiencies which existed in the former recital, besides alluding to occurrences of more recent date which materially affect the welfare of the Platine States, and are explanatory of the late depreciation in the value of their securities. As regards Brazil, it cannot be said that she has sustained any injury from the commercial and financial crisis which has passed over so many foreign countries—her onward course having been characterized by more steadiness and caution. A "twice-told tale" is not always agreeable; but inasmuch as the scenes in a play are constantly shifting, so it may apply to the countries herein described. The sketch given of events since the writer last visited those countries, in 1870, will serve to illustrate his meaning, and he trusts be an apology for again intruding himself on public notice.

The portrait of President Avellaneda, affixed to this volume, is a tribute of respect due to a ruler whose decision of character, united to a conciliatory spirit, has done so much to extricate his country from the difficulties into which it had fallen, but from which it is now rapidly recovering. That of the Viscount do Rio Branco represents a statesman who has rendered important services to his country, both as a diplomatist and a legislator, to whom Brazil is greatly indebted for having succeeded, in accordance with the feelings of the Emperor and the wishes of the people, in carrying through the General Assembly the law for the freedom of birth, which in another generation will completely terminate slavery in the Empire.

BRAZIL AND THE RIVER PLATE

IN 1870.

SOUTHAMPTON, June 9th, 1870.—"Once more upon the waters, yet once more," but this time on board the Royal Mail paddle steamer La Plata, one of the most old-fashioned ships of the Company's fleet, but thoroughly good and comfortable for passengers. She was originally intended for the Cunard service, but bought by the Royal Mail Company, when they lost the Amazon, destroyed by fire at sea, a very terrible event, now almost forgotten. The La Plata was built by Mr. Wood, of Port Glasgow, and has engines of immense power, with of course a large consumption of fuel. The ship herself must be a mass of timber to bear the strain of such an enormous weight of machinery, and I believe on recent official inspection she was found to be perfectly sound—sound "as the day she was built," to use the technical term for such things. There can be no doubt, however, that the modern iron-built steamers possess many and great advantages over these

B

comparatively antique specimens of naval architecture, both as respects economy of space and fuel consumption, while excelling in relative speed; so that the old La Plata class will ere long be a *rara avis* in steam navigation.

Southampton looks very lively on the departure of two or three steamers the same day, ourselves and the Cape Mail being of the number. The new joint stock hotel, which had been closed for some time, is re-opened. The town is more or less a place of transit only, so far as strangers are concerned, passengers by the steamers not lingering much longer than they can help. It was a beautiful warm morning, and a more than usual number of " leave-takers" accompanied the tender on board the La Plata, creating an amount of bustle, and to some extent of confusion, incident to these occasions. The tide was low, and Southampton Water did not show to great advantage. At 2.30 the mail came off, and certainly nothing can better show the enormous increase of trade with South America than the formidable number of letter bags and newspaper bags, &c., which came on board, notwithstanding that in this case the Falmouth steamer of the 3rd instant took replies to communications received by the last mail. There are now some half-a-dozen mail contract steamers a month to Brazil and the River Plate, all taking their quota of correspondence, and yet some of us are old enough to remember when the Falmouth sailing packets once a month only took half-a-dozen bags of letters—a fair complement in those days. It may be observed the postage was then 2s. 7d. under the half-ounce, and even now it is 1s. under the half-ounce. I will not enter into a disquisition on foreign postage rates, beyond remarking that as a rule a reduction has always been found to recover the perhaps temporary difference in gross receipts, as it induces more frequent writing and less economy in the use of paper.

We are steering down Channel with moderate weather, but the temperature very cold. Yesterday, when embarking, it was quite hot and even sultry, indicating thunder, but towards evening the wind backed to the north, and after dinner it was a question of bringing out robes, coats, and cloaks of all shapes and sizes. Our passengers are not numerous, and less mixture than usual, but amongst them is the second brigade of Mr. Henley's colonists, including some of England's best blood and breeding, going out to seek their fortunes in the pampas of South America. The first lot went out with Mr. Henley himself, by the Royal Mail steamer of the 9th May, consisting of some 50 colonists and 20 camp followers or servants; the number by this one consists of 16 first-class and a few second, a third lot following next month, so that altogether Mr. Henley will muster a force of 100 young, active spirits, to commence farming operations with in the neighbourhood of Bellville, near to the Central Argentine Railway, where already there are numerous English settlers, constantly multiplying. On the results of this experiment of Mr. Henley much depends; for if it is successful this class of settlers in the Argentine territory may be indefinitely extended, to the great advantage of the government, and to the more rapid development of the country, for they become so many landed proprietors, requiring the employment of manual labour to assist in working their farms; and the only fear is that a portion of these English youths, so soon as the novelty is worn off, may become disgusted with the monotony of a camp life; but for those who make up their minds to endure hardships for a season, to keep steady, and above all things sober, I quite believe there is a very hopeful future. Numerous disappointments have been experienced by Englishmen who have invested their little capital in sheep farming, and the alleged lawless state of the country is another potent argument against Englishmen settling in the Argentine Republic; but the one is accidental, and owing chiefly to the great fall in the value of wool; the other cannot be said to be chronic. I have great faith in the Argentine Government removing the causes of mischief, so far as practicable in a new country, with a mixed, heterogeneous population, and I dwell a little on this topic because it is of importance both to ourselves and to countries where energetic young Englishmen are ready to settle if sufficient encouragement is given and local protection afforded them. The rising generation of the middle classes in England require an outlet almost as much as the labouring classes, and there is ample scope for them in the River Plate.

Amongst other *agremens* on board the La Plata there is a thoroughly good band of music, which plays morning and evening, and there is a stalwart bugleman who announces feeding time, one of the never-ending occupations on board all passenger vessels; but here everything is certainly done in very good style, and we must be fastidious indeed to find fault with the bill of fare provided. The Royal Mail Company are no doubt catering more for traffic than in the good old times of monopoly—when no other "canoes were in the field;" but it is quite a different case now, and they are prepared to go with the stream; the reduced rates of passage money have also been a considerable inducement to travel, and a trip to South America is now looked upon as one of the new "sensations" of which people are fond. Both goods and passenger traffic have multiplied enormously, and if the Argentine Government should decide to give "assisted passages," not only would they get a fair share of our industrial population, but also the steam lines derive a share in the advantage by being enabled to carry the emigrants out at a moderate rate.

Noon, Friday, 10th June.—Just rounding Ushant, at a distance of about three miles. I have never seen it by daylight before—a precious wild looking spot it is, the sea breaking over the numerous rocks about the lighthouse. We are now fairly in the "Bay of Biscay," a steady westerly breeze and fine weather; some fore and aft canvas set.

Sunday, 12th June.—Beautiful weather after a fine run down the Bay, and hope to be in the Tagus to-morrow morning early. It is over 16 years since I visited Lisbon before, nor from all accounts has it progressed much, but I well remember the beautiful scenery after passing the Burling Rock, the Mafra convent, Cintra, the lines of Torres Vedras, and other interesting associations, which of course remain engraven on the mind. Unfortunately, Portugal does not march with the times, and the complaints then made as to the impediments thrown in the way of commerce and communications with the outside world remain, I believe, more or less stationary. Doctors of law and medicine, quarantine and sanitary dogmas hold undisturbed sway, unless the Government of the Duke de Saldanha sweeps some of them away, for which his lease of life is hardly long enough. Portugal, in fact, responds in a large degree to the familiar title of *pés de chumbo* (or leaden feet), by which the people have long been known.

Tuesday, 14th June.—After the excessive heat of Lisbon yesterday, the change to fresh breezes and cooler weather is very agreeable, and we are favoured with a fine north-easter, bowling along at the rate of ten knots an hour, with square canvas set, which is the more fortunate as the steamer is heavily laden, having received a considerable addition to her cargo at Lisbon, besides coal. A good many passengers landed at Lisbon, but were replaced by others there, so that our number remains pretty much the same, say about 100 first and second class—a small number for a ship of such capacity. As usual, there was any amount of bustle and clamour of voices around and on board, which, combined with coal dust, renders a steamer anything but an aquatic paradise during these necessary operations at calling ports; so the comparative peace and quiet following is fully appreciated.

There is apparently little change in the appearance of Lisbon as seen from the Tagus since my last visit, beyond its evidently great increase in size, the extension of wharves, ferry-boats flying across, and other indications of improved communications; but it being one of their innumerable saint days (or holidays as they may more properly be called) everything had a dead-alive look on the river. The city itself seems to be all the better for sanitary regulations and an absence of those offensive odours one used to experience. It was too hot to expect much locomotion, but the churches were well attended and the markets busy with customers, it being the fruit season, with any quantity of melons, figs, strawberries, and cherries, but we saw no grapes—rather too early for them. We found the Douro steamer had arrived on Saturday, the 11th, with a large number of passengers, 120 of whom had been deposited in the Lazarette buildings for a week or ten days on the flimsy pretence of yellow fever lingering at Rio (though there was not a case of sickness on board) to the great discomfort of passengers and evident loss of traffic to the place, as many prefer going on to Bordeaux or England rather than undergo incarceration of this kind; but, like the laws of the Medes and Persians, the sanitary dogmas of Portugal undergo no change. To show the absurdity of the thing, it may only be noticed that, during the prevalence of cholera in England, passengers by steamers were subjected to quarantine, whilst those coming by land were allowed to enter, it being rather too serious a business even for the Portuguese faculty to draw a "cordon sanitaire" round the frontier. Lisbon has now the benefit of a submarine cable to Falmouth, which places the city in prompt communication, not only with England, but with the far East, and before long it will no doubt be extended to Brazil and the River Plate. Even the present facility will be fully appreciated, and, I have no doubt, be largely availed of for commercial purposes. We hoped to have had a peep at the Channel iron-clad fleet, either on the Tagus or cruising near, but were disappointed, there being only a Yankee frigate and two or three Portuguese men-of-war lying at anchor.

Reverting to occurrences on board, I may mention the muster of the crew on Sunday, before prayers were read in the cabin by the commander. It was very gratifying, showing the discipline and order which prevails in the company's service, as they are able to keep good men in constant employment, and not obliged to ship a new crew every voyage. Indeed one of the great comforts, and, I may add, the safe navigation of ships belonging to large and well-organised companies, is not only the regularity with which the service is performed, but also the comparative security which an efficient staff of officers carries with it, in proof of which I need only allude to the long and successful career of this very line to Brazil and the River Plate. Other ships and commanders may be quite as good, but the *prestige* rightly due to a perfect organization is an advantage that travellers soon find out, provided things are more or less on a par in other respects. A wholesome competition is good for the general public, and the greatly increased and still increasing traffic in such countries as Brazil and the River Plate has had to be provided for through other channels, to meet which competition the Royal Mail Company (by which title it is best known) has had to come down from the high scale of charges formerly existing, and accommodate itself more to the circumstances of the times. I have said that so far as is possible on the "ever restless ocean," the comfort of passengers is amply provided for, and the attendance good, by trained servants. We hear of grumbling occasionally as to the treatment of passengers, but our experience in this way is, that, as a rule, it is satisfactory in most services which make passenger traffic a study, and that generally there is a superfluity. Occasionally, when a steamer is very full of passengers, it may be difficult to please every one, and due allowance should then be made for the pressure on the *cuisine*, as well as on the stewards, who have often a very hard task to perform. As an instance of the treatment on board the La Plata, I copy the following bill of fare, premising that the hours for meals are:—Breakfast at 9; lunch at 12 (rather close together); dinner at 4.30; tea at 7. Sandwiches *ad libitum* after 9 p.m.

Breakfast.—Haddocks, fresh fish, eggs, bacon, omelettes, mutton chops and cutlets, beef steak and onions, salt fish, cold ham, currie and rice, tea, coffee, &c.

Dinner.—Soup, broth, fish, salmon and anchovy sauce. Entrées—joints, mutton and caper sauce, roast pork; salad, cabbage and boiled potatoes, &c. Pastry, plum pudding, custards and savory cakes. Dessert—Oranges, Brazil nuts, figs, wine biscuits, almonds and raisins, olives.

I may add that the bill of fare is varied as much as possible, and the cooking leaves little to be desired, and he must be either an excessive gourmand, or wanting in that best of stimulants, a good appetite, who cannot be satisfied with such a table.

Off Teneriffe.—Passing between the islands, with a splendid view of the grand old peak, some 12,000 feet above the level of the sea, on which the full blaze of a mid-day sun is shining; for the weather, which has been generally cloudy and very cool since we left Lisbon, brightened up as we approached the land, and it is beginning to feel much more genial. A sight of land is always a source of excitement on board a passenger ship, making a break in the monotony of daily life. We have also just passed an Italian barque, Violentina, bound from Genoa to Monte Video, crowded with emigrants. We are looking out for the Pacific steamer Araucania, which ought to be at Lisbon not later than the 20th, but she has a strong northerly wind to contend against.

St. Vincent, Monday, 20th June.—Came in here early this morning—"coaled" and left again at 1.30, with a fresh trade wind and fine weather. Found my friend Mr. Miller, who is again out here for a few months for the purpose of extending his coaling facilities, the strain on which has much increased with the numerous lines of steamers running from Italy and Marseilles—some half-a-dozen companies, besides the English and French lines—altogether, we summed up some 16 to 18 steamers a-month from Europe to Brazil and the River Plate. They do not all coal at St. Vincent, but the exceptional ones are often compelled to call on their way home, and this month the following steamers have followed each other in succession:—Douro, for Southampton, on the 4th; City of Buenos Ayres, for Falmouth, on the 6th; Poitou, for Marseilles, on the 8th; Araucania, for Liverpool, on the 11th (with 460 passengers on board); Newton, for Liverpool (with damage to her machinery). We have, therefore, no chance of sending letters but by a postal steamer, daily expected at St. Vincent, bound for Madeira and Lisbon. However, we shall catch the Royal Mail steamer, homeward bound, at Pernambuco. Mr. Miller is building a wharf for the shipment of ballast, as every vessel bringing coal is obliged to be supplied with ballast, there being no cargo whatever for them at St. Vincent. The ballast will come down to the wharf from the mountain range just above it, composed of loose rock and debris—a very suitable material, much better than the common sand ballast the ships have hitherto had to take; and at a less cost.

21st.—Steam and canvas fully at work, fine weather, and passing ships bound southward. Pernambuco passengers looking forward to their arrival at the port on Monday morning next, the 27th; not a very agreeable prospect for them if the steamer has to anchor in the open roadstead, where there is always more or less swell. There is also about 120 tons of cargo to be landed there, which will occupy an entire day. Pernambuco affairs are discussed on board, and amongst other things the railway, which appears to be in very bad odour, and looked upon as a useless waste of national resources. It is contended that, for the same expenditure or less, some 400 miles of excellent roads could have been made, that would have developed the varied resources of the Province, whereas the railway leads nowhere, and can never be made a paying concern. People who know the Province well are unanimous in this conclusion, as well as in their opinion that the whole affair is a monument of jobbery, ignorance, and folly, the Government being greatly to blame for ever sanctioning such a project, and still more in allowing the original estimates to be exceeded. Certainly the condition of English railway enterprise in Brazil is not encouraging, or flattering to those who conceived and projected it; and I have always contended that the most sensible course for all concerned was to get the Government to take the existing railways and work them, giving the shareholders railway bonds at a moderate rate of interest. The tramway is a success, because it traverses the very suburb where the railway ought to have been made, which contains most of the out-residents of the city, and is a great local convenience. Projects for extending Pernambuco harbour, and making docks are spoken of, but it is all moonshine. All that the harbour really requires is dredging and deepening, with a sufficiency of moorage laid down with screw spile, instead of vessels having to anchor with the risk of constantly getting foul of each other's anchors and chains, often causing considerable confusion. I allude to these matters, because it embodies the views of local people, strongly interested in the real progress of Pernambuco, but not advocates for extravagant theories or wild chimeras, such as those indulged in by concession hunters; and I must say my own reminiscences and knowledge of the place lead me fully to concur in these opinions. Many far-seeing, able Brazilians contend that railways are altogether out of place in a country like Brazil, and that making efficient common roads would have been a far more judicious application of national resources, as well as in the end more remunerative. Railways, they contend, are luxuries, to be indulged in only by countries already wealthy and populous, or in such cases as that of the Argentine Confederation, where nature herself points to railways as the most economical and effectual means of overcoming the difficulties of distance, and linking the outlying provinces with the centres of population.

Saturday, 25th.—We are across the line, with the fine clear weather usually prevailing in the southern hemisphere. The wind is as yet well to the southward, and of course against us, but it affords a good draft for the engines, which do their work all the better. The amusements of the week have been diversified by dancing, but we have only a small sprinkling of lady passengers. Last night, on the occasion of crossing the line, an amateur play was got up by some of the juveniles, assisted by two or three veterans on board, and the following is a copy of the programme issued :—

NOTICE.

THEATRE ROYAL, " LA PLATA."

On Friday, June 24th, the amateurs of the Theatre Royal, by kind permission of Captain Hole, intend to commence the season with Lacey's screaming interlude, entitled :—

Courting a Cook.—In 3 Acts.

Silas Hopefield ...	"Swell out of Luck" ...	Mr. *Dickenson.*
Farmer Grief ...	"A jolly old Farmer" ...	Mr. *H. Cuthbert.*
Imp ...	"A Broken-down Tailor"	Mr. *Unknown.*
Patience ...	"Bailing" ...	Mr. *E. B. Whisk.*
Susan Grief ...	"A Cook in the City" ..	Mr. *Carden.*
After which— ...	"A Sword Dance" ...	Mr. *Saidens.*

The whole to conclude with a series of songs, recitations, and comic sentiments. To commence at 7.30 ; doors open at seven o'clock.

N.B.—Children in arms not admitted.—" Vivat Regina."

One side of the spacious main deck was portioned off with canvas, ornamented with flags and lighted with lamps, lanterns, &c., the audience being seated aft in front of the stage. The performance was given throughout in a very creditable manner, considering the short time there had been for rehearsal, and afforded much amusement to all who witnessed it. These little events break the monotony of a voyage, but are only attainable on board a large ship, with a band of music, and all the accessories for carrying them out properly. The sea was smooth, the night cool, the heavens alive with a galaxy of brilliant stars, the milky way intersecting them, and the southern cross shining brightly a-head; altogether a most enjoyable evening, and one to be remembered by those especially who for the first time gaze on the beauties of the southern hemisphere. The weather is beautifully clear and fresh again to-day. Monday morning will bring us to anchor off Pernambuco, from whence I shall send off my budget.

PERNAMBUCO TO RIO DE JANEIRO.

After a tug against a strong southerly wind we came to anchor in Pernambuco Road about 9 a.m. on Monday, the 27th June. A rough, rolling sea on, which rendered the prospect of landing anything but comfortable. The sea was beating over the reef as usual, and the old familiar buildings in sight reminded one of days when it was regarded by the writer as a privilege to visit vessels outside or to accompany them a certain distance in order to give friends a "bota fora," as it is called. After a lapse of forty years, boating in such a place as Pernambuco Roadstead does not offer much attraction, and there is the coming on board again, it may be with a good ducking, and generally under difficulties; so, after looking at the prospect before me, and reviewing the subject on its merits, rather than as a matter of feeling, I came to the conclusion it was wiser to remain quietly on board, sending my despatches on shore for the next homeward mail. The temptation to go on shore in other respects was great, and there was ample time, with so much cargo to discharge. Only the passengers bound to Pernambuco landed here, although a good deal was talked about it, and haggling with boatmen carried on for some time.

After being at sea a certain period, the ports of call are a great relief, affording fresh topics for conversation, and renewing as it were relations with the world, although it may be a new one, such as Brazil is to many of our younger passengers. A week from Lisbon to St. Vincent, and another week from St. Vincent to Pernambuco, are short periods compared with the dreary existence on board of former sailing ships on this route. Still the human mind assimilates itself more or less to the progress of things, and at the end of the fortnight the desire becomes intense to renew our intercourse with the outer world. We have probably exhausted the tasks we set ourselves in the interval, and thus the expectation of reaching Pernambuco became an object of much interest to all on board, not excluding those belonging to the ship.

A sight of this place always brings back old reminiscences and calls for a few comments. At that time (I speak of my first residence here, when Brazil was comparatively in its infancy, and only shaking off the trammels of colonial rule), Pernambuco was looked upon as one of the most spirited go-a-head provinces of the Empire. For some years after the establishment of independence, it gave the Central Government much trouble by its political bias towards a republican form of Government. That feeling, however, gradually subsided, and Pernambuco has since remained loyal and contented, but has hardly maintained the reputation for enterprise it formerly held. The fact cannot be gainsaid that of late years the Southern provinces of the Empire have taken the lead, and their proximity to the capital gives them local advantages; but the slow progress of Pernambuco must chiefly be attributed to the fact that some of the Northern provinces, which previously sent their produce to Pernambuco, and drew their supplies of manufactured goods from that city, now do their business direct with Europe, and have lines of steamers running to and from Liverpool.* Another difficulty both Pernambuco and Bahia are now subjected to, is the want of labour, a large portion of their slaves having been sent to the

---

* The low price to which cotton and sugar have fallen are also greatly against the Northern provinces.

South and not been replaced by free labour to any extent. No doubt the Province of Pernambuco is a productive one, and the Pernambucanos possess considerable spirit and enterprise, but without an increase of population they cannot materially extend their productions; and where is this to come from? The attempt to introduce a railway system has not been so successful as was anticipated, and it will require many years to improve or extend communications with the interior of the province in such a way as to tell effectively on the prosperity of Pernambuco as a commercial city. All trade in these countries is, of course, a matter of reciprocity, as without exports the consumption of imported goods must be limited, or more or less in proportion to the former; hence the urgent necessity that exists for the whole Empire to look seriously and steadily at its labour question and to the means of augmenting free population. A cheap, practical railway, running into the heart of the producing districts of Pernambuco, would have done something towards economizing an import of labour, but a couple of millions sterling have been thrown away without attaining this end, and the country cannot bear further inflictions of this kind. The success of the little tramway may lead to native enterprise of the right sort, and in the right direction, and the sooner the provincial government gives its attention to these industrial objects the better.

As regards Bahia pretty much the same observations will apply as in Pernambuco. It has a splendid bay, with great facilities for an extensive shipping, but trade is limited. It has a railway, which has cost £1,800,000 for a line of 75 miles, and, like the Pernambuco one, it goes nowhere, the traffic barely paying working expenses. An attempt to make a tramway in another and more populated part of the province has broken down, owing chiefly to want of sufficient capital to start with; so the province is left in a great measure to its own natural resources, which are doubtless great, but require the presence of labour in order to develope them. After all, we come back to this question of questions to Brazil, which both local and central Governments will have to turn their early attention to, if the country is to progress as its best friends could wish. That there is a practical solution of it no one can doubt, but it requires to be studied and grappled with firmly by those who have the administration of the affairs of the Empire. An example is presented to them by English colonial legislation, and the large importation of coolies that has taken place of late years into the British West India Islands, the Mauritius, &c.*

Knocking about in Pernambuco Road for a whole day is not the most agreeable mode of spending time, although a certain degree of excitement is kept up by boats coming off from the

* See Supplement.

shore, some with fruits and other articles of local production. Discharging the cargo into large lighters, towed out by screw steamers, is a very laborious, difficult task, particularly with so much sea on, and it is impossible to prevent some of the packages getting wet. I almost wonder the company undertakes to land goods here, as the expense of doing so must be very great, to say nothing of delay and wear and tear of the ship's tackle, hawsers, &c. A new four-inch hawser snapped like a piece of thread, and the lighter had nearly got adrift. They succeeded in loading two lighters before dark, but the remainder of the cargo intended for Pernambuco had to go on in the steamer as she could not spare another day to discharge. It was 8 a.m. before we got under weigh; still squally, with rain, and every appearance of bad weather; during the night we signalled the Oneida, homeward bound. This morning, Tuesday, the 28th, we dropped off Maceio, a jangada that had been hoisted on to the sponson of the steamer as a dispatch boat with special orders. A jangada is simply a raft composed of from three to five logs of a light, porous tree, with a sail stuck in the middle and a paddle to steer by. They are used by fishermen on the Northern coast, who lead a very adventurous life, and may be said to be a substitute for telegraph wires, which are still wanting on the Brazil coast. It is a debatable point whether electric cables will pay here; certainly not without a subsidy from Government, to whom of course they would be very useful in keeping up communications with the provinces. Whether this can be accomplished most cheaply and efficiently by land or sea has yet to be determined, but of course Brazil cannot long remain behind the world in this respect. We expect to get into Bahia early to-morrow (Wednesday), when we shall have a few hours' respite from the rocking and tumbling of the last few days.*

Wednesday, June 29th.—We got into Bahia about 10 a.m., and had the whole day for a ramble on shore—visiting some old friends. It was one of their holidays—St. Peter's day—characterised by masquerading about the streets, which towards afternoon were alive with people (as also the windows and balconies of the houses), all in holiday attire, evidently enjoying the fun. There is a curious mixture of colour, from the " irrepressible negro" to the pure white, the number of juveniles and little children (some running about *au naturel*) being something wonderful on these festive occasions. It was a bright sunny day, with a cool wind, and Bahia looked its best after the rains which have lately prevailed. The city has enlarged its borders considerably, and two tramways have just been opened, one running on the high ground from the square in front of the theatre, and across the Campo, a distance of about three miles, to

* See Supplement.

the end of the Victoria. It is a rough and ready sort of affair, the cars drawn by mules, and in places passing some very sharp curves, but on the whole it is a great convenience, and seems to have plenty of traffic. The second line runs in an easterly direction towards Bom Fim, a point on the bay where people go for a change in the hot season, but I had not time to see this tramway. Both have been constructed by our Yankee cousins, who are foremost in works of this kind in Brazil. The population of Bahia is said now to number about 200,000 souls. It was dark before we got away, when the gas lights of the city had a very imposing appearance, extending for several miles along the heights up the bay; but the gas company has been very badly managed, and does not yield anything like the return it ought to have done under other circumstances. The old cadeiras (or Sedan chairs) have not disappeared, and are, to me, a most enjoyable luxury, being taken up on the shoulders of two stout blacks from the lower town up the steep hill to the Victoria. As you ascend the breeze comes fresh upon you, until on the hill you get into quite another atmosphere; there still exists that fine, stalwart race of negroes, both male and female, for which Bahia has long been remarkable. The oranges were, as usual, delicious, with plenty of other fruits, which grow here in abundance. The Yankee steamer bound to New York, *via* Para, was at anchor in the bay when we arrived, but sailed during the day; she is no beauty—a short wooden-built paddle-wheel steamer, which had already done service in the Panama and Pacific line, with what is called steeple engines, working high above the deck. She was deep in the water, with apparently much lumber on deck, and by no means a tempting looking conveyance to make a passage in. It appears a Yankee firm has got the contract for conveying Government mails up the coast, from Rio to Para, and Messrs. Lamport and Holt for the Southern route, say from Rio to the River Plate, calling at intermediate parts, and also up to Matto Grosso.*

Advices received from Rio and the River Plate are, on the whole, favourable. The reign of Lopez Jordan in Entre Rios promises to be a very short one; and although the weakness and vacillation of the Government at Monte Video enables the Blanco party to maintain a hostile position, it is not supposed they can succeed in regaining power in Monte Video, but the state of anarchy existing in the Banda Oriental is greatly to be deplored. Legislation in the Argentine Confederation appears to be in the right direction, money being voted for the extension of railways, telegraph wires, and other useful undertakings, and the veteran Mr. Wheelwright is again in the field with a tender to construct a railway from Cordova to Tucuman, a distance of 360 miles, in conjunction with his partners, Messrs. Brassey and Wythes. I should

* See Supplement.

think there was little doubt as to his getting the contract, the cost to be paid for in bonds, and the line to be the property of the Government.

We passed the Abrollos last night, which have now a good revolving light on them, to be seen at a considerable distance, and as we expect to be in Rio de Janeiro harbour in good time to-morrow, this letter will close the first series, comprising the voyage out, to be resumed at Rio.

RIO DE JANEIRO.

There is quite a revolution in things since I was here two years back, both politically, socially, and financially. The successful termination of the Paraguayan war has immensely strengthened the party now in power, and the best results are following the removal of the incubus that hung over the financial position of the Empire. Whatever may be advanced to the contrary, there can be no doubt that the resources of Brazil have proved equal to the demands made upon them, and have exhibited an elasticity for which the best friends of the Empire hardly gave it credit. Mr. Consul Hunt, in his recent report to the Foreign Office, is decidedly at fault when he says there is a want of accumulated capital in this country; otherwise how could it have been possible for the Government to find the large sums called for by a long protracted and expensive war without the aid of foreign loans. This fact, together with a steady maintenance in value of the national securities, is sufficient to controvert Mr. Hunt's statement, besides the irresistible evidence of authoritative statistics. If Mr. Hunt had delayed his report until the war was really at an end he would have seen reason to alter materially his opinion as to the true financial position of Brazil, but he has evidently taken a prejudiced, one-sided view of the case. As to the productions of the country having reached their maximum, such a conclusion is at utter variance with results, except in those provinces where a scarcity of labour exists; but even in those cases the opening of roads to facilitate the transit of produce to the sea board would undoubtedly largely augment the exports.

The next noticeable feature—that of a local revolution—is the establishment of tramways, which have reduced locomotion to a mere question of a few pence, instead of shillings and pounds as formerly, and people move about in shoals, to the great profit of the tramways themselves, as well as the saving of time and money to the entire community. The traffic must be seen to form a correct idea of its extent, and it comes nearer to our own Metropolitan Railway than anything I have seen, with the advantage of being on the surface instead of underground. The fare for the full distance of three or four miles is a uniform rate of 200 reis, or about 4½d. sterling.

The city of Rio de Janeiro is pre-eminently suitable for tramways, as it admits of starting from a common centre, to run in opposite directions, dividing the city into two longitudinal sections, each being supplied by separate companies, and does not interfere with the narrow streets running down from the tramway terminus to the Customhouse. In another year the whole of the suburbs will be supplied with tramways, and only an occasional omnibus be seen to some distant quarter, where there is but a very small traffic. The first company is realising fabulous profits, known only to the few partners concerned in it, and the shares of the second company (both being promoted by Yankees) are, I believe, at 60 to 70 premium. Talk of railway dividends after such a result!

There are many other notable improvements at Rio in the last two years, such as the Customhouse quays and landing places. Building is extending itself in all directions. What remains in *statu quo* is the miserable Exchange and the absence of clubs or conveniences which are usual in large mercantile cities; half-a-century has made little or no difference in this respect, and the mercantile community appear utterly apathetic, content to pass the greater part of their lives in a dark, dingy place, more fit for a prison or wine store than for merchants to congregate together. I believe the proprietors of the Exchange have now got possession of the land on which it stands; so they have the opportunity of improving their position if they think proper to do so.

There is a great controversy now going on as to the rate of Exchange, which certain parties contend has been driven up by speculation, and that commercial transactions are now at the mercy of the banks, which rule the markets. When last here the Exchange was down as low as 14d. per milreis. Since the conclusion of the war it has been at 24d., and is now fluctuating between 21d. and 22d. The rise must have been greatly in favour of legitimate commerce, and the nearer it reaches a steady par value the better in this respect, although it may not suit the views of speculators in produce. That the banks should take advantage of the position to recoup some of their past losses is natural enough, and much better that they should exercise a proper and legitimate control over speculative transactions in produce. It is asserted that much larger sums have lately been drawn for on Europe than are represented by the value of produce shipped, which only proves that a speculative movement exists in the Exchanges themselves in the way of drawing and remitting;- all fair enough, so long as a proper check is kept on the class of paper negotiated. There were grumblers enough when the Exchange was down to 14d., and ruin was said to be staring every one in the face, but now there are grumblers because the Exchange has gone up too fast. It is in fact a kind of fight between the "bulls" and the "bears" of Exchange.

The season has been unusually dry in this part of Brazil, and unusually cold in the Province of San Paulo, where a large portion of the coffee crop is said to be injured by the frost; but less so the cotton trees. Such severe cold has not been experienced for the last 28 years. Now rain is falling here, and it will do much good.

There is not much political excitement in Rio just now, beyond the discussions of the Chambers, which possess no great interest. Signora Carlotta Patti has come here from the United States to divert the current of opinions, and amuse the Rio fashionable world. She made her *debut* last night, which was unfortunately one of pouring rain, but the attendance was good and her reception enthusiastic.

6th July, *via* Bordeaux.—The accounts from the River are conflicting; Lopez Jordan appears to have destroyed some unfortunate little place, with its inhabitants; but the fact of his being gradually surrounded by the national troops is undoubted, and he deserves to suffer the fate of his namesake. A little shooting and hanging of these disturbers of the public peace would produce a salutary effect, but in too many cases criminals are allowed to get off scot free, after having inflicted all the evils they can upon others.

My last letter noticed improvements in the city

during the last two years, and particularly the social revolution caused by the establishment of tramways, which will shortly traverse the entire suburbs. It does not, however, appear to have diminished the number of private carriages, but rather to have multiplied them, as also the general movement, which is now very remarkable, probably owing in some measure to the coolness of the atmosphere inducing people to stir about more than usual. The crowded state of the streets is, however, no doubt owing to the facility with which people can now come into the city by the tramways. The Custom house and the warehouses attached to it are progressing fast, the whole intersected by tramways, with every possible convenience for receiving and delivering goods; and when all is finished it will be the most complete fiscal establishment in South America.

Some improvement has been made in the postal department, but the building is a terribly cramped one for the enormous increase of business. I understand this department has now obtained possession of a site for which it has been for some time in negotiation, and when the post office is removed to it there will be thorough reform in the system, including the abolition of the privilege at present enjoyed by the British post office of having a branch here for the use of its contract mails, creating in fact a little *imperium in imperio*, which is most objectionable. The French Government has a postal treaty with Brazil, and the letters by their contract mails pass through the Brazilian post office, but ours is still an appanage of the British Consulate, which acts as agent for the post office at home in direct opposition to the law of nations, which claims for each the exclusive right of conducting its own fiscal affairs. It is indeed a wonder that Brazilian statesmen have so long endured this infringement on national rights arising out of past traditions. Complaints are made as to the manner in which the British postal agency is managed, and the sooner it is done away with the better.

A great want in Rio is a really good hotel, something on the principle of those in the United States, and, having so successfully inaugurated the tramways, it is to be hoped some enterprising "citizens" will undertake to get up an hotel here on a comprehensive scale, for which there is ample scope. There are many hotels scattered over the city, some with more or less pretension, but none of them afford that degree of comfort so essential to a large city like Rio de Janeiro. The most spacious and comfortable hotel out of the city is the "Estrangeiros," generally filled by Englishmen and other foreigners. The situation is good, and the views of the bay from it lovely; the tram cars to and from Botofoga and the city pass the hotel door every five minutes from 7 a.m. till midnight. At present Carlotta Patti is here with her suite, and at times, when practising, her warbling and the wondrous shakes of her voice echo through the house. The great increase of steam traffic to Rio renders it more than ever necessary that there should be some good hotel in the city where the wants of passengers can be promptly attended to, forming also a general rendezvous for them. As I have before remarked, conveniences for commercial purposes and the transacting of business are more or less on a par with what they were half a century ago, and in this respect Rio is far behind the age.

That the commerce of Rio de Janeiro has greatly augmented of late years the statistics and the revenue collected fully show, and our own Board of Trade Returns indicate the large share we have in that commerce. Still it cannot be denied that in many articles of consumption foreigners are not only competing with us, but excluding us from the market. French and German manufactures are now largely imported, particularly in light, fancy goods, and native manufacture is also making some progress. Hats, which formerly were largely imported, are now made here of various patterns and qualities, and a cotton manufactory is about to be established under Government sanction; but in this particular line it will require a long time to make much way, both from the absence of skilled labour and other natural drawbacks. Tolerably good beer is brewed on the spot, and in time it may supercede the well-known English brands of Bass and Allsopp; indeed, there is no reason why native industry may not by degrees supercede some articles hitherto exclusively imported. As a rule, however, Brazil is essentially a producing country, and to this the attention of both Government and people should be mainly directed. It is of course a question of labour, as the capabilities of the soil are boundless, and will meet any amount of cultivation that can be directed towards it.

July 8th.—The great event—a *Te Deum*—to celebrate the termination of the Paraguayan war is to come off on Sunday the 10th, and preparations are making for it on a very extensive scale, in the immense area, or square called the Campo da Acclamação. The Legislature has voted 200 contos, or about £20,000, towards the expenses. I have received an invitation to attend the ceremony.

July 9th.—Went to the top of Candaleria church, where a grand ceremony was being performed in hoisting up to the tower the last of eight images of saints, placed at the summit. The central tower is being completely renovated, and a long series of temporary wooden staircases were erected to enable people to ascend the tower, which was decorated with flags of all kinds. The statues are all cut out of solid marble, and brought, I believe, from Lisbon; quite works of art, of colossal size. The street in front of the entrance to the tower was strewn with laurel leaves, and the ceremony collected together a large concourse of people. The view of the city, the bay, and the surrounding mountains from this elevation was magnificent, and gave the best possible idea of the extent of the city, which can only be realised from such a central position, owing to the windings and turnings of the hills about it. The clear atmosphere, the blue sky, and the varied landscape formed a panorama not easy to be found in any quarter of the globe. It would make the fortune of any artist capable of doing justice to so extensive and beautiful a picture.

Sunday, July 10th.—Ushered in by a dense fog, rather an unusual occurrence in this country, nor did it clear up before 10 o'clock, soon after which the grand *Te Deum* commenced in the newly-erected Temple in the Campo da Acclamaçao, constructed of wood, plastered over, the design, I believe, being taken from some Grecian temple, and in the form of a cross with four entrances. The building is a series of open columns, with an altar placed in the centre, under the dome; tastefully decorated, where high mass was gone through. The arrangements were under direction of the War Office, and a certain number of tickets were issued for the morning ceremony, which comprised the dignitaries of State, Ministers generally, and the corps diplomatique, who assembled at the top of the portico by which the Emperor was to arrive. This he did with his usual punctuality, accompanied by the Empress and other members of the court, the Count d'Eu and the Princess being already there to receive their Majesties. The display of gold lace and orders of various kinds was very striking; but, apart from this, the simplicity and ease of the royal reception must be patent to anyone accustomed to the stately ceremonial of European Courts. The Emperor is always very affable and gracious, and he looked remarkably well; but of course the chief object of attraction was the young Count d'Eu, who is tall, good looking, with an open countenance and manner anything but French. In fact, without any disparagement to his origin, he looks more like an Englishman than anything else; and his campaign has only imparted a more decided, manly expression to his young face, for he is yet only 26 years of age, but is unfortunately afflicted with deafness. The Princess may well be proud of her consort, and the Emperor of his son-in-law; and it would, perhaps, be difficult to find a more united, happy family. The Empress has rather a careworn but, at the same time, a very amiable expression. Not many ladies were present, and the extensive platform was only scantily occupied; but after the *Te Deum* was partly over the outside public were admitted, and soon filled it with very orderly, well-conducted people. No crushing or confusion, so that after the ceremony was over the Royal party took their departure with the same greetings to those around them as before. The open windows of the Mint and some other large buildings facing the Temple were filled with well-dressed ladies, and booths were erected near it to accommodate a considerable number, but they were not availed of for the morning service. Troops of various arms were assembled in the square—infantry, cavalry, and lancers—making a good military display, and altogether the muster was an imposing one. This afternoon the attendance of the public is expected to be great, and the illuminations at night will be attractive. Much difference of opinion exists as to the necessity of this ceremonial after the demonstrations which accompanied the return of the Count d'Eu and the volunteers; but, at all events, it proceeded from a good motive on the part of the Emperor, who, I believe, is always happy in having his people around him. Party spirit, too, was enlisted on the occasion, and a waste of public money alleged, when the resources of the country are required for other more pressing wants; but there are grumblers in all countries, and such is the case here. Before the ceremony was over the fog had entirely cleared away, and the sun shone brilliantly, but with an agreeable temperature; indeed, it has been one of the coolest seasons known in Rio for many years, with short frosts on the table lands. A friend writes me from San Paulo as follows: "We have had the severest frost known since 1842. Thermometer down, between Jundiahy and Campinas, to 24 degs., and at my chacara to 27 degs. Fah. My servant brought me ice in bed nearly a quarter of an inch thick. The coffee plantations have suffered, many of them severely; but the accounts are exaggerated and conflicting. One man at Campinas is reported to have lost 15,000 trees. One consequence is, if the reports are anything like the truth, that cotton will be planted for a year or two on a large scale until the coffee trees have time to grow again, as the fazendeiros must employ their hands; and perhaps this severe lesson of nature may show the Paulista planters the folly—to use a homely phrase—of "putting all their eggs into one basket." I may add that the temperature of Rio since my arrival has been between 60 and 70, the former early in the morning.

July 14.—We were surprised on going into the city yesterday to find the French boat Amazone had arrived the previous evening in eighteen days from Bordeaux, and she sailed again for the River to-day with a considerable number of emigrant passengers. She is a splendid vessel, nearly 400 feet in length, with great power (steams 13 or 14 knots), and low in the water, looking more like a huge blockade runner than anything else. The French have adopted the screw, like most other countries. I am told that they are very comfortable sea boats, with good passenger accommodation, and well appointed. In her case some of the berths open out of the main saloon, which,

I think, objectionable for many reasons. The sleeping berths should be away from the main saloon, as in the La Plata and the Pacific boats; but there is no mistake about the improvement in speed of these new boats over the old ones of the Messageries Imperiales. The Humboldt also arrived yesterday, 23 days from Liverpool, which, considering the greater distance than from Bordeaux, is a very good passage, and the reputation of the Liverpool line is kept up. We shall now be having several steamers homeward bound, and it is a pity they should come so close together. I may mention that very few English newspapers were received viâ Bordeaux, and it is supposed that they arrived there too late, a not unfrequent occurrence.

July 19.—A disappointment in the arrival of the Liverpool steamer Newton (advertised to leave on the 17th ult. with the contract mail), which has been due from the River Plate. She appears to have broken down on her outward voyage, and had been unable to repair the damage in time to start on her homeward trip with the mails. There is some confusion in the arrangements for the contract mails homeward coming too close on each other; for instance, after the departure of the French mail from Rio on the 6th, the next one should be the Liverpool mail on the 17th—an interval of eleven days; then comes the Southampton mail, on the 23rd or 24th, according to the number of days in the month; the Falmouth mail and the pacific at the end of the month; so that the four mails generally arrive in England during the space of a week. It may be difficult to arrange it otherwise, as the steamers have to wait in the river to discharge and load cargo, and the weather often interferes materially with them; but certainly the public is inconvenienced by this uncertainty of departure from Rio. Accounts from the River are looked for with some interest, from the unsettled state of politics and the civil war going on there, besides the large amount of financial operations that have been carried on from thence during the war; but these must now be drawing to a close. The negotiation of remittances from the River Plate has been a source of considerable profit to speculators, and has tended to support the exchange here, as also to keep down the value of gold. The manner in which Brazil has managed her financial business during the long period of pressure reflects great credit on the Ministry, though it has disappointed what may be termed the " bear" party here. The chief interest felt in the discussion of the Chambers lately has consisted in the comments on the speech from the throne, which still continue. It has afforded the much-abused Duke of Caxias an opportunity of defending himself from the ceaseless attacks made upon him by the Liberal party, and which he has done with great ability and success. I shall give a few extracts from his speech in a separate article as extracted from the report published by the *Diario do Rio de Janeiro*.

July 20th.—The grand ball given by the National Guard to the Count d'Eu came off last night at the Palace of Baron de Itamarity, who lent it for the occasion, and a splendid affair it was, at least 1,500 persons being present. The building itself is a truly palatial one, sumptuously fitted, regardless of expense, and the liberal-minded owner of it must have been highly gratified at the admiration which was expressed on all sides and the enjoyment afforded. The Emperor and Empress, with the Count d'Eu and the Princess, arrived in state about half-past nine, and there was a gorgeous display of uniforms on the occasion, all the distinguished generals and officers during the late war being present, including the Duke de Caxias, who was the observed of all observers and looked remarkably well. The Imperial party entered the large saloon and dancing soon commenced, being kept up to the small hours of the morning. At first the rooms were rather inconvenietly filled, but, as the evening wore on, the guests became more distributed in the ante-rooms, where dancing parties were also formed, as well as in some large rooms in the lower part of the building, and in others there was card playing. Nothing can more forcibly illustrate the progress made in the capital of Brazil and its social advancement than the contrast presented by this ball with what was witnessed twenty years ago. At that period there was much stiffness in Brazilian society, and such gatherings as these were chiefly remarkable for the presence of many dowagers, not all of the purest blood, glittering with diamonds; but on this occasion there were hundreds of good-looking, handsomely-dressed young ladies, who would have graced the balls of any capital in Europe, evincing an ease and self-possession only acquired by mingling with the world, as a majority of the Brazilian educated ladies have done. No London or Parisian toilettes could have exceeded those present in taste or splendour, amongst which diamonds and Brussels lace figured conspicuously. There was a simplicity and freedom in the intercourse between the guests and the Imperial family not often seen in such an assemblage, and the Emperor walked about the rooms conversing with all he knew, or who were presented to him, in a manner the President of the United States might have envied. In fact, there was all the glitter and pageantry of a Court without any of its attendant formality, a *mélange* of Royalty and Democracy probably not to be found in any other country in the world. Another remarkable feature was the absence of crowding or crushing; all seemed quite at home and to enjoy themselves in their characteristic manner. The music was good and refreshments abundant, the rooms being decorated with the choicest flowers. The large garden of the palace was tastefully decorated with various coloured lamps, the representation of a military encampment with tents, and altogether it was a brilliant and gratifying scene. Outside the building and in front of the entrances there was a considerable assemblage of persons, but of a most orderly kind, and no policemen were required in spite of the numerous vehicles which occupied the spacious streets, and the large area formed by an adjoining square. All were civil and in good humour. As the Chambers are sitting, every province of the Empire is represented on these occasions, with, in numerous instances, the presence of the wives and daughters of the deputies. Another grand ball is to be given on the 26th, at the Public Assembly Rooms, which are on a large scale, and very handsomely fitted up. Not a word appears in the journals to-day on the subject of the ball, but I dare say those of to-morrow will give a description of it, from which I may take an extract. The New York steamer arrived to-day to her time, but she brings nothing new, telegrams by the last French mail from Lisbon being quite as recent. The sea cable from Falmouth to Lisbon will be an additional advantage to the mail steamers calling there, as news can now be transmitted so quickly through that medium.

I have just seen a letter from Pernambuco,

addressed to the manager of the Pernambuco Railway, now in Rio, stating that the net working of the railway for the last six months had exceeded the government guarantee by some 800 milreis, and he expresses a confident opinion that the additional amount of capital guaranteed by the government will soon be covered by increased traffic receipts, which ought to be an encouragement to proceed with an extension of the railway further into the province, a measure of great moment, with a view to an increase of its products. The La Place sailed to-day, taking on the mails brought from the River by the Newton, which arrived here yesterday.

July 24.—The La Plata came up from the River, with a good passage, but brings no particular news beyond a confirmation of the taking of Conception by Lopez Jordan, which is an ugly episode. She proceeds on to Southampton on the morning of the 24th, and her mails will doubtless reach home before any others, thus causing the old-fashioned lapse of a fortnight since the arrival there of the French mail. As I have before remarked, it is a pity that the contract mails cannot be so arranged as to ensure a weekly arrival both ways, but this seems impossible, taking into account the difference in the speed of the steamers employed in conveying them.

July 24th, 1870.—The great nautical event here after all is the departure of the "Royal Mail" steamer, by which the old company has been so long known, though in reality most of the steam companies possess the same title, so far as postal contracts are concerned. The "Royal Mail (Southampton)" is, however, the only subsidized line, responsible to the Government as well as the post office, and is generally looked upon by the people in Brazil as a superior and more reliable conveyance from being subject to more stringent conditions. To a certain extent this is undoubtedly true, and it accounts for the preference given to the Royal Mail steamers in the despatch of letters as well as passengers. The La Plata left this morning with as much cargo as she required, a fair complement of passengers, a considerable amount in specie, and very heavy mails, the accumulation of the last fortnight's correspondence. She takes no particular commercial or political news; business being quiet and exchange steady. Affairs in Paraguay are in train of settlement, but the unfortunate revolution in Entre Rios is not put down, and was a source of much anxiety when the City of Rio de Janeiro left on the 17th inst. This fine steamer proceeded to Falmouth on the 26th, and it is expected she will run the La Plata very close.

The Jockey Club, formed in Rio for the promotion of horse-racing, had their meeting to-day, at the race course, a few miles by the Don Pedro Segundo Railway, and a large concourse of people attended. The result is said to have been very satisfactory. Festivals of this kind in Catholic countries are generally held on Sunday. Complaints were made as to crushing at the railway stations, and damage to ladies' dresses, &c., so I fear the Brazilians are rather getting into our rough mode of treating the fair sex, although, as a general rule, they are not usually demonstrative in this way. The breed of horses does not appear to be much improved here, mules being generally preferred both for carriages and travelling, as they are much more hardy and better suited for rough usage. They are used entirely for the tramway (a pair to each car), and I was much pleased to see the evident care taken of them by this establishment. The mule is a most valuable animal in countries like these, where endurance is required and difficult roads have to be traversed.

The question of intense and all-absorbing interest here is that of emancipation, which also serves as a handle for the Liberal party in their attacks on the Government; but, as the latter very justly retort, their opponents have advanced no practical solution of the difficulty, involving so many momentous considerations. That the feeling against a continuance of slavery is rapidly gaining ground is undeniable, but it requires nevertheless most cautious legislation in a country, situated as Brazil is at present, without a substitute for slave labour. A way out of the difficulty will no doubt be found, but not by political clamour and abuse. As to the necessity of bringing foreign labour to the country all parties are agreed, but hitherto attempts in this direction have been only spasmodic, and wanting in some of the primary elements with which alone it can be carried on successfully. Coolie labour has been discussed, and the Government has entered into a contract with some parties to import Coolies, but on terms and conditions not easy of accomplishment; likely enough to fall through altogether, as the concession amounts simply to an exclusive permission to bring them.

July 26th.—Quite an influx of foreign steamers. The Brazilian, belonging to a Hamburg Company, came in on Sunday; the City of Brussels from Falmouth yesterday, with a good passage of 22 days; and in the afternoon the Nova Scotian, extra ship of the Pacific Company, was announced off the harbour, bringing telegram from Lisbon to the 8th July, with a cock-and-bull story of the proposed election of a Prussian Prince as King of Spain, and a threatened rumpus with France in consequence—all which I have no doubt will be dissipated by the Douro accounts, expected on the 30th instant. However, the rumour at once sent up the price of sovereigns and lowered the rate of exchange. There is a striking proof of the advantage in telegraphic communications arising from the new sea cable to Lisbon, the last two telegrams from London having reached there in about an hour and a half, notwithstanding the messages have to be sent first from Belem to the city by the Government line. This new cable to Lisbon is sure to be largely availed of by Brazil and the River Plate, bringing them in fact two or three days nearer to Europe than before, and the Indian Submarine Company's revenue will soon show the wise policy of going to Lisbon. Whilst on the subject of telegraph cables, I may as well mention that the general feeling here is that no cable can now possibly be laid to Brazil except with the aid of a Government subvention or guarantee, for which things are hardly ripe or the necessity considered urgent. Communication with Europe and the United States may possibly be established, via Panama and West Coast of South America, but eventually there will no doubt be a direct cable from Lisbon. In the meantime the Government are prosecuting their land lines under difficulties, and have already got some 1,200 miles of cable and wires laid; but the public mind requires to be educated in this respect, and it will hardly be believed that the country is yet without a code of telegraph laws, nor does it possess any compulsory powers or right of expropriation in order to lay down their lines, being subject to the caprice of landowners and liable to actions for trespass. There is a telegraph board, with a manager and inspector, but they have not as much authority as a parish vestry at home.

The dog nuisance here is great, half famished, miserable looking animals prowling about the streets in all directions, and at night the chorus of barking and howling is enough to wake the seven sleepers. All have dogs about their houses or in their grounds, the latter to prevent theft, but the remedy is almost worse than the disease. It reminds one of Constantinople, only the unruly members of the canine species there are worried and discipline enforced. As local taxation in Brazil is now at its height, in order to liquidate the heavy expenditure arising out of the war, I wonder they do not impose a tax on these noisy animals. People appear to bear the infliction of taxes patiently enough, and it is to be hoped a long period of peace will enable the Government gradually to reduce them, as well as the import and export duties, all which press heavily on the industry of the country.

A VISIT TO THE CANTAGALLO (COCK-CROWING) RAILWAY.*

July 28th.—His Excellency Viscount de Barbecena kindly invited me to accompany him on a visit to this railway, of which he has been the promoter and is now managing director. I gladly availed of so favourable an opportunity to make myself acquainted with the only railway in this part of Brazil I had not already gone over. We started by a small steamer from the Petropolis Station at 8 a.m.; a fine morning, but not a breath of wind stirring. Passing amongst the many vessels laying at anchor in the harbour, and one of the huge floating cranes belonging to the Government arsenal, we were soon steaming across the Bay, and sat down in the low dark cabin to a substantial breakfast of fish, stewed beef, &c., cooked Brazilian fashion and very palatable, to which I did ample justice. As I have before remarked, Rio has improved its

* This rather singular name appears to have had its origin, according to tradition, in a man, who had violated the old mining laws of Brazil, taking refuge where the present town of Cantagallo stands. The soldiers sent in search of him heard a cock crowing, surrounded it, and found the object of their search. Hence the present Cantagallo.

waterside facilities, but there is still a good deal to do in this respect. One effect of the war has been the erection of floating pontoon wharves to facilitate the embarkation of troops, and they are extending the quay walls from the arsenal upwards. Everything went on pleasantly until we got within a short distance of the entrance to the River Macacu, where, owing to the low spring tides, we grounded on the mud, and remained there a couple of hours, until the tide flowed again and enabled us to enter the river—steaming up it some 11 miles to what is called Villa Nova; but, in fact, the Cantagallo Railway Station. The islands in the Bay of Rio have so frequently been described that it is unnecessary to do so; but that of Paquetà, with its white houses glittering in the sun, looked very pretty, and I believe many wealthy inhabitants of Rio reside here during the hot season, a steamer calling at the island daily. The railway comes down to the river bank, the station being covered with a large shed, under which are the offices and a substantial warehouse; from which, in a kind of creek, the small schooners are loaded by means of short stages, thus economising labour. These schooners carry about 400 bags of coffee, which they deliver in Rio the next day.

After the passengers were booked and all in order, we started from Villa Nova Station about one p.m. Passing through the usual kind of woody countries here bordering on rivers, we came to the first station, a distance of six miles, which was formerly the terminus of the railway until it was extended to Villa Nova on the River Macacu already alluded to, and which must be an immense convenience to the traffic of the line. Porte das Caixas appears rather a large straggling place, but with the through river access its importance has diminished. There is a good station here, and a large receiving warehouse for coffee, now rendered unnecessary unless the traffic of the railway increases so much as to bring these roadside facilities into operation. On leaving Porte das Caixas Station we had to mount a short but steep incline of one in sixty, and go through a short tunnel under the road. The distance of 19 miles to the next station of Santa Maria embraces very pretty mountain scenery, with districts of cultivated land, although some churches more or less in ruins showed where large plantations had formerly existed with a considerable population, but which are now comparatively deserted. Santa Maria is a station of importance, having also a large receiving warehouse for coffee or other produce. From this to Cachoeira, a distance of eight miles, the road winds through the mountain passes with many sharp curves, and cultivated country; Indian corn and sugar being the principal products, as both grow very luxuriantly. Houses and cottages spread about on each side of the road. After skirting the river for some distance we crossed it by an iron bridge and soon reached Cachoeira, a distance from the river terminus of 33 miles, beyond which the rails are not at present laid; but a line is being constructed from Cachoeira to the top of the mountain, a distance of 24 miles and at an elevation from the sea of 3,600 feet, to be continued from thence to Nova Friburgo and Cantagallo, a further distance of 30 miles, thus forming a continuous line of about 90 miles.

Until this visit I was under the impression that the Cantagallo Railway was a very insignificant line leading to no particular point, instead of which I found a first-class line, substantially made, with all the accessories for the development of a valuable traffic in connection with one of the great coffee producing districts; sugar mills being also in operation on the lower lands bordering on the line. Quite a little colony has been formed at Cachoeira by the railway. It is beautifully situated amidst mountain scenery. The river running past it is traversed by a modern bridge, and a temporary railway extension bridge is in process of construction. A more picturesque spot it is difficult to imagine—quite a park-like open space, with trees scattered here and there, and cattle and mules feeding. The surrounding mountains, clothed with virgin forests from top to bottom, are one mass of foliage, and many of the trees are 80 to 100 feet high, and mostly covered with innumerable parasites. The air was deliciously cool, and I have rarely spent a pleasanter day in any country. There is an hotel here on rather a large scale, called The Cantagallo, with suitable entertainment for man and beast. Being the station before ascending the mountain towards Nova Friburgo and the town of Cantagallo, it is the rendezvous of all the troops of mules bringing down produce or taking up merchandise; and hundreds of these patient, hard-working animals are tethered about, creating much activity. Passengers bound in that direction generally pass the night at the hotel, so as to ascend the mountain early in the morning, a distance of 24 miles to the summit. There is another large receiving warehouse for produce here, and the company have a good repairing shed, with all modern implements; in fact, they have all the requirements within themselves for carrying on their business. One important feature also in connection with this railway is its cheap construction, the whole 33 miles from Villa Nova to Cachoeira having cost only £240,000. After this it cannot be said that cheap railways are impossible in Brazil. The whole concern is evidently under good control; and I had the pleasure of meeting old acquaintances in Mr. Jell, the traffic manager, and Mr. Williams, contractor, who I believe is also interested in the extension now making. Senhor Capenema, the manager of Government telegraphs, accompanied us from Rio to Porte das Caixas; he is an active, intelligent man, and speaks English fluently. He has a deal of trouble with the telegraphs, owing to there being no law respecting them, and people not yet appreciating their value. The wires are about to be laid on the Cantagallo railway, with an improvement which, I understand, enables the guard of a train to communicate from any part of the line by applying a connecting wire having the necessary apparatus inside.

Friday, July 29th.—I awoke early, and after getting a cup of coffee—always ready in such places—I rambled along the mule road which skirts the river on the left. It was a lovely morning, the sun rising over the mountain tops and gilding everything below. A mass of foliage of every description met the eye, dripping with dew, as the latter must have been very heavy. The air was cool and refreshing, one side of the road skirting hanging woods, the river murmuring and rippling over its rocky bed. There has been little rain for some time, otherwise it is occasionally converted into a mountain torrent. A perfect galaxy of ferns lined the banks by the roadside, which was intersected here and there by little streams of pure delicious water. I could have gone on some distance, but as we were leaving at 9 a.m. I was obliged to return, and met a black boy in search of me to say that breakfast was ready. If anything, the return trip was pleasanter than that of yesterday, the clear morning sky showing the outline of the grand mountain chain more favourably, and the fresh pure air blowing as we were whisked along at the rate of about 20 miles an hour. I should mention, too, a great advantage in the carriages, that they have a small platform outside in front and rear, where a few passengers, who wish to see what is passing around them, can stand in safety; moreover, by the same means the guard can traverse the train throughout—a great improvement on our stupid boxed-up system. The passenger carriages comprise first, second, and third class; and they are very solidly built on the American plan, with seats at the side and a passage up the centre. At present there is only one passenger train up and one train down each alternate day, the goods traffic being carried on daily and as circumstances require; but when the line is made up the mountain (it is to be on Fell's system) the passenger traffic must greatly increase, particularly should the contemplated extension from Villa Nova to Nethirohy (opposite to Rio) be carried out, thus avoiding the tedious uncertain passage by water to the former place. What has been accomplished so far is very creditable to native enterprise; and much praise is due to the late Baron de Novo Friburgo and the Viscount de Barbecena, to whom I am indebted for the opportunity of making this little recital of his enterprising spirit, evinced in the case of this Cantagallo Railway, as well as in connection with many other undertakings which will contribute to the development and prosperity of his native country.

Aug. 3rd.—The excitement caused by the war news has sobered down a little, but still leaves on the mind sensations such as are often created by an ugly dream, which this European war would really seem to be if it were not for the stern reality pictured in every face as to what may come next, or how many complications may arise to affect the current of business on which Rio de Janeiro is so entirely dependent. If the subject of ocean telegraphy had been forgotten it now comes up with double force, as events may be transpiring in Europe compromising the well-being of many foreigners out here who can now only wait the course of mails. The meeting of the two Pacific steamers here for the first time, the extraordinary passage of the Araucania from Lisbon, and other circumstances affecting the communications with Europe, would have been subjects for discussion; but now the all-absorbing question is the war, and what next? These steamers sailed to-day, one north and the other south, the Patagonia taking a large number of passengers; and to-morrow we may look for the homeward French steamer Amazone, to whose rapid movements I before made allusion.

To turn to lighter subjects, such as amusements, Carlotta Patti has been warbling forth to the Brazilians, and soon intends, I believe, going to the River Plate. Opinions differ as to her vocal powers; but, as the French say, " contentement est assez," and so I leave the critics of Rio to ruminate over their verdict. Other performers are now in the field catering for public support—a blind fiddler and his wife, without any disrespect to either be it said. Mr. and Mrs. José and Ada Heine came up from a professional visit to Buenos Ayres, and are about to appear before a Rio audience. Mr. Heine was born blind; but this privation has only enlarged some of his other organs of sense, that of music being predominant, and certainly there is the touch of a master hand in the few strains I have heard, whilst his wife is an accomplished pianist. It is an interesting, though a painful sight to see a wife leading her husband about at all times; but, to judge from his cheerful tone and manner, the want of sight sits lightly on his mind, which is attuned to harmony. I sincerely wish them every success on their adventurous tour.

A lecture was given the other evening by a Mr. N. F. Zeba, a Polish exile, who went to England some 38 years since, on a new method of teaching history by means of a chess board looking plan, subdivided into compartments, embracing a period of 2,000 years before the Christian Era. It is so arranged as to assist the memory by being able to point at once to any particular event by the aid of colours and other visible guides on the plan. Two Brazilian boys were brought forward, who had only received a fortnight's instruction, by which they appeared to have benefitted sufficiently to be able to answer questions put to them; but the system requires more elucidation before it can be appreciated by the general public, who are invited to attend some further lectures. An explanatory book is also to be published by subscription.

Aug. 4th.—The French steamer, Amazone, came in from the River to-day, and leaves again to-morrow afternoon; only a short notice, but it matters less on this occasion after the recent departure of other steamers homeward bound, and transactions being necessarily limited by a European war. Another steamer, the Italo-Platense, also came in from the River; in fact, the movement of steamers here has become so general that scarcely a day passes without arrivals or departures, foreign or coastways. I went on board the Amazone, which is certainly a splendid vessel and admirably adapted to this particular trade, having large capacity for passengers of all classes, with sufficient space for cargo to work within the time she has to devote to the voyage.

Not an inch of room is lost in her arrangements and fittings, and her speed is unquestionable, averaging 13 to 14 knots. Her engines are 600 horse-power, three cylinders of 200 horse-power each, worked upon a simple plan; but it must be rather warm work for the stokers. She is a long narrow boat, and will be difficult to catch by any Prussian cruiser.

August 6th.—A comparative calm prevails since the departure of the French Mail yesterday; waiting for the next accounts from Europe, with a shadowing forth of the portentous events likely to take place there and their probable influence on commercial transactions. What a valuable thing an ocean telegraph cable would now be and what a handsome revenue it would be deriving. The absence of it may be attributed entirely to the injudicious manner in which such enterprises are dealt with here, and to the loose way in which concessions are given; otherwise there can be no doubt a direct ocean telegraph cable would now have been in operation to Brazil. When and under what circumstances this most desirable mode of communication will be carried out is very problematical, as nothing short of a substantial Government guarantee would now provide the requisite capital at home. The mere permission to lay a cable amounts to nothing. The unlooked for prospect of a war in Europe has certainly raised the question in a practical form, and in the meantime the Government is paying more attention to land telegraphy, pushing on their lines gradually north and south, and I believe powers are to be obtained in the chambers to facilitate the laying of wires. The published reports of the manager of the telegraphs are not very favourable to the spirit of enterprise in this country as regards the desire to avail of such facility, which may be attributed in a great measure to its scanty population; and the kind of "jog-trot" habits people have got into will make it a work of time to change them. With an ocean telegraph in existence, however, I believe a different feeling would be gradually instilled into the country, as most people are imbued with the importance of a close connection with Europe, such as can be attained by no other medium, and it would certainly revolutionise commercial transactions.

We have had a strong southerly wind for the last four days, with a good fall of rain, which was much wanted for a supply of water to the city; but it is said the country can do without it until the coffee crop is gathered. The temperature keeps very cool for Rio, and it is trying for the natives, who suffer from these changes.

The fleet of steamers in the harbour has latterly been much augmented by the return of the ironclads and steam transports, which are now lying up in ordinary, many of them requiring repairs. Amongst the ironclads which did good service during the war are those built by Messrs. Laird Brothers, of Birkenhead, the Bahia and Lima Barros. The old blockade runners converted into transports are easily recognised, conspicuous among which is the Isabel, with her four funnels, having lately brought up between 600 and 700 men and officers. She came out from Liverpool in 17½ days. Some of the old Brazilian vessels of war which were engaged in the celebrated action of Riachuelo are also here, so that Brazil has now quite a formidable little fleet. They occasionally exercise their heavy guns by firing at a target in the bay, and I believe are mostly in a state of efficiency.

Reverting to the manner in which the French Mail service is performed, great complaints continue to be made. The Amazone, for instance, arrived here from the River on the morning of the 4th instant., and was immediately posted to sail on the 5th at 5 p.m.; the mails closing at noon on that day, which caused considerable confusion, and they were only kept open an hour or two longer from sheer necessity arising from the pressure at the Post Office. The company profess to allow 48 hours here, which is little enough for a place of such commercial importance as Rio; but to curtail this limited time is inconvenient and improper. Our own mails also require better regulating, and Sunday ought to be made a *dies non*, not to count at all in the time allowed whether proceeding southward or returning home. As it is, Sunday is made quite a working day at the English Post Office on the arrival and departure of contract mail steamers. The Praça or Exchange here is closed on Sunday, and so ought the English Post Office to be; otherwise, having an English Church and paying a chaplain is almost a work of supererogation, and sets a very bad example; in fact, the Brazilians look upon us as little better than heathens from the manner in which our only day of religious observance is desecrated. Catholic churches have always some outward or visible sign of religious observances going on, and a large number of people attend them on Sunday or on church festival days, but our only Protestant place of worship is, as a rule, very thinly attended. So long as the Mail service is carried on at the Brazilian Post Office we have nothing to do with it, but the anomaly of an English branch Post Office being open on Sunday is a reflection on the action of St. Martin's-le-Grand that ought to be represented. It appears the latter establishment is about to make some change in the rate of postage allowed to the contract mail steamers (the Royal Mail from Southampton has, of course, a Government subsidy), and the Falmouth line has availed of it to throw up their contract; so the City of Brussels lately arrived here will be the last to carry a contract mail, and I suspect the Liverpool line will follow their example. The fact is that, with the restrictions as to time and heavy penalties of the Post Office, these steamers cannot make it answer their purpose, as they are more dependant on cargo and general traffic than the regular subsidized ones. So I suppose there will again be changes in the days of departure, and that the steamers of the non-subsidized lines will only carry ship letters under former regulations. It may make little difference to the Liverpool Pacific line, as they depend mainly on their West Coast cargo traffic, picking up passengers here and at Monte Video.

August 10th.—The Poitou, arrived a few days back from Marseilles, brought no further war news, so we are still in the dark as to what is going on. The following melancholy accident is recorded in the Rio papers:—The steamer Purus, of the Upper Amazon Company, steaming down the river, about two o'clock a.m. on the 8th July, was run into on the port side by the steamer Arary, belonging to the Amazon Steam Company. The latter was on her way to Manaos. The accident occurred off the heights of Paraque-quaru, and resulted in the total loss of the Purus, with some 150 souls, only 73 escaping. This calamity is attributed to the carelessness of the pilot of the Purus, who is said to have been intoxicated and away from his official post on the steamer. The Amazon has been so long navigated in safety by the steamers of the Company that this unfortunate accident will throw a damper on their proceedings, although it appears from the statement to have arisen entirely from carelessness. People in this country are not so go-a-head or so venturesome as the Yankees, and such a serious loss of life makes an impression not easily effaced.

August 13th.—After an interval of ten days of anxiety, enlivened only by the arrival of a large French iron-clad, the Alma, and some of the Liverpool steamers to and from Santos, the arrival of the Hamburg Company's steamer Santos, under the English flag, brought telegraph news from Lisbon to the 21st July, with a confirmation of the preparations for war and various surmises as to the attitude of European states; but more important news is hourly looked for by the French mail steamer from Bordeaux, now quite due, as she will bring telegrams to the 29th July. Business is almost entirely suspended as regards shipments of produce or negotiation of exchange, which is nominally 21d. Some few speculative transactions take place in sovereigns, which maintain their value.

Sunday, August 14th.—The French steamer came in this morning, closely followed by the Tycho Brahe mail contract steamer from Liverpool. The news is bad enough, though its effects will not appear for a day or two, as to-morrow is one of the very close holidays—a religious festival in honour of "Nossa Senhora da Gloria"— when there will be very grand doings at the church of that name; a procession, and other ceremonies, attended by the Emperor and his suite. Some of the old-fashioned holidays have been done away with, but enough remain to render them a serious interruption to business. At one period of the history of the Catholic Church the institution of holidays in connection with these religious festivals was all very well, as time was then of so little value; but in these days of prompt action and worldly excitement they are a great nuisance, and only engender lazy habits. One of the three French vessels of war, a small screw corvette, went out of the harbour this morning, having no doubt received instructions by the mail; and I conclude she will be cruising about in quest of prizes so soon as the time allowed to Prussian and German vessels expires.

Monday, August 15.—A perfect *dies non*, all places of business closed; the city and suburbs alive with holiday seekers dressed in the gayest attire, and it is curious to see the fondness for bright colours exhibited by coloured ladies, from the black girl upwards. The day is remarkably fine, cool, and pleasant, so it is largely availed of by the population. The church on the Gloria Hill, where the festival is being held, is decked with flags of all kinds, and a constant stream of pilgrims (if such they can be called) are visiting the shrine of "our Lady of Glory." The French mail leaves this afternoon for the River Plate,

F

taking down Carlotta Patti and suite to exhibit her vocal powers before the rather critical taste of a Buenos Ayres audience. I believe she has met with tolerable success here, but not excited a *furore*. I suppose Mr. and Mrs. Heine will now come before the Rio public to exhibit their musical powers.

August 16.—The Copernicus is in from the River, so we have a mail conveyance home at last. She brings no particular news from that quarter beyond the fact that the excitement of a war in Europe seemed to divert attention for the moment from the serious position of things in Entre Rios, where Lopez Jordan remained master of the country for the time, but how long he may retain it is another matter on which opinions differ. It is satisfactory to find the other Argentine Provinces remain quiet. Being the dull season for business, financial affairs may be less affected in the River than here. There is some interesting matter published in the *Standard*, which will repay perusal.

August 17.—The Copernicus sailed to-day, and her letters ought to reach before the Douro, to sail 23rd instant. An important document has been issued to-day, namely, the report of the committee appointed by the Chamber of Deputies to consider the question of slavery—and a very satisfactory document it is. The opponents of Government asserted that referring the question to a Committee of the House was tantamount to shelving it; but such has not been the case, as the prompt production of the report testifies. The leading principle recommended is freedom of birth and a gradual diminution of slavery by means which appear both sound and practical, going indeed much further than might have been supposed from the difficulties surrounding the case, and the various conflicting interests mixed up with it. No doubt the struggle now going on here for political power has accelerated the anti-slavery movement, but it is to be hoped the Legislature will not be driven into any crude or ill-defined measures for solving the great problem of slavery. All may at once agree that there shall be no more slaves born in the country; but the process of emancipating those already existing involves much more serious considerations than appear on the surface, or than can possibly be understood by those unacquainted with the social condition of the Empire.

August 18.—I looked in at the Senate to-day, where a very tame discussion was going on. The building is a wretched one, and not nearly so convenient or well-ventilated as the Chamber of Deputies. It seems strange that better accommodation has not by this time been provided for the legislative body, and still more so that the two Chambers should be a mile apart from each other, which must be a great inconvenience and hindrance to public business, particularly in a warm climate. The concentration of state offices with their various departments does not seem to have been studied here, as they are scattered all over the city, which involves a large amount of trouble as well as of locomotion. The practice of interrupting speakers is a great drawback to oratory; and renders the ordinary proceedings of the Chambers little more than a running discussion similar to what exists in the United States. They would do well to follow the example of our House of Commons in this respect, although in both cases a deal of time is taken up with mere verbiage. A considerable sum is paid for reporting and publishing the proceedings of both Houses, which only appear after an interval of some days, but still I believe they are read extensively. One advantage they certainly have over the Chambers at Buenos Ayres is that the speakers stand up, and consequently can be both better seen and heard.

August 19.—I went over to Praya Grande (the opposite side of the Bay) or the City of Nitherohy, which has just been lighted with gas; and a new ferry has been established, with large American ferry boats, the latter affording additional facility to communications, calculated to materially improve the prospects of the place, which has for some time been rather in a declining state. It so happened that the Emperor was going over to visit the gas works this evening, and to see the city lighted, and great preparations were being made for his reception at the ferry and the gas works, both of which were extensively decorated with flags. We took a drive round the neighbourhood, which is very pretty and picturesque, with many good-looking houses scattered about, where families come to reside during the hot season, for which there is an extensive sea beach of the purest white sand. House rent is much cheaper here than in Rio, and living also, I understand. We inspected the new gas works, which are rather in an unfinished state; but, when completed, it promises to be a compact little concern, well built, with all modern improvements. The contract has been carried out by Messrs. Burton, Sons, & Waller in a solid, substantial manner, under the inspection of Mr. Neate, as engineer, and the buildings erected by Mr. Boullman, Mr. Buck being now the resident manager. The works are rather too far from the city, and with only shallow water for discharging coals. The scattered nature of the lighting will require a large amount of main pipes; but altogether, if well and economically administered, it ought to be a paying concern. The steamer from New York came up as we were crossing. I should not omit to notice the improvements making at the market, to which they are building an upper story, with ample convenience for storing the products brought for sale, and much more cleanliness is observed. A few years will make a great change for the better in this respect throughout the city, which is apparent to those who have known it in former years, more so probably than to those who are constantly on the spot.

August 20th.—The Douro came up early this morning from the River with a fair complement of passengers. She has the honour of taking home the Count d'Eu and the Princess. Various surmises are afloat as to the object of their visit to Europe under present circumstances, most of them arising from political feeling, but I dare say most of them very wide of the truth. They will carry with them the sympathy and good wishes of all loyal Brazilians, who think very highly both of the Count and the Princess; nor do I believe they have any enemies. It is stated that the Emperor will positively visit Europe next April, by which time the Count and the Princess are expected to return, and that I take to be the reason of what may appear a hurried arrangement. To judge by the language of some River Plate papers, the state of affairs in Entre Rios and in the Banda Oriental, serious as it undoubtedly is, only affords food for editorial merriment, or at all events they seem to be tired of treating things *au serieux*. The most extraordinary rumours are circulated from day to day, simply, it would appear, in the absence of any events worth recording, and for the time the war in Europe absorbed public attention. National bonds were weak, though money was plentiful and rates of discount easy. In fact, they have evidently retained a considerable portion of the gold sent down from Rio during the progress of the war.

August 22nd.—No appearance yet of the steamer Germany, extra ship of the Pacific line, most anxiously looked for, and the Falmouth steamer is also due in a day or two. There is no political or commercial news of importance, but a fair amount of exchange appears to be negotiating at about 20 to 20½ for bank paper, and 21 to 21½ for private paper; but under present circumstances transactions are irregular, depending much on the nature of the paper offered.

August 23rd—The Douro sailed to-day under a Royal salute, having the Count d'Eu and the Princess on board, a fair number of passengers, nearly a full cargo, and £4,000 of specie. Went to visit the Immigrants' Home, an institution supported by Government. It is beautifully situated, on an eminence at the extreme end of the city, commanding a fine view of the bay and the shipping. The house was originally built by a rich Brazilian, afterwards converted into an hospital, called the "Casa de Saude," which name it still bears, and it is admirably adapted to its present purpose, being large and spacious, with plenty of ground about it for exercise and recreation. Only women and children were the occupants, the men lately there having gone out to work some land in the neighbourhood of the city, recently bought by the Government for this purpose. They appeared to be well cared for and the children looked reasonably healthy—indeed it is one of the healthiest positions about Rio. We arrived just at dinner time, and certainly there was nothing to complain of in the food they were partaking of, which consisted of soup, good fresh beef, beans, and farinha, a repast which any labouring man ought to enjoy. The occupants were chiefly Irish, which accounts for the place not being kept as clean as it might be; otherwise, with so many able-bodied women, there is no excuse for discomfort. The building is capable of holding a large number, and, I believe, as many as 500 emigrants have been located there on a pinch, but latterly not more than 100. If emigration becomes systematized and the establishment is properly looked after, it must be a very valuable adjunct. Speaking of emigration, the attempts hitherto made to promote it have been very crude and spasmodic, nothing like a regular, well organized plan having been adopted; otherwise there is ample scope for prosperous colonies in this and the adjoining provinces. There has been no unity of purpose between the Government and those who have brought out emigrants, failure in such cases being the natural consequence. It is the injudicious choice of localities for placing the emigrants and not providing for their comfort at the onset that has caused so much dissatisfaction, nor can success be attained without proper arrangements being made beforehand, such as exist in countries much less favourably endowed than Brazil for all the requirements of an industrial population. I ought not to omit mentioning that there is an English benevolent institute here for relieving distressed British subjects, some £500 per annum being expended in this praiseworthy object; as it is difficult to imagine a worse place than Rio for this class of people, not speaking the language and finding it impossible to obtain suitable employment.

August 24th.—The Donati arrived to-day from Liverpool with two or three days later advices, which only increases the desire to know more relative to the extraordinary state of things in Europe, and the progress of the gigantic struggle which appears inevitable. In the face of what may be called conflicting statements as to the probable duration of the war, and the complications which may arise out of it, exchange has been rather firmer, with more business doing; but of course everything here is contingent on the tenor of advices from Europe and subject to daily fluctuations, as opinions change with regard to the probable future.

August 25th.—The Germany is up to-day, with Lisbon telegrams from London to the 5th instant, advising a commencement of hostilities between

France and Prussia, together with other information not favourable to a prompt settlement of existing difficulties; but rather the contrary, that the war will be a long one, and may bring about complications with other States. However, people here seem to have made up their minds for the worst, and it is discounted.

There are rumours here to-day that the Emperor is determined to have the slavery question brought forward this session, and that if the present Ministers will not do it, he will try to find others. It is difficult to believe that a measure involving such vital consequences to the Empire is likely to be hurried forward in this fashion; but moderate people think there would be no harm in legislating upon the report of the committee lately presented to the Chambers, and that it would tend to allay irritation. The arrival of Senhor Paranhos from the River Plate is anxiously looked for, as it is thought his great influence would be exercised in bringing about a satisfactory solution of the present political crisis, if such it can be called.

August 27th.—The movement of steamers continues. The Poitou, of the Marseilles line, arrived to-day from the River, bringing papers to 20th inst., and the Montezuma, belonging to the Havre line, also sailed for the River. At Buenos Ayres attention appeared to be concentrated on the advices from Europe, and internal troubles forgotten for the moment. Dr. Tejedor had been appointed Minister for Foreign Affairs in place of Dr. Varela, who goes to England to recruit his health, and he is highly spoken of as a man of character and ability. Señor Riestra had also been unanimously chosen a Senator. In Entre Rios a forward movement on the part of General Gelly y Obes was looked for; and matters in Uruguay are culminating to a point that looks very like the Blancos obtaining possession of Monte Video, in which case the old struggle between them and the Colorados may last for years, to the destruction of a fine country. By a Government decree the Cordova Exhibition is again postponed to the 15th March, 1871, which must be a source of great annoyance and of some loss to those who have been making preparations for the opening in October next. No reason is assigned for this step, which I conclude arises from events connected with the revolution in Entre Rios; but, whatever the cause, the delay is much to be regretted, and will be very prejudicial to the exhibition itself.

The prosperous state of Brazilian finances is exciting general attention. The Government has a large surplus in the Treasury, and has recently reduced the rate of interest on its bonds (apolices), as well as on other securities, all of which are gradually rising in value. All expenses connected with the late war will now soon be liquidated, and it would be a judicious step to make some reduction in taxes levied to meet the expenses of the war, particularly the export duties on produce, which weigh so heavily on the industrial interests of the country. On the other hand, the Government is asking very large sums for railway extension, the making of roads, navigation of rivers by steam, and other enterprises identified with the progress of the country. A judicious outlay in this way, so as to reduce the cost of transport of produce to the seaboard, is of all things wanted, and most desirable, calculated to encourage agriculture and assist emigration.

The much abused Duke of Caixias has just been presented with the order of Dom Pedro I., one of the oldest of the Empire, and very rarely bestowed, in a manner that must be very gratifying to him, many of his companions in arms having united to pay him what I consider a well-deserved compliment. The future historian of South America, and of Brazil in particular, will yet do justice to the services of this distinguished soldier, and the more the hardships and trials the Brazilian army had to go through in the Paraguayan campaign become known, the more will the fortitude as well as the tactics of its commander be appreciated. In fact, few soldiers but those born in the country could have stood the severe physical ordeal they had to go through. Amongst his most conspicuous opponents may be ranked those who advocated at one time an ignominious peace, and prognosticated a collapse and ruin of the country if the war was continued, instead of which it is rising superior to its former condition, both politically and financially.

August 31st.—The Cordillera arrived from the Pacific yesterday—very punctual, with a large cargo and a considerable number of passengers for Europe. She sailed again to-day. Things in the River Plate remained pretty much in *statu quo*, except that a report prevailed of General Gelly y Obes being about to move forward in Entre Rios; but the Buenos Ayres papers do not speak very hopefully as to the result. The formation of a National Bank, with Señor Norberto de la Riestra at the head of it, and under the auspices of Messrs. J. Thomson, T. Bonar and Co., of London, is announced rather at an unfortunate time, with a European war and internal troubles; but there seems to be great monetary ease at Buenos Ayres. The names are a guarantee for able and prudent management on both sides. National Bonds were declining, as well as Exchange on England, under the influence of European advices. The Oneida is anxiously expected here. The Brazilian mail coasting steamer arrived here last evening, brought accounts of the Pascal having reached Pernambuco with some news of French defeats, but not much reliance is placed on such indirect rumours.

September 2nd.—The Oneida came up yesterday afternoon, having been groping about in a fog, and not signalized, so she took every one by surprise.

The rumours alluded to, brought from Pernambuco, about the war, proved not only correct, but far below the estimate, and set people wild with excitement and surprise. Every one asked, what has become of the French grand army, about which the world has heard so much of late years? It seems to have "melted into thin air," and the cause of Louis Napoleon is regarded here as quite hopeless. The commercial and financial news comes also more cheerful, which has restored a degree of confidence, and produce is more freely operated in, with a steadier rate of exchange. All the German vessels in harbour hoisted their flags yesterday on receipt of the news, but not a French one was to be seen. Events crowd on each other so fast now-a-days that it is difficult to keep pace with them. There will be later news by the Pacific steamer, due to-morrow or the next day, the telegrams from Lisbon being the only things cared for, although on this last occasion several were missing, amongst them the usual ones for the Praça do Commercio, for which people are at a loss to account. I am leaving for the River Plate tomorrow, by the Royal Mail steamer Oneida, so my narrative will now take a wider range, and embrace the state of affairs there, which by all accounts is not very satisfactory. The homeward French mail is looked for on the 4th, and an announcement is made that in future they will give fully 48 hours after arrival for letters to be posted.

RIO DE JANEIRO TO THE RIVER PLATE.

Sept. 4th, 1870.—Again on board one of the Royal Mail Company's ships—the Oneida—an old acquaintance of mine, having been under my charge at Constantinople whilst employed in the Transport service during the Crimean war. She has undergone considerable alteration since that time, having had new engines, and been built upon so as to adapt her for passenger traffic. She is a faithfully-built ship, having been originally constructed for private owners, under very close inspection; but she is probably behind her day when contrasted with the magnificent new steamers now running to Brazil and the River Plate; still, she is a fine ship and a comfortable sea-boat, and has always done her work remarkably well. The comments I have before made as to the organization of the Royal Mail Company's service in the case of the La Plata apply equally to the Oneida; being well-navigated, with every arrangement on board that can conduce to the comfort of passengers, and a first-rate *cuisine*. On leaving Rio yesterday, the place was in a state of considerable excitement, caused by the arrival of the Magellan, bringing dates from England to the 19th August, telegraphed from Lisbon, with continued accounts of Prussian victories and of the Prussian armies marching on Paris. We have on board a *Times* of the 15th August, the contents of which, coupled with the later telegrams, would seem to place the cause of France and the reign of Napoleon III. in a very precarious condition.

The weather in Rio before our departure had been very dull and unsettled—not a glimpse of sunshine for two or three days; and it continues the same now, with occasional showers of rain, little wind, but a heavy southerly swell, which causes the ship to roll a good deal, leading us to think that it has been blowing hard in these latitudes, nor is it possible to imagine a more gloomy day in the chops of the English Channel. No observation possible, so we are running by the log —difficult to believe we are in the "sunny south." The Magellan was to leave a few hours after us, and it is possible her superior speed will enable her to reach Monte Video first, which would be a disappointment to our commander and his officers, who have all the *esprit de corps* about them appertaining to rival services. However, the "race is not always to the swift nor the battle to the strong," and we still hope to take down the first news of the recent stirring events in Europe.

A sense of relief will be felt in Brazil and the River Plate by the more cheerful tone of commercial advices just received, and the recovery both in commercial and financial affairs at home, however much the drawbacks and disasters caused by the war may affect local interests. Moreover, there appears to be less chance of continental complications, and it is believed the decisive nature of the struggle between France and Prussia may lead to some mediation by other Powers that will bring about a speedier peace than could at one time have been supposed possible.

Amongst the passengers on board the Oneida are a further small detachment of "Henly boys," from which it may be supposed that Mr. Henly is not yet "snuffed out" as some people suppose. By the last accounts published in *The Buenos Ayres Standard* he appears to have purchased land a few miles from Rosario, where he was establishing his colony—and it is to be hoped he will be successful; nor do I see any reason why this should not be the case, if they only work cordially together. Of course much will depend on the calibre of the settlers themselves; and unfortunately the habits and ideas of some of them are not very promising, but these will probably be weeded out. It is a singular propensity amongst a certain class of young Englishmen of good families, well-educated, and who ought to know better, to conduct themselves in a foreign country and amongst strangers as if they were entirely devoid of these advantages. Such conduct creates a prejudice against them, and it is exceedingly offensive to quiet-going passengers on board the steamers which bring them out, who are often obliged to witness behaviour and to hear language that would hardly be indulged in by members of the swell mob. The general impression as to the behaviour of fast young Englishmen is not favourable even at home ; but society keeps some check upon them there, which cannot well be exercised under the circumstances alluded to. There may be good and noble qualities in the race, but these are sadly obscured by a prevalence of very vicious ones. As a rule the class of emigrants or settlers in a new country ought to be steady, sober, hard-working people, who will look their position boldly in the face, determined by patience and perseverance to overcome any drawbacks or difficulties that may attend it. Whether "Henly boys" possess these qualities remains to be seen. A life of easy indulgence and folly is not the best suited for dealing with the stern realities of an adventurous life in the pampas of South America.

September 5th.—The prognostications of some friends in Rio that the late misty, disagreeable weather would be followed by a southerly blow has been realised. It came on strong yesterday afternoon from the south-west, dead in our teeth of course, with rather a heavy sea, causing the steamer to pitch and roll considerably; but, on the whole, she is as comfortable as any ship well can be under such circumstances, and more so than a great many. To-day has been bright and sunny, but still blowing fresh from the same quarter, reducing our speed to the minimum, with the prospect of a longer than usual passage. It is not the first time I have experienced such weather in these latitudes; and, as I have maintained, the worst part of the passage is generally between Rio de Janeiro and the River Plate. The Bay of Biscay is sometimes bad enough; but a south-wester, or Pampero, are not to be despised. As a set-off the air feels fresh, cold, and invigorating—very different to what it has been of late about Rio, where a damp cold has been so prevalent. The thermometer ranges about 60 degs.

September 6th.—Wind gone down, but the heavy swell has continued, retarding our progress, and we have only made 215 miles since yesterday. On the other hand, the weather is delightful, bright sunshine, with a cool breeze—something like a fine day in England.

Monte Video, 8th of September.—We came to an anchor here about 11 a.m. and found the Magellan had preceded us by a few hours; the

City of Buenos Ayres was here, and the Cassini, belonging to the Liverpool line, also came up from Buenos Ayres, having taken in a large portion of her cargo at Rosario, the first steamer loaded there direct for Europe. It was a beautiful sunny day, and on going on shore we found it was one of their holidays, " Nativity of the Virgin." Ships and places of business all closed, with flags flying in various directions, nor could any stranger have imagined that a rebel army was encamped within two miles of the city, threatening it with assault at any moment. It is true the place wore a dead-alive sort of aspect, and I believe many families have left the City for Buenos Ayres; but those who remain in it appear indifferent as to what is passing around them. Things are evidently in a hopeless state of confusion. It matters little which party gains the ascendant, as the country is utterly ruined, the Government without means or resources, and the whole affair is a sort of wind-up to a long period of anarchy, where plunder is the order of the day as long as there is anything to divide. What a curse that so fine a country should be in such miserable hands; but there is no help for it at present. The wonder is how people get their daily bread, or in what way the political and social machinery is kept in motion at all. Whilst there, Government troops, said to number some 2,000 men, marched out with the intention of attacking the rebels, and as we left numerous rockets were fired ; but whether they will come to close quarters and bring things to a crisis remains to be seen. The telegraph wires are cut, so the news of passing events will have to be brought over by the daily steamers. The accounts I received as to the state of things on both sides of the river are very discouraging ; but, as regards the Argentine Republic, I shall know more on arrival at Buenos Ayres. It is a lovely night, with a full moon, but a keen, searching air, which makes the cabin much more preferable than the deck, and two or three recent copies of *The Buenos Ayres Standard* post one up as to what is taking place there. Several of our passengers were left behind at Monte Video, chiefly " Henly boys," who appear to have found the city rather attractive, as there was ample time for them to have returned on board; besides which, the steamer fired three guns after the time appointed for leaving, nor does it do to trifle with a large steamer in such a ticklish navigation as that between Monte Video and Buenos Ayres. It may teach them a lesson for the future, and certainly no blame whatever can be attached to the Captain of the Oneida.

Buenos Ayres, 11th of September.—We anchored in the roadstead, some twelve miles from the shore, early on Friday morning ; very inconvenient distance, but a small screw steamer took us in close to the mole, whence we had to be transhipped into a boat, the luggage having a third process to go through, that of being put into carts and landed at the end of the mole for examination, &c., which, however, is gone through promptly, and with much courtesy on the part of the Custom House officials. All the drawbacks of landing remain, nor will it be an easy task to remove them, unless a temporary facility is afforded by extending the mole. The intention, I believe, is to run a double tramway on the mole, and only make the latter accessible by ticket; thus doing away with the trouble and expense of having everything conveyed by peons, who scramble for the luggage like so many hungry wolves. A more systematic plan of managing these things would certainly be a great comfort and relief to passengers, many of whom are very helpless on such occasions. No particular improvement struck me on landing, if I except the institution of tramways, and building of some large fine houses, which becomes more visible on traversing the City—now so easily done, contrasted with former times. The streets themselves were still bad enough, the more regular paving of the tramways only showing the deformity of the other portion of the street, rendering locomotion by carriages even more difficult than before. The tramways don't appear so well laid down or so compact as those of Rio de Janeiro; and another singular process is that of a man on horseback riding a little distance before the carriages, blowing a horn, the object being to prevent collision with other vehicles when passing the cross streets, which are of course very numerous from the plan of building in squares. A serious drawback here to the otherwise great conveniences of tramways is that they do not run continuously or in succession, but collect together at a starting point to the number of six or eight carriages, which leave at the same time, causing much delay, and when they do start, what with the blowing of the horns and the passing of so many tram carriages in close proximity, it creates quite a *furore* in the streets, something like that of a grand cavalry charge, or the passing of an artillery train. Being single lines of rails, the carriages are obliged to return the same way; but I believe it is intended, before the system is complete, to improve on this kind of "confusion worse confounded." Certainly the tramways as at present worked are a positive nuisance to the city, and whether they are likely to be paying concerns there is no data yet to go upon, except that the cost of construction has been heavy and the working expenses must be great. The rumbling omnibuses have nearly disappeared, to give way to a modern and much more agreeable conveyance, to say nothing of the great saving in expenses of locomotion. No doubt one result will be that of people living more in the suburbs, and less crowding in the city. Beyond a supply of water, which is a great boon, sanitary improvements remain in *statu quo*. The weather has continued fine and bright, but still cold, necessitating fires in the evening to those who wish to feel comfortable.

As regards the political and social state of the country there is much to be said; but I shall reserve my comments until a more lengthened inquiry enables me to arrive at a truer estimate of the actual condition of things. On the surface all appears to go on as usual, but there is an under-current of mischief caused by the very freedom of its institutions, which to a certain extent paralyses the Executive. As in the United States, the working of the federal system is found to be defective, inasmuch as each province exercises a separate power, with the interference of which there is great jealousy, so that virtually the National Government is under control of the Chamber of Deputies, whose action is often slow when a prompt decision is necessary to be arrived at. To this cause may be ascribed the prolongation of the Entre Rios rebellion, and the difficulty the Government experiences in passing measures of much importance to the general welfare of the Republic as a body. The action of the President is limited and circumscribed, and the views of Sarmiento are said to be much in advance of the majority of his countrymen. The general opinion is favourable to an early settlement of affairs in Entre Rios, as a portion of Lopez Jordan's army has been signally defeated, and a decisive action is daily looked for. Meanwhile, this rebellion causes a large drain on the national exchequer at a time when its funds are urgently required for the prosecution of railways and other useful purposes, besides occupying the attention of Government and distracting public opinion, which requires rest after the excitement of the last few years. A great misfortune in the settlement of affairs in Paraguay has occurred by the abandonment of that portion of the triple alliance which had for its object a definition of the boundaries—each party being left to establish its own—which may give rise to future trouble. There has been too much sensitiveness in the matter here, from a feeling of not taking advantage of the powerless condition of Paraguay, and the Brazilian minister was reluctantly obliged to abandon the point. A kind of incipient revolution has just occurred at Asuncion, resulting in a change of the governing body; but this is of little consequence, and it may not be the first by a good many changes before Paraguay assumes anything like a settled government. From Monte Video we hear of the Blancos being defeated in an engagement outside the city, which may somewhat change the aspect of affairs. The telegraph wires are being constantly cut, which is a great annoyance to people here, and a serious loss to the company. It seems a most wanton piece of mischief on the part of the Blancos, as the telegraph can have no possible influence on their movements—just at this time, too, when the anxiety for news from Europe is so strong. The Oneida takes home a large amount of specie from here and Monte Video, and it is believed this will be considerably augmented at Rio de Janeiro. She has also a fair complement of passengers.

14th September.—Nothing new to-day; weather windy and cold; fires very acceptable.

Buenos Ayres, Sept 15th, 1870.—The Oneida takes on a supplementary mail from Monte Video to-morrow morning, but there is no news to-day worth recording. A continuance of splendid weather, less mud, and warmer to-day. Visited the Southern Railway Station and went on to Barracas, where much activity prevails; more shed accommodation, many new covered waggons built and building on the spot, the iron work being sent out from England. The goods traffic has not been so heavy of late, owing to the dull produce markets; but the passenger traffic keeps steadily increasing, and both will experience a great development when the extensions southward, now in process of making, are available—particularly that across the River Salado, which is a stopper to the old bullock traffic. Few foreign railways have been so uniformly prosperous as the Great Southern, which has built up a traffic for itself that must go on increasing and multiplying with the development of the province, and act as a great stimulus to railway enterprise throughout the republic. Of this fact the Government appears to be fully sensible, and money is freely voted by the Chambers for constructing railways. At the same time it requires judicious handling, in order that the lines should be carried where they are most likely to be productive, and become feeders for existing traffic, as well as that which the railways themselves will create. Another very essential requirement is that population should keep pace with railway advancement, which is impossible unless adequate encouragement is afforded; nor do the Government or people yet appear alive to this great want and necessity of their position. They think because a certain number of Basques and Italians come out spontaneously, that a portion at least of the surplus population of Northern Europe will migrate to their shores, and some go so far as to argue that they don't want immigration at all. The response would soon be a stationary exchequer and an uncultivated territory. The real and permanent wealth of a country must emanate from its soil and from its natural products, and without population there can be no progress. Even with the influx of emigrants for the last few years the census of the Argentine Republic is ridiculously small.

The more I see of the working of the tramways here the more objectionable it appears; and unless some great change takes place they can only be a standing nuisance to the city, besides interfering very materially with the paying nature of the traffic. To be of any real use there should be constant regular departures every few minutes, instead of half-a-dozen or more carriages starting together at intervals of hours or half hours, the collection of so many carriages creating moreover a great interference with the regular traffic of the streets, which are generally too narrow to admit of a double line, or even sidings; the crossings might be allowed in some places. Then the fellows on horseback, blowing their horns, and galloping before the carriages, with the generally crowded state of the streets, causes a scene of indescribable uproar. What the Government or Municipality ought to have done was to allow tramways to be made only through some of the leading streets, up one and down another in regular succession, as there is not room for curves. Something will have to be done in order to mitigate the existing evils, which really neutralise a great portion of the advantage tramways are intended to afford. A London population would not allow such a system of tramways to exist for twenty-four hours, but Argentines are a very patient people in some things. As regards the condition of the streets themselves, I can say nothing more than that they are a perfect abomination and a standing disgrace to the many noble buildings in them. The brute creation are the worst off, as the flagged parapets admit of bipeds getting along with tolerable comfort; but it would break the hearts of the Society for the Prevention of Cruelty to Animals to see the way in which the poor horses are treated here. The next provincial loan raised ought to be specially devoted to the paving and sewerage of the streets—the latter becoming annually more urgent, if the city is not to be converted into a pest house. I understand Government is about to undertake this necessary work themselves, the tenders for it having differed so widely in amount as to render it almost impossible to do it by contract. Governor Castro has got his work carved out in this and other respects for the entire period of his office, and confidence is felt that he will prove equal to the occasion. Considerable sensation prevailed in the city yesterday, in consequence of the assemblage of a large number of people at the Government House to demand (for it could be called nothing else) the pardon of a wretched criminal, who was to have been executed to-day for the barbarous murder of his wife. The movement was set on foot by *The Tribuna*, the leading journal here; and the well-known editor, Mr. Hector Varela, addressed the Governor, who, after retiring to consider or consult his colleagues, consented to commute the sentence of death. This is one of the mischievous results of what may be called mob government and outside pressure; but, as it has become the fashion at home, we need not be surprised at its exercise here. It is the more to be regretted, as the two late executions of murderers had afforded satisfaction, as an earnest that they would not be allowed to escape scot-free in future. It may be, as it is contended, that the sentence on this wife-murderer was a severe one; but a pardon under such circumstances will tend to encourage the sickly sentimentality of those who protest against capital punishment, but can tolerate the perpetration of crimes for which the death of the culprit is the least atonement that can be offered. To do away with capital punishment in countries like these would be virtually to condone, if not to encourage assassination.

I went to take a look at the Boca and Barracas railway to-day, where the new viaduct has been lately erected, running a mile in length from the Custom House along the margin on the shore, which was subject to injury from the flood. It is constructed entirely of iron, the numerous columns screwed down, with a double set of girders at the top, on which the rails are to be bolted. The rest will be quite open, and only space for the carriages to traverse, conveying a sense of danger, though not so in reality. It is a single line, which is now being continued on from Barracas to Ensenada, the latter looked upon as the future port of Buenos Ayres; but it will require a long time before that project can be carried out, as the vested interests in property in the city are too strong to admit of such a change, however beneficial it might be to shipping. Various schemes for making docks and improving the port are projected, but the amount of money involved is too considerable to be easily dealt with, and other urgent requirements, such as paving and sewerage, are a primary consideration. The Boca line is valuable in connection with the traffic of the port, and it will no doubt eventually be joined to the Northern Railway, having a central station somewhere on the beach.

Monday, September 19th.—The city has been wild with excitement to-day in consequence of the arrival of the French steamer at Monte Video, whence telegrams have been passing all day, one contradictory of the other; but the letters and newspapers to be delivered to-morrow will give more or less a real statement of affairs. So far as can be made out of the telegrams from Lisbon to the 29th August, it looks like a siege or occupation of Paris. At the same time people do not believe the French cause is hopeless. There are so many French and Germans here that it is like "fighting the battle over again," and all must be decided whilst they are speculating on the event. Local politics and local troubles sink quite into the shade contrasted with such portentous events in Europe, but it cannot be denied that the National Government have quite enough on their hands in Entre Rios and the uncertainty as to the struggle in the Banda Oriental. This may account for the extraordinary rejection by Congress—for its postpone-

ment to another session is tantamount to that—
of the very advantageous offer made by Messrs.
J. Thomson, T. Bonar and Co., of London, to
establish a National Bank in the country, which
one would have thought so congenial to the professed views of progress; but "truth is stronger
than fiction," and at the very time Congress is
voting millions of money for railway extension
they deprive themselves of an institution so
eminently calculated to assist them in carrying
out projects of this kind, some of which, in my
humble opinion, are of very premature conception,
one in particular just passed—called the Santiago
Railway Concession—being looked upon as little
better than a joke. If the legislators of the
Argentine Republic do not exercise more judgment
and discretion in the passing of measures they will
seriously injure themselves in the eyes of European
capitalists, who are quite able to "separate the
tares from the wheat" in such cases as these. There
is sadly too much personal intrigue at work, which,
like the dog in the fable, leads occasionally to
dropping the substance for the shadow. I believe
the Government were most anxious to have carried
this National Bank project, and very wisely, as an
influx of foreign capital must be of great benefit
to the country. The labours of the session will
now soon close.

September 20th.—People have been busy to-day
digesting the war news received by the French

mail, but without feeling much wiser as to the final result. There is a report that the Emperor had destroyed himself, but it cannot be traced to any credible source, and is not believed. A grand ceremony at the Cathedral to-day, celebrating the obsequies of the late Archbishop of this Province, who recently died at Rome. A very large attendance, the President and Governor Castro, with all the *élite* of the city. The ladies muster very strong on these occasions, all dressed in black, with their characteristic mantillas. The display of carriages was great, that of the President reminding one of the Lord Mayor going in state, only the ornaments were silver gilt instead of gold.

September 23rd.—The Pacific steamer, homeward bound, is expected at Monte Video on the 24th, so I leave my despatches to be forwarded by her. The outward bound one is due about the same time, but the telegraph wires are again cut, and news is only brought over by the steamers which leave Monte Video in the evening. It is looked for with feverish impatience, as likely to decide the future course of events in Europe, where two immense armies are only waiting the signal to recommence their mutual slaughter. It is a sickening subject, and the world will rejoice to see it at an end. Whilst I am writing at the Hotel de la Paix the clatter of the bells of "La Merced" church, which is close to, is enough to drive all coherent thoughts from one's head. Two or three times a day, and for an hour or more in succession, does this frightful jingle go on, in connection with the ceremonies of the church, I suppose; but in no Catholic city in the world did I ever hear such a prolonged nuisance, which ought to be put a stop to. Some half-dozen bells, great and small, go hammering as hard as they can, without the semblance of time or tune, but simply to make as loud and discordant a noise as possible.

I am leaving to-morrow for Rosario and Cordova, from whence I hope to send some interesting details respecting the Central Argentine Railway, its condition and prospects, as also a brief account of the progress making in colonization. I shall also be able to form an impartial judgment as to Mr. Henly's colony, about which so many different reports are current; but "seeing is believing." He has had many unforeseen difficulties to contend with, but, so far as I can judge or know of his movements, he is honestly endeavouring to fulfil the engagements he entered into at home.

Rosario, 25th September.—We left Buenos Ayres yesterday by the San Fernando Railway at 10 a.m. for the Tigre. Mr. Crabtree, the manager, kindly afforded every facility. I was glad to observe the improved condition of the line, the station works being enlarged and evident signs of progress in traffic arrangements, with several new carriages costing £1000 each, whose services were only occasionally called into requisition; so the public cannot complain that the company does not strive to meet their requirements. In this case, as in many others, patience is likely to be rewarded; and the line must become a valuable property, especially if the company will afford facilities to steam traffic by extending their rails to the Lujan River, thus overcoming the difficulty of the little creek which at present cramps the movements of steamers. Want of means was a sufficient reason when I was last here; but this cannot now be pleaded, nor does it require more than common observation on the spot to show how much the Northern Railway Company would gain by the proposed extension to the Lujan, a matter of a few hundred yards. We embarked on board the new steamer Capitan, a fine paddle-wheel boat, built by Messrs. Robertson and Ely, of Glasgow, expressly for passengers and mails, as she carries no cargo. Her engines are of 120 horse power, oscillating cylinders, and capable of great speed; more so in my opinion than the navigation to Rosario requires, as a night must be spent upon it under any circumstances. Nothing can be more comfortable than the accommodation on this boat, which is commanded by an old Birkenhead acquaintance, Captain Davies, who has been here since the year 1854, having brought out the steamer Menai (as engineer), belonging to the then South American Steam Navigation Company, which may be truly said to have been the pioneer of steam navigation in the river. Passing over the line from the Retiro station I observed many new buildings, and an extension of country residences, forming in fact a continuous suburb of Buenos Ayres, and if the railway is rendered subservient to the wants of the locality it must prove a very lucrative concern; but, if this enlarged view of things is not taken by the company, opposition may arise that would seriously interfere with its traffic receipts. The main station will shortly be on the beach, near to the Plaza Victoria, the Western Railway having already their branch line made, extending in the same direction; and these, uniting with the Boca and Barracas line, will form the future central termini of Buenos Ayres railways.

Navigating through the Capitan (after which the steamer is called), with the waters so low as at present, is not an easy task, requiring time and patience; but all obstacles were finally surmounted, and we emerged into the wider Parana. It is curious to see, at this period of early spring here, the willow trees in full leaf for miles, overhanging the narrow tortuous channel of the Capitan, while the trees of a larger growth are entirely bare and apparently dead; but the first fall of rain, followed by sunshine, will bring them into vitality, and the islands then become one mass of verdure. We stopped at the Parana entrance to the Capitan to send off a boat with a beacon to be laid down to mark it, being so extremely narrow and hidden that if the weather be at all thick it is difficult to distinguish it.

Up the Parana to Rosario has been so often described as to render repetition unnecessary. After a capital dinner I came on deck once more to gaze on its still waters under a bright starlight, but the cold piercing wind soon sent me below. We had a considerable number of passengers on board, amongst them some old aquaintances, including Colonel Mansilla, Major Rickard, and Mr. Grigor, the latter two gentlemen going up to Santa Fe in connection with the colonization enterprise of Messrs. J. Thomson, T. Bonar & Co., lately alluded to. The large English element out here may be easily judged by the number of passengers travelling in this direction. At daylight we landed passengers at San Nicolas, and at 10 a.m. on Sunday morning we moved alongside the new ground (for it cannot at present be called a wharf), which has been covered in since I was last in Rosario in 1868. It saves all trouble of boating, and a few years more will see a fine pier extending the length of the harbour of Rosario. Vessels of all nations were at anchor, and Her Majesty's steamer Beacon came in soon after us. On the high ground near to Rosario is Dr. Alvear's very fine "quinta," possessing a large estate behind it.

In 1853, when I first visited Rosario, it was little more than a village; in 1868 it had become a very large town; and now its borders are again greatly enlarged, the streets being all well paved, lighted with gas, and buildings erected, or in course of erection, quite equal to any in Buenos Ayres. No doubt the war in Paraguay and the large traffic carried on from Rosario have contributed to this prosperity, combined with the opening of the Central Argentine Railway through to Cordova; but there must be an inherent vitality in the position of the place that has led to such great and notable progress. The streets are wider and better paved than in Buenos Ayres, although it must be admitted that the traffic over them is much less. The drawback just now is the long prevalence of dry weather, which makes dust in the ascendant, and the surrounding country looks brown and dried up, the river also being lower than most people remember it. The gas works, which had partly tumbled down when last I was here, have been resuscitated, and are now in full swing; in fact, "go a-head" has been the order of the day. The civil war in Entre Rios exercises a prejudicial effect on everything just now, otherwise there would be much more activity both here and in the upper provinces. The weather here continues very dry and terribly dusty, and the camp I fear will suffer much unless rain comes soon. The river keeps falling, which must render navigation difficult, and the islands in front of Rosario look very brown and bare of vegetation. This place now swarms with Englishmen, a large number of whom are connected with the Henly colony.

ROSARIO TO CORDOVA.

Cordova, September 28th.—Arrived here last night, and drove to the Hotel de la Paz. A peep outside this morning was enough to satisfy me that I was in the centre of South America. The number and antiquity of the churches, convents, and other religious establishments, the unpaved, sandy streets, the type and costume of the people, with a large mixture of Indians and Gauchos, all marked the difference which a few hundred miles from the sea coast makes; at the same time the sound of the railway whistle is heard here at last, together with the presence of the telegraph wire; and close to the hotel is a tramway laid, I fancy in the direction of the railway station, but which I have yet to explore. Unfortunately the long continuance of dry weather converts the sand into fine dust, and makes locomotion rather disagreeable, and it is a hot sultry day; otherwise I believe the atmosphere is generally pure and healthy. The silence that reigns, as contrasted with the noise and bustle over the paved streets of Buenos Ayres and Rosario, presents a remarkable contrast, and it is a rest to the nervous system.

We started from Rosario at six a.m., having the advantage of being accompanied by Mr. Cooper, the railway manager, and his family; a bitterly cold morning. There was only one passenger carriage, with some twelve or fifteen covered waggons and trucks conveying merchandize, as there is not yet sufficient inducement to run passenger trains only; but no doubt this will come, and a journey of 250 miles, that now occupies some fifteen hours, will be done in little more than half that time. To the right of the line, a short distance out of Rosario, Captain Thompson (who is established in business there, and acts as Vice-Consul during the absence of Mr. Hutchinson) has built himself a very pretty cottage, looking over and down the river, and numerous other buildings have been erected near to the station since my last visit. At Roldan station we had some detention, to discharge cargo, amongst which was a pipe of wine, requiring rather delicate handling. Soon after, we passed the new colony of Bernstadt, belonging to the railway, where some hundreds of Swiss emigrants are now established. The colony covers a considerable space of ground, laid out in squares, after the custom of the country; the clergyman's residence is conspicuous amongst the numerous buildings already erected, and a good deal of work is going on—such as making ditches and fences to keep off the cattle, ploughing, planting trees, &c.; but it will take some time before there is any great show for the money expended. Flags were flying from several houses about the head-quarters of the colony, which altogether wore a cheerful aspect, and I believe it is progressing most favourably. The quality of the land is evidently such as will reward the labour of the husbandman. After passing the colony we launched into the open camp, or sea of land, as it is very appropriately called, the usual number of cattle, horses, and sheep roaming over the immense space; but I noticed a diminution in the number of flocks of sheep, for the simple reason they will not pay. At Carcaranal station a new building is in course of erection, and several new estancias are to be seen along the lines. Approaching the station of Canada de Gomez the excellent model farm of Mr. Krell is seen, with its numerous buildings, and abutting on the road is a crop of wheat well up and very forward for the season. We here left Mr. Wheelwright's housekeeper, with two of the maid servants, coming to spend a few days at Mr. Krell's farm; and much they appeared to enjoy the prospect of their out. The station of Canada de Gomez is unaltered; but the stationmaster, who had been long here, and was building a good-sized house to serve for an hotel, died only a few days back, leaving a wife and family, who, I believe, will remain on the spot. He was an old sea captain, and is very much regretted. The breakfast of roast partridges, which I had looked forward to with so much interest, was missing, the reason alleged being that it was not the season for them; so we had to be content with some good coffee, home-made bread, and very good cheese made in the country. Tortugas station is still a very miserable one. Afterwards comes the dreary distance to Leones station, between which we saw some ostriches, and in many places the camp grass was on fire—an operation which the dry weather facilitates, new grass afterwards springing up of a better quality. At Frayle Muerto (now called Bellville, and a large, complete station) we stopped to partake of a very satisfactory travelling dinner, and learnt by telegram the war news, announcing a continued defeat of the French, the surrender of McMahon with 120,000 men—that Napoleon was a prisoner, Bazaine routed, several French generals killed, and Paris invested by the Prussians. It appears scarcely credible, such a succession of disasters never having befallen any great nation in modern times. Speaking of telegrams, the company have now got the wires through to Cordova, the National Government are about to put up their own, and the Transandine Company are progressing with their wires across the Andes to Chili; so the link between the Atlantic and Pacific will soon be complete. After Bellville we came to Ballesteros, where a new station is also being built, and arrived at the now extensive station of Villa Maria, to which place only the line was opened when I was last here, and then called Villa Neuva, where I spent a very pleasant day, visiting the farm of Yucat, described in my book. This has become a place of very considerable traffic,—indeed grown into a small town, about which numbers of bullock carts are collected to convey merchandize to the adjoining districts, after bringing in their produce. A large number of people were collected on the platform, and the train stopped some time. Leaving Villa Maria, the line traverses an extensive forest, after which there is a dead level plain, like a chess-board, to Chanares station, so called from the kind of trees growing near. Between this and Laguna Grande it became dark, so I leave a description of this portion of the line for my down trip. At the Rio Segundo station, where there is an iron bridge upwards of 1,200 feet in length, we were detained some time, but finally reached Cordova station soon after nine p.m., where we found plenty of carriages in attendance, with the usual bustle of a terminal station.

THE CITY OF CORDOVA.

A day's ramble over Cordova does not impress one favourably. There is much of the antique, with few modern innovations at present; and the churches one has heard so much of are clumsy masses of architecture, mostly in an unfinished state. As to the sierras, or mountains, they were not visible to-day for the dust, and it requires an elevated position to see them to any advantage. The shops are poor, and the merchandize in them, so far as one could judge, is very old-fashioned. Some good two-storied houses have been lately erected, amongst which figures conspicuously that of the Argentine Bank and the Hotel de la Paz. There is a tolerably large square, which seems to be in course of renovation; and the famed Alameda, or public walk is pretty, with its water and willow trees. The middle of the day was hot and sultry, followed by a thunder storm and a few drops of rain—the latter being sadly wanted to impart freshness to vegetation. The preparations for the exhibition, about which there has been so much disappointment, are progressing; but I shall judge better on going over them and the grounds tomorrow. It is close to the Alameda, and if the intention is properly carried out it ought to be of much benefit to the old city by an infusion of new ideas, as well as bringing people from distant provinces to meet together, compare notes, and exhibit their different productions. I hear the serenos (watchmen) calling out the hour (10 o'clock), reminding one so much of the old "Charlie" nuisance, being also as useless probably as those worthies were in the early part of the present century. In other respects "a solemn silence reigns."

October 1st.—We had an expedition yesterday, accompanied by some friends in a carriage and on horseback, to visit an estancia some ten miles distant, at the foot of the Cordova range of hills, called the Soldan, belonging to Señor Don Martin Allendi. The first thing on leaving the city is to cross the River Primero, now very low, but at times it must be difficult to ford. The bottom of the river is strewed with loose stones, as well as for some distance on the other side of the Barranca, after mounting which we come upon the open camp, where only a few stunted trees were to be seen, with some few ranchos, or cottages, scattered at intervals, very like gipsy encampments. The road, which is good enough for equestrians, is rather trying to carriage springs, and the team or horses required no small amount of skill on the part of the driver to keep the vehicle out of mischief. We rather skirted the sierra to the right, an hour and a-half's drive bringing us within sight of a large, low, white building, prettily situated, which proved to be our destination. Our visit was quite unexpected, but we were very cordially received, shown over the estancia, and soon sat down to a good and ample breakfast, for we had started early to avoid the heat of the sun. The house is built on a slight eminence, close to the stream which winds round it, and on the left bank is a splendid walnut tree, not yet fully in leaf, affording an agreeable shade. After irrigating the lands near, the stream falls into a deep gorge amongst rocks, forming a cascade, which in the wet season swells into a torrent, and joins the River Primero on its way to Cordova. From the front of the house is a fine view of the sierra, stretching away north and south, respecting the metallic formation and auriferous nature of which I shall have more to say. After spending some hours rambling about and enjoying ourselves in real pic-nic fashion, we returned to Cordova, of whose numerous old churches we had a fine view, and a splendid sunset behind the mountains.

Cordova, 2nd October.—Reverting to my trip to Soldan Estancia, I omitted to notice the crops in the ground, which looked very strong and healthy, and they also grow very good tobacco. Indeed, there is hardly any agricultural produce, either European or tropical, that cannot be grown here with a little care and attention. It is only a short time since this estancia has been in possession of its present owners, who have done a great deal in the way of fencing and enclosing the land, and certainly they have great advantages in the way of irrigation; but the defect you generally meet with in this country is the want of practical farm labourers, the natives being born and bred to pastoral pursuits or to live on horseback. On the way to and from the Soldan we met many bullock carts, as well as troops of horses conveying produce to the city, or merchandize up the country. The railway has not been open long enough to test the amount of traffic likely to find its way to it, but there can be no doubt that it will increase and multiply as railway facility becomes better known and appreciated at a distance. Already it is making a quiet revolution against which ignorance and superstition must vanish. No city in the world has been more under the influence of the latter feeling than Cordova, having been almost excluded from what was passing in the outer world; but this enemy to progress is about to give way before the onward march of the iron road. It is a pretty sight to look at Cordova from the high tower of the Hotel de la Paz, surrounded by an amphitheatre of hills with a back view of the mountains. The Jesuit founders of this city were excellent judges in the way of selecting a *locale*, nor was it possible to make a better choice of site. There is wood, water, marble, and every requisite for founding a city and affording it the means of subsistence; a fine climate, with a pure temperature, although hot at certain seasons of the year. Now the great want is rain, which prevails from this to Buenos Ayres. There are twelve churches in the city with the cathedral, which is an immense pile, some with monasteries and nunneries attached, possessing household property and large tracts of land; but the tide of progress is sweeping onward, and will soon overtake this former stronghold of priestly sway. Religious ceremonies are, meanwhile closely observed, constant services going on, with ringing of bells; and yesterday there was a procession through the streets of one of the images, attended by the troops; in fact, the chief business of the place seems to be carried on in the churches; but, as I before observed, the railway whistle is now heard through the city, and the electric wire has reached it. Its future lies in these two modern pioneers and the influx of foreign labour.

Speaking of the railway reminds me to record my visit to the station, which for the present consists of a wooden shed about 200 feet long, the

CITY OF CORDOVA.

north end being used for a booking and telegraph office, the remainder for merchandize. The ground on which it stands is a raised bed of sand several feet high, forming (with additional space, also to be covered) the site of the permanent station, which will be on a scale commensurate with its importance. At present all is bare and awkward, simply a temporary makeshift, like what existed at Rosario when I was there in 1868. The position of the station is convenient, having the river on one side and the city close to on the other. The line takes a sharp curve a few hundred yards after leaving the station, crosses a gap by an iron bridge, and then goes through a deep cutting, with a rise of 1 in 50 until it reaches the top of the barranca or bank, and has a straight course to the Rio Segundo, about twenty miles distant. The site of the station appears to me admirably chosen; but, owing to land difficulties, it cannot be carried on quite far enough. Railways in this part of South America are a novelty, nor do people readily part with their land to assist their movements, however valuable its proximity is to them hereafter—like many other Shylocks at home, they want their pound of flesh. Traffic has been slack since the opening of the line, owing to various causes, amongst which may be noticed the civil war in Entre Rios, and the great butchery now going on in Europe between civilized nations, which produces its effect even in these remote regions, paralysing business transactions. There can, however, be no doubt as to the future; and as regards passengers, it appears to me that it would be good policy to run a passenger train once a day between Rosario and Cordova at reduced rates, so as to encourage travelling, which at present is only undertaken from necessity. The opening of the Cordova Exhibition would be a good time to try the experiment, as it is likely to bring the line into more general and familiar use. At present, to travel 247 miles in fifteen hours, for £3 first-class and 32s. second-class, appears high for the country, although there is a deduction of 25 per cent. for return tickets. It is just a question of policy, and to run a passenger train through once a day may come under this category. No doubt all these things will be duly considered and weighed by the directors and managers of the line, as they have better data to go upon than I have; only, as a topic of outside conversation, I think it as well to allude to the subject. Starting at six a.m. and arriving at nine p.m. involves many inconveniences in a country like this; at the same time the railway managers have to look at the financial part of the case. Of course produce and goods constitute the chief receipts, passenger traffic holding at present quite a secondary position in the scale. Another alternative would be to make a two-days' easy journey of it, goods and passenger train mixed as at present, and building a good, roomy hotel at

Villa Maria or Bellville; then passengers could take their time and enjoy themselves; and certainly travelling at night on these open lines is not unattended with risk.

I now come to an inspection of the new exhibition ground and buildings, which are deserving of a special notice, not only from the public interest attached to them, but also their intrinsic merit. The site selected is close to the Alameda, itself a very picturesque spot. It was, I believe, once a garden and orchard, having the advantage of grown-up trees. The space occupied is between 14 and 15 acres, lying close behind the high barranca (or hill) which forms the south side of the enclosure, with a pure mountain stream running through its whole extent, affording every facility for irrigation and any amount of water power. At the west end there will be a building for foreign exhibitors; next comes the great central hall for native productions, about 500 feet long by 75 feet wide, with central projections. The height is considerable, with plenty of light and ventilation, but very little glass, which in this country is expensive. The roof will be of zinc, and on the whole the effect, when completed, will be very pretty. As the building is entirely wood every possible precaution is taken to guard against fire, by means of forcing pumps placed under the floorings, ready at any moment to be put in operation, besides several fire engines about the grounds. Next came the ornamental works, such as a large glass conservatory filled with choice plants, a large aviary, ornamental fountains, and other things we are familiar with in Europe, but never before seen in this country. There are shady walks, grottos, bowers, and all sorts of agreeable surprises, terminating at the extreme end in a rustic-built refreshment room, near to which is a space of ground to be set apart for dancing, an enjoyment of which all South Americans are fond; but I do not know what the numerous priesthood, monks, and nuns may say to such innovations. The whole south side of the enclosure is a high, and at present, rough-looking bank that will be laid out to suit rustic ideas; and at the top is to be placed the observatory about to be erected by Mr. Gould, the American astronomer, in the service of the Argentine Government. The people of Cordova and its visitors will be astonished at the terrestrial paradise provided for them; and it is to be hoped the collection of the native and foreign productions will correspond with the efforts made to show everything off to advantage, in which the services of Mr. Henry Zimmerman and Mr. Shaw are conspicuous. Mr. Shaw is the son of the former worthy manager of the City of Dublin Company, long since retired into private life. I ought to allude to the beautifully green grass plots, all sown with English seed, and kept fresh by means of irrigation during this very long continuance of dry weather. Great taste has been shown in laying out the ornamental grounds, as well as in the construction of the buildings attached to them; the large one, undertaken by a Yankee contractor about 21 years of age, had everything brought out ready-made to be put up.

October 6th, 1870.—The more one rambles over this old city the greater the surprise at the massive nature of its buildings, particularly the churches, convents, monasteries, &c., some few of which are in ruins, others never completed; but those which have been completed remain as wonderful monuments of Jesuit industry and perseverance, for these edifices and institutions are worthy the work of that remarkable body of men who laid the foundation of civilization in South America. Where the labour or the money came from to raise such huge piles may well be asked, and so many of them within so small a space; the buildings themselves being sufficient to contain even the present population of Cordova, and the bells all within sound of each other. Where could be the requirements for a dozen churches in so limited a city? The only explanation is that the people absolutely lived in the churches, monastic buildings, or nunneries, and the few outsiders who carried on the ordinary business of life were obliged to conform to the general rule. I paid a visit to the university attached to the old church of the order of Jesus, belonging especially to the Jesuit order.

The outside of this building is in an unfinished state; but the inside consists of immense vaulted roofs, all gilded and ornamented after the fashion of the time, and they present quite an imposing appearance with the highly-ornamented altar at the extreme end. Below the church is an extensive vault, where the remains of the brotherhood were deposited. Outside are the Jesuit arms. The university is a large building founded by Dr. Don. Frai Fernando Trefoi Zambria, of the University of San Carlos, in Cordova, in the year 1613; and his portrait is hung in the lecture room, where also the examination of pupils takes place. It is a very good-sized room, with every accommodation, and a raised pulpit in the centre for the president. The university is under extensive repair, with a new library, to which the old volumes are being removed. It contains many old valuable works, and when completed will be a credit to the city. We visited the different schools of instruction where the boys were at work, one of design and painting, the professor being an old Portuguese, who has resided here for twenty years. He is now engaged on a large allegorical picture representing the downfall of Lopez, the Dictator of Paraguay, on his way to a certain unmentionable place, the foreground being occupied with numerous figures, showing the triumph of the Argentines, a locomotive engine drawn up in the square fronting the cathedral and the old Cabildo, now used as the

CITY OF CORDOVA.

Government House. The picture is not without merits in design and colouring, but of course somewhat high flown in character. The busts of General Mitre and President Sarmienta occupy the top of the picture. There are departments of science, with numerous modern instruments, such as large galvanic batteries, barometers, thermometers, and instruments of various kinds. Considerable sums of money must have been expended in this way, and it is very creditable to the city to have initiated such institutions for the advancement of the rising generation. Some very old houses are being modernized, and active building operations appear to be going on throughout the city; but, as a rule, there are few people who can be called rich as regards ready money, although they own large tracts of unproductive land. On the other hand, there is a large amount of poverty and wretchedness visible in the numerous hovels on the Barranca which skirts the city, which is said to contain 30,000 inhabitants, though I can scarcely believe in that number. The climate is changeable, in winter severly cold and in summer very hot; but the air is generally clear, except when clouded with the dust of the city. The moonlight nights just now are very beautiful and cool contrasted with the heat of the day. The want of rain is of course a great drawback, otherwise in this season of spring it would be much more agreeable. It looks like a continuance of dry weather, which must be very injurious to the growing crops. To-day the sun is scorchingly hot, but the thermometer not much above 70 in the shade, which shows the temperature must be influenced by the cool breezes from the mountains coursing over the plains. It is a dry rather than a moist heat, causing less perspiration than in Brazil, though I question if the climate is more healthy, as the death rate of this city is very high—as much as 75 to the thousand at times; caused, I fancy, by the want of proper food and nourishment, as well as the miserable hovels so many of the population live in.

Strange enough Madamoiselle Patti, the singer, with her corps, are expected here to-night, to give a few performances. We have followed in her track, and have been in the same hotel ever since our arrival in Brazil; but we hardly expected to have fallen in with her here after her having returned from Rosario to Buenos Ayres, as it is a long way to come back, some 500 miles, for two or three more concerts. Perhaps she wishes to see the far-famed city of Cordova, and I hope she will not be disappointed; but I understand the theatre is a wretched little place. Quite an ovation is preparing for her at the Hotel de la Paz, where we are staying. The train was late this evening, but Patti arrived at the Hotel amidst a shower of rockets, with a band of music accompanying her on an omnibus and sundry carriages. The people rushed into the hotel with her *en masse*, as they do not stand on much ceremony here, and there was quite a scene of confusion; but all is now settling down again, and the songstress will be allowed to take a rest in the heart of South America, after her long journey. A splendid night, cool, and with a temperature strongly in contrast to the heat of the day.

October 7th.—To-day has been a most disagreeable one—blowing a gale—a regular pampero. The city was enveloped in a cloud of dust, at times so great as to obscure the churches, which are such conspicuous objects, towering far above other buildings. The clouds gathered, and it looked very like a thunder storm, but it passed over without the much-required rain. The heat was intense, as all doors and windows had to be closed to keep out the dust, which nevertheless finds its way, and covers every article of furniture. I expect we shall hear of a storm at Buenos Ayres. Considering that this is a quiet-going kind of place, the noises are remarkable during the day, and even before daylight the church bells are always at work, and at night the screech of the owl-like watchman disturbs one's slumbers. Then at daybreak and sunset the drums and bugles of the soldiers add to the chorus, together with the crowing of innumerable cocks, so that one is literally dinned. The garrison comprises some 300 recruits or volunteers, who are tolerably well drilled and exercised amid clouds of dust. Their uniform is a dark blue, the arms and accoutrements clean, with glittering bayonets, altogether a respectable turn out. I was amused on one occasion to see the commanding officer seated on a chair in front of his house, watching the marching past. Telegraphic news arrived to-day, with the account of France being declared a Republic, the names of the new Government, and that Thiers was appointed Minister to the Court of St. James—what a change in a few months! It also stated that 300,000 men were marching to defend Paris, but everything leads to the conviction there would be an early peace.

There are two large enclosed markets, north and south of the city, with an extent of accommodation much greater than is required at present, the display of wares being very meagre, even of vegetables or fruit; which is the more surprising, as every species of the latter can be grown within easy reach of the city. The fact is, that hitherto there has been no incentive to industry, the sleepy system pervading everything and everybody. That the people themselves are naturally industrious and hard-working I quite believe, from the symptoms visible, but they have never had encouragement to exert themselves, or any stimulus to industry; consequently the advantages bestowed on them by nature are not turned to account. Of their honesty and quiet disposition there can be no doubt, as

CITY OF CORDOVA.

strangers can travel through the country with perfect safety, treasure itself being conveyed without an escort. It is true that until recently the Indians have been troublesome in some districts, but the measures of government, and above all, an influx of population, will soon put a stop to their incursions. As civilization advances, barbarism must give way, and the Indians themselves fall into its track. The manner in which a few Jesuits converted and rendered them subservient to their own purposes is a proof of what may be done with a simple-minded people, dealt with in a proper spirit. The enormous masses of buildings in South America, such as churches, convents, and nunneries, were chiefly raised by Indian labour, under a species of coercion or slavery it is true, but this became greatly mitigated, until finally entire freedom was established throughout the old colonies of Spain.

October 8th.—The dust storm and great heat of yesterday were followed last night by rather a heavy thunderstorm, with some rain and hail, sufficient only to lay the dust, but bringing about a cooler state of the atmosphere, which renders locomotion much more agreeable. Indeed, it is a beautifully fine day. The lightning was very vivid and the thunder occasionally loud, but nothing to what prevails in some parts of Brazil. It is almost day, and the bells are going furiously. I believe I alluded to the tramway laid down from the exhibition buildings to the railway station, which traverses the whole length of the city from east to west, and is very substantially made. I conclude it will be used for passenger traffic during the exhibition, as it would be a great convenience in this way. I also notice that most of the large warehouses for the deposit of produce and merchandize have a narrow gauge tramway, with small trucks running through them to facilitate moving goods about—a great saving in labour. We might imitate some things in England to advantage. There is not much outside show in the shops, but some of these will bear looking over. I have come to the conclusion that the reason one sees so few of the male sex issuing from the churches is that they remain at home to mind their business. They are certainly very industrious, as whenever I pass the tailors, shoemakers (for which latter Cordova is famed), or other places of labour they are always hard at work, early or late, and shopping itself seems to be chiefly carried on in the evening. The numerous operations now going on must occupy many labourers, who are anything but idle; indeed, I see less of this propensity here than any place in South America I was ever in.

THE SIERRAS OF CORDOVA.—This range of hills, which rises abruptly a few miles to the westward of the city, extends nearly north and south for a distance of some 300 miles, forming a picturesque background to it. They stand out quite alone, and distinct from any of the Andine chain, as, after crossing them, the level plains continue more or less as before towards the province of San Juan. That the hills abound with valuable minerals has long been known, but very little has been done towards exploring them. Iron in a very pure state has lately been found, and copper; latterly some excitement has been caused by the discovery of gold, a number of young adventurers having gone to the "diggings," but with what result is not yet known. I have seen several specimens of the gold, which leaves no doubt as to its existence; but the question resolves itself into the cost of working. The presence of valuable minerals so near to a railway terminus is of course a great encouragement, and it may probably lead to some mining experiments being tried on a larger scale than heretofore. One traffic has long been in operation connected with the Sierras—that of lime, made from marble, of which there are extensive hills—and it is proposed to form a small company in order to work them to greater advantage. The quality of the lime made from marble is superior to any other, as proved when trying to make holes or windows in some of the old buildings in Cordova, which are found to be as hard as adamant. There is plenty of water power to work both these or any other mines, and attention is naturally being turned towards mining development in the district. There are several fine estancias within and about the mountains, where any kind of European fruit or vegetables can be grown, and cultivation is only limited by the absence of consumption. With the railway to Cordova, and the consequent increase of population there, the mountain districts are certain to be largely developed and availed of for country residences, as the situation is a very healthy one. Already a short railway is projected, with a sanitarium proposed to be established, under the auspices of Mr. Hutchinson, British Consul at Rosario, to whom the Government has ceded a small portion of land, which, I believe, is to be appropriated to this object. The few miles intervening between the city of Cordova and the mountains renders the latter easy of access, and a railway might be made at a very moderate cost. After travelling the long and dreary pampas, it is a great relief to sight the Sierras of Cordova, and a short sojourn amongst them must benefit both the body and the mind.

October 9th.—A very quiet Sunday, all shops closed, and no work whatever going on. An excursion train started this morning for the Rio Segundo, about 20 miles distant, I dare say many persons making a trip for the first time. It is again hot and sultry, likely to be followed by thunder, being full moon to-day. Carriages are driving about with parties, who seem to have the same taste in this way as at Buenos Ayres. Before the opening of the railway I believe there were only two or three carriages in the place, and now there are dozens. I went down to meet the train this evening, expecting a friend, and was astonished to see the number of persons there, the greater part from curiosity, and very orderly. It was a beautiful moonlight, which might induce many to go, but it is clear the novelty has not yet worn off. Many of us can remember when a similar curiosity to see the arrival of a train was evinced at home. This feeling is much preferable to stolid indifference. Both old and young thus learn to familiarize themselves with the wonders of the iron road, and certainly, as the train came thundering down the incline, with the bright lights of the locomotive, it was a sight calculated to impress itself on the minds of a sensitive people so long excluded from the benefits of modern invention. As a sign of progress I may mention that there are three daily papers published here, the *Eco de Cordova*, the *El Progreso*, *La Prenza*, and also an evening paper called the *Ferro-Carril*, the first one well edited, and all containing a certain amount of useful information. Congress has closed its labours at Buenos Ayres, one of its last acts being to vote a sum of 16,000 dollars, or £3,200, towards the expenses of the President visiting the exposition here, and for which purpose a holiday of 40 days is to be allowed him. The National Legislature, as in other countries, can be lavish enough in some things and parsimonious enough in others, but the sum voted appears reasonable enough. It also evinces the degree of interest attached to this national festival, for such it may be called, as well as an occasion for a general gathering of the provinces to exhibit their respective productions. The more I look into the subject, the more satisfied I am of the great benefit the Argentine Republic will derive from it, particularly under such favourable circumstances as the ground and the buildings will present. I notice amongst the stores in the city one belonging to Temple & Co., wherein are to be found ploughs, and other agricultural implements, besides a variety of articles suited to country and other puposes. The chief requirement is more demand for such things, which an increased population can alone bring.

Monday Evening.—I paid another visit to the Exhibition ground this afternoon, which was a scene of much activity and the work progressing fast. During the day some fine animals had arrived from Bolivia, amongst them a llama, some alpacas, several guanacos, deer, &c. Two troops of mules had also come in with productions from the distant provinces of Salta and Catamarca; in fact, before the time for opening I should not be surprised that they will have as much as they can manage.

CORDOVA TO ROSARIO.

October 12th, 1870.—We left the quaint old city of Cordova at 6.30 yesterday morning, after being called an hour too soon, and having to wait at the station three-quarters of an hour for the real time of starting. It was a glorious sunrise, the churches and church steeples glittering in the light, which also gilded the tops and sides of the mountains. Ascending the steep incline from the station, the scene behind us became very fine, of which a traveller arriving by night is deprived; the whole valley of the river Primero spread out, with the city in the centre. It is, in fact, a complete basin. The cutting is long and steep, with an incline I think of one in fifty, but once reaching the top it is again almost a dead level. Between Cordova and Rio Primero there is a good deal of wood. The bridge over this river is some 1,200 feet long, and a fine piece of workmanship. The river is now dry, but after heavy rains becomes much swollen. Our train was a light one, and we had almost a gale of wind behind us the greater part of the way, with a glaring hot sun and plenty of dust. I need not describe the other part of the road. At Bellville

Station, which we reached about 1.30, we found the up train arrived, the two together creating quite a bustle; but this did not prevent our getting a very good railway dinner at a moderate cost. We reached Rosario about 9 p.m., and found a hospitable reception at the residence of Mr. Wheelwright, where Mrs. Krell, his daughter, still remained, previous to joining her father and mother at Buenos Ayres by the steamer of to-day, when all the family embark for England. As the Fates would have it, however, we were disappointed, the steamer not having yet arrived, and we fear may not leave till to-morrow, which loses a day when most wanted. It appears the water was too low for her to get out of the little insignificant Tigre, an additional argument for the railway being extended to the Lujan, where there is plenty of water at all times.

I availed of the opportunity early this morning to visit the railway station with its numerous buildings and workshops, most of which are very solidly built, and I think I have before mentioned that the station is nearly three-quarters of a mile in length, a considerable width, walled in on the land side and the two ends, but open to the river frontage, where there is deep water. To cover this large area of ground is a work of time; but already a great deal is done, and when finished it will be by far the finest station in South America, as well as the most convenient. The carriage sheds are the first entered, comprising a treble roof, where I counted seven large carriages in a row, preparing for work. They come from the United States, are handsomely fitted up, and hold about 60 passengers each. The company has twelve passenger carriages, twelve locomotives, and a large amount of rolling stock, for which it is to be hoped there will soon be ample use. The general passenger station and offices will be built in front of the sheds, close to the main entrance. On the right, nearer to the river bank, are the temporary wooden sheds for goods, where the covered waggons discharge and load, connected by sidings with the main line. On the left are the workshops for carpenters, mechanists, engineering, repairing; in fact, everything required to keep the locomotives and rolling stock in order. There is a steam engine, with engine-house, on a very solid scale, and my old friend, the brickmaking machine, occupies the extreme end of the station, the latter doing its work I believe in a very satisfactory manner. There is a large collection of material on the ground, such as rails, iron sleepers, timber, and coal; indeed, all that can be required to work a first-class railway of 247 miles long, dependent almost entirely on the resources within itself. It will probably be another year or two before all is in perfect order, as regards station accommodation, and that at Cordova will be an affair of some magnitude; but in the meantime the traffic will keep growing, and the revenue of the company be gradually developed. I repeat the conviction I so often expressed, that this main trunk line going to the heart of the Republic is calculated to yield immense advantages to the country, and that it will also turn out a very profitable investment to shareholders. Difficulties naturally arise in working out an enterprise of this kind, where the Government itself is a large shareholder, and differences of opinion may exist as to tariff charges, but there is nothing to affect seriously the interests of the railway. I must not omit to allude to the beautiful garden attached to Mr. Wheelwright's house, which produces European fruits of every kind in perfection—apples, pears, peaches, strawberries, grapes, and figs, of which there is now a wonderful show. As to roses, it is impossible to describe their size and beauty; two or three trees, such as are now in full bloom, would carry off the first prizes at a London flower show. And all this is the work of a few years; vegetables in abundance. Towards evening rather a heavy pampero came on, preceded by clouds of dust, thunder and lightning, and then heavy rain. It was magnificent!—the dark masses of clouds and dust advancing over the plain, illuminated by constant flashes, the rushing wind, the growling thunder, and finally heavy rain, which lasted for an hour, when the storm cleared, and the night became fine, with innumerable stars. The rain will do good.

MONTE VIDEO TO RIO DE JANEIRO.

Sunday, October 16th, 1870.—We left Buenos Ayres at 6 p.m. yesterday, after receiving on board the mail and a large quantity of specie. Fine calm night, and anchored here at 7 a.m. Another Sunday's work for post office agents and writing for the mail, which might just as well have been closed and the bags ready to put on board this morning, and save just 24 hours, as we only proceed at eight o'clock to-morrow morning. It is a sheer loss of time without any object whatever, as people know exactly when the steamer will be down, and could always be ready. On calling at the Consulate I found it besieged by parties posting letters, the Consul himself and his assistants having their hands full for the day—a great hardship when so miserably paid, to say nothing of violating a national feeling against Sunday work, which even the natives of the country will not do after their fashion. "Thou shalt do no manner of work" is completely ignored in these countries by our post office arrangements. Precept and example are at direct variance, and the sooner some independent member of the House of Commons takes the matter in hand the better, separating the post office from the consular department and leaving the latter time to attend to official duties. In the case of Monte Video there are eight British postal mails to be made up during the month, namely, the Royal Mail twice a month, the Pacific Mail steamers four times a month, and Lamport and Holt's line twice; all subject to Sunday work, and the agents are miserably paid for their trouble. On the other hand, Major Munro, who so long filled the office of Vice-consul, is now made a full Consul; having, moreover, a large portion of diplomatic work to do in the absence of either a Resident Minister or Chargé d'Affaires, for all which he only receives £950 a year, a sum totally inadequate to meet the necessities of such a position in one of the most expensive cities of South America, or probably in the world. Major Munro is an old and faithful servant, has a large family, and it is a disgrace to the British Government that he should be allowed to exist on so miserable a pittance, under existing circumstances, in a place frequented by so large an amount of British shipping, and where so large an amount of British property is held, constantly exposed to the risks of civil war and to political contingencies enough to weary the patience of any man. The Consul at Buenos Ayres receives £1,500, with much lighter work, there being always a Resident Minister or Chargé d'Affaires; but this sum is little enough for Buenos Ayres, where the cost of living is also enormous. These considerations appear to have little weight with our cheeseparing Treasury; but it is to be hoped the force of public opinion will compel them to do justice to the representatives of the British nation in such expensive and difficult countries, where so large a number of our countrymen are located.

October 17th.—Reverting to Monte Video, it was a lovely day with a smooth sea, and we prepared to go on shore after breakfast to attend the English church; but suddenly a heavy fire of musketry was heard near the city, and knowing what are termed the rebels—or, in other words, the "Whites," who are out of power and want to get in—were encamped close to it, we feared some skirmish might be going on between them and the "Reds," who are in possession of Monte Video; we awaited further information, when we found the firing only proceeded from a body of Red volunteers, who were being exercised. On going on shore we found all quiet, the citizens taking advantage of the beauty of the day to ramble about; the toilettes of the ladies in particular were something stunning—velvet dresses (the favourite) in every colour, crimson, green, and blue. High Mass at the cathedral was just over and a large number pouring out from it, chiefly across the Plaza in front, where the leaves of the trees were just out, and a handsome allegorical fountain is nearly completed, but still boarded round. Inscriptions of various kinds commemorate the achievements of the Banda Oriental, but no black tablet to record the endless civil strife, or the bloody scenes with which its annals have been disgraced. No casual visitor seeing the cheerful aspect of the city could possibly suppose that fighting was constantly going on outside, or that the Government *de facto* had not a dollar in its coffers and was glad to raise a small sum for pressing wants at home at 30 per cent. interest! Yet this is the fact, and this state of things has existed more or less since the murder of General Flores, chief of the Red party, whose reign is supposed to be short. They have managed to enlist a considerable number of volunteers, and it is believed the city cannot be taken; but *quien sabe*, as they say in these countries, what to-morrow will bring forth? A compromise is spoken of, but I fear it will be a case of "Kilkenny cats;" meantime the country is being devastated by the contending parties, and commerce reduced to the narrowest limits—a sad spectacle in one of the finest spots of South America, and which with peace and quietness would be one of the most prosperous. By rather a strange coincidence we have on board, as passenger, one of the sons of the late General

Flores, who is not allowed to land at Monte Video, nor do I know his destination. His ingratitude and treachery to his father are said to have contributed to the murder of the latter, and now neither party will have anything to do with him. Whilst at anchor yesterday several friends came off to see him, amongst them his widowed mother and other relatives. Several men of war are lying in the harbour, amongst them American, French, Austrian, Brazilian, and a small English gunboat. Coming out of the harbour this morning we passed a fine French frigate under canvas, also several sailing ships. It is a beautifully clear day, with rather a fresh breeze, at present right a-head, and the atmosphere decidedly cold. Last night it was a question of great coats and cloaks, and promises to be the same to-night. We are pleased to be on board our old friend La Plata, as comfortable as ever, with the same commander and nearly all the same officers and crew. The band of music and the bugleman for meals go through the same routine, all which makes one feel very much at home. It is not the season of the year for passengers to Europe, so we are few in number, amongst us Mr. and Mrs. Wheelwright and their daughter Mrs. Krell. My departure from the River is rather hurried, having to be at Rio to complete some important business; otherwise it is now a fine season for the River, but if anything rather cold. At Rio the temperature will no doubt be warmer than when we left it. Just passed between the Island of Lobos and the mainland; several vessels sailing up and down.

October 18th.—Came on to blow fresh last night from the north-east, which still continues, with constant rain and a nasty head-sea, rendering everything as dreary as can well be imagined, and a very shy muster at the breakfast table. We passed the Agamemnon (Liverpool mail boat of the 20th September) this morning, bound to Monte Video and Buenos Ayres, with a few days' later dates. We shall hear the news at Rio, about which anxiety does not diminish, as it is feared that complications may arise with other nations if Prussia persists in taking advantage of her victories to crush the life's blood out of France.

We have a young Englishman passenger on board who has been settled some years at Bahia Blanca, where a colony of some 100 Englishmen was formed. It is interesting to hear the graphic account he gives of their first trials and difficulties, which were gradually overcome by patience and perseverance, until they now find themselves in a satisfactory position, the chief drawback being the Indians, who make occasional inroads, carrying off cattle and committing other depredations. There is only a detachment of some 20 soldiers in the little town of Bahia Blanca; but, when occasion requires, they are joined by volunteers, and they lately defeated a large body of Indians, recovering the cattle. There is a garrison of 500 men on the frontier, and the Government has promised to afford additional assistance so soon as the war in Entre Rios is over, in which case the settlement of Bahia Blanca, which now numbers about 100, promises to become a flourishing one, as other English settlers of a good class are going down there. When we contrast the success of this little colony with the failure of others in the Argentine Republic, started under so much more favourable circumstances, the conviction that it is the fault of the colonists themselves is very strong; in fact, too many have treated it as a toy or plaything instead of the serious business of a new vocation, in which personal endurance and hard work were the primary elements of success; *aide toi et Dieu t'aidera* is assuredly not the general motto of Englishmen who come to seek their fortunes, or to make a living in these countries.

October 20th.—Yesterday proved as disagreeable as before; constant head wind and sea, with misty weather, but to-day it has cleared off and looks more natural. Still our progress has been considerably retarded, and we shall not get to Rio harbour before Saturday evening, making five full days—nor could any vessel have done it in less without hard pushing. A strong current has accompanied the north-east wind, and in a small steamer it would have been a very uncomfortable work. River Plate traffic has gained immensely by the large steamers going down there, as all experience proves that this is the most unreliable part of the passage. I have met with worse weather and as bad a sea between Rio and the Plate, on the average, as I ever did crossing the much dreaded Bay of Biscay. Even after the wind has gone down there is a heavy head sea, which retarded our progress coming down in the Oneida; the wind was just as bad the other way, S.W., dead in our teeth.

Rio de Janeiro, Sunday, October 23.—As usual, nothing but Sunday work, the English community engaged in preparing papers for the La Plata, which leaves to-morrow morning, the 24th. We got into the bay early yesterday morning, and found nothing particularly new on shore—all going on quietly—although the new ministry is not expected to be very long in office; a kind of intermediate one, to announce certain measures with reference to the great question of slavery, and then to be followed by a stronger body to carry them into effect next session. The Cordillera is in with later advices from Europe; but the interest in events there is evidently diminishing, as most people consider the cause of France utterly lost, and that she will now dwindle down to a second or even a third class power, whether for the future peace and advancement of the world remains to be seen.

VISIT TO THE EMPEROR'S PALACE OF SANTA CRUZ.

I had often heard of this Imperial domain as a place well worth seeing, and Viscount de Barbacena having kindly offered to accompany me there, we left on Thursday afternoon, 27th October, at 4.30, by rail for Sappabemba, in order to avoid having to get up in the middle of the night, as the train leaves at 4.30 a.m. The weather had been wet and looked very doubtful, but we determined to risk it. At Sappabemba Station is the sugar estate of Baron de Maua. Here we got into a diligence, which landed us at a small village called Campo Grande (large plain), a distance of four miles from the station. There is rather a tumble-down barracks here, and close to a little Shoeburyness for trying heavy guns. We got tolerable quarters at a small one-storied "Casa de Pasto," with a picturesque little church in front, and after some supper took possession of a room with two sofa beds and slept soundly until daylight, when the noise of those well-known country waggon wheels, drawn by oxen, awoke us. It was so cold and damp when we arrived, we were glad to sit in our cloaks; but we found the temperature warmer in the morning, although the hills in front were loaded with moisture. Our host provided us with a really good breakfast (at which a little pig intruded itself Irish fashion), after which we started in a light carriage with four mules over a tolerably good wide road, but very sandy and heavy after the rain. The road winds amongst mountain scenery, and occasionally a large fazenda (or estate) appears in view—relics of old times, when a plentiful supply of slaves enabled the owners to cultivate large tracts of land; but the glory of most of these places has departed. At San Antonio, where a large church stands on an eminence near to the road, we changed mules, and again dashed along at a good pace until we reached the entrance gate of the palace after about two and a half hours' good driving. During the reign of Don Juan VI., when the royal family fled from Portugal, Santa Cruz was his favourite residence, the roads in those days presenting generally a scene of considerable bustle and excitement, having also large league stones placed instead of mile stones, and which still exist to mark the distance. There are eleven of them between Rio and Santa Cruz, equal to about 44 English miles. Now the route is very little travelled over, the palace never having been patronized by the present Emperor, whose only son had died here. Entering the palace gate there is a wide avenue of some length, over undulating ground, which terminates in front of the palace, forming a large open square, having rows of cottages ranged at the sides, with the palace forming the background—conspicuous from two belfrys or towers which belonged to the old Jesuits, who were driven out of Brazil by the Marquis de Pombal. The church is the centre of the palace, and remains intact as a private chapel, being built in so as to form a square mass. The position is very fine, on an eminence surrounded on three sides by beautiful green meadows, which appear to terminate at the foot of the mountain; the other, or front view, being undulating ground backed by other mountains. The full effect of the scenery comes suddenly upon you on reaching the palace, and it fully justifies the selection and taste of the Jesuit fathers who understood so well the advantages of locality. They not only built their church and settlement for their people, but drained and brought under cultivation four square leagues of land—unequalled in Brazil for fertility if it were made a proper use of. The palace has no external pretensions, but contains a large amount of accommodation, with some spacious rooms, the whole in simple, good taste; the few rooms still furnished showing what has been the general character of the interior of the building. The basement floor is entirely devoted to household or other purposes, the upper range forming a complete suite, with the chapel in the centre. We were shown over it by the keeper, a Portuguese, who has occupied his post nearly half a century, and the cleanliness and good order of the rooms certainly do him credit. Like all such important personages, he dilated without intermission on the grand doings of the old Court during his residence here, its glory having now departed. Alluding again to the view—nothing can be finer than that from the palace windows, commanding an extensive prospect over vast meadows terminated by mountains, with every variety of scenery. In the distance can be seen the village of Itagoahy, and a peep at the ocean to the left. The estate belongs to the Emperor, being held in fee simple by the royal family, to whom it is, however, quite unproductive. Formerly it possessed upwards of 2,000 slaves, but many have been liberated. The females have a peculiar custom of covering the head with a piece of black cloth, which all ages wear, together with a red petticoat, giving them much the appearance of gipsies, whom they resemble also in other respects. The superintendent of the estate, Senhor Saldanha de Gama, was absent shooting when we arrived, but we were immediately accommodated with a room on the basement floor of the palace;

and, on his return home in the afternoon, we dined and spent a very pleasant evening with himself and family.

The Jesuit fathers appreciated the advantages of early rising, if we may judge from an insignia at the top of the chapel—a cock; and certainly it is an agreeable sensation to rise with the sun in such a climate, to enjoy the cool refreshing breeze, particularly in such a situation as Santa Cruz. The bell rang at daylight, and about six o'clock the slaves began to muster in front of the "Armazen" or depôt, whence the rations are distributed to men, women, and children. After waiting some time the superintendent came round and the distribution commenced, lasting upwards of an hour when we visited the depôt; there are hospitals and other offices connected with the establishment, all of which are in first-rate order; but the hospital is on a large scale for so healthy a place, and it contained very few patients. There is a manufacture of red earthenware on the estate, a large collection being ready for sale, consisting chiefly of various shaped vessels to hold water, all of a porous material. This appeared to be the only industry carried on. The inspection over, we breakfasted with Senhor Saldanha and his family, and at 10 a.m. we started in a light carriage drawn by two mules (one an outrider) for the village of Itagoahy, distant about eight miles, the road being a raised causeway with a deep ditch on each side, running straight through the meadow land of the estate, crossing several modern bridges over the rivers which intersect the property. Cattle and horses were grazing on very fine, well-drained pastures, capable of containing large quantities, but at present only about 4,500 head were there. The Jesuits are said to have had some 13,000 head of cattle here. Leaving the Santa Cruz estate we came upon a long strip of deep sand, which extends to the sea, filled with shells, and leaving an impression that the sea once covered this immense track of reclaimed meadow land. The jungle became thick, and continued until we reached the village of Itagoahy, where we called at the house of a Brazilian, who formerly carried on a large business in forwarding coffee by sea to Rio, but since the railway was opened this trade has left the place. I was surprised to find such an excellent house, furnished in such good style and taste, in this remote spot. It belongs to Senhor Manoel José Cardoza, with whom we promised to dine on Sunday on our way back from Mr. Coates, which is about six miles distant from the village and the limit of our present excursion. We started in the carriage through a very rough road, but were obliged to leave it half way and mount on horseback, as it was impossible to proceed in safety over the delapidated wooden bridges, the whole district being intersected with water and running streams. We soon reached the hospitable cottage of Mr. Coates, situated on the margin of a little inlet from the sea, in the midst of pretty scenery; and here I will pause to revert to the estate of Santa Cruz.

As I have before observed, there is probably not a finer spot in all Brazil for a model farm than Santa Cruz. It is at present not only quite unproductive, but rather a drain on the private purse of the Emperor. It has been suggested to make a railway from the Sappabemba station, which could be done at a moderate expense, have the supply of cattle for Rio de Janeiro grazed here, and the abatoir removed from San Christovao—where it is an utter abomination—to Santa Cruz; the supply of meat for the city could then be taken down and easily distributed. No doubt the estate is capable of doing all this and much more in the way of agricultural production; but it requires to be dealt with on an entirely new principle, and the slaves to be replaced by free labour of some kind. Looking to the early prospect of emancipation, some such scheme may possibly be carried out, and the estate be rendered subservient to the great object of supplying the capital with fresh meat, as also setting an example for practical farming. At present neither cereals nor vegetables are grown even for local purposes, which is most extraordinary. Pity the taste of the Emperor does not run in the direction of agriculture, so much wanted in the country.

Saturday 29th.—Curious enough, the origin of Mr. Coates' residence here was a small salt work, established here nearly half-a-century back with one good-sized pan, brought out from England, enclosed in a solid building. Rock salt was sent out from England, melted down, and then boiled as in Cheshire. Later on the import of salt into Rio from Europe reduced the price, so as to render this little manufactory unprofitable; and, moreover, the people actually gave a preference to the dirty composition made from salt water. The salt pan exists still, of course totally useless. Mr. Coates established a sugar mill close to it, which he now works. He has got a corrugated iron-roofed house, and has drained and improved the land near to him, where he grows sugar-cane, rice, &c. When I state that Mr. Coates is in his 91st year, with the enjoyment of all his faculties and personal activity; that he goes to the city once a month, and has lived in the country upwards of half-a-century, it is a strong proof of its salubrity. To-day we took a ride to a sugar estate of Baron Maua, a few miles distant, which I believe has not been very successful. The great drawback of the district, like many others, is superabundant vegetation and want of drainage; but I believe there is good land when cleared, with every facility for drainage to the sea, which encircles it. Towards evening came on a heavy storm of wind, rain, and lightning, which does not bode well for our return journey, as the road becomes flooded after heavy rain.

We left Mr. Coates after breakfast this morning on horseback, to join the carriage waiting for us between this and Itagoahy, where we stayed to fulfil our dinner engagement. We looked over a very solid structure built here nearly a century back by a sovereign of Portugal, as a kind of model sugar manufactory, but which has not been used for the last thirty years, the improvements in making sugar since that time having quite superseded the model. Still it is a curiosity, and shows how desirous the mother country was to instruct her colonists in sugar-making. Going up to the church, which is on a considerable elevation, and commands a fine view of Santa Cruz, with the surrounding mountains, as well as of the sea, visible from the tower of the church, there is a pretty cemetery adjoining the church, with some monuments of a superior class, evidently by European sculptors. The church itself is simply adorned, but beautifully clean; and the whole indicates a presiding genius, capable of appreciating the "mighty dead." The cultivated land around and good houses indicate what has been the former condition of this village, now more or less abandoned, until its fortunes are revived by direct railway communication, which cannot be long delayed.

We returned here last night, being delayed

by missing a train at Sappabemba. The Douro is in this morning, and some further comments on my late visit to Santa Cruz and neighbourhood must be left over for the next opportunity.

If the Bishop of London and Her Majesty's Postmaster-General could have been present at the British Consulate last night (Sunday), they would have been greatly edified, the first at the desecration of the Sabbath by a branch of the National Post Office, and the Postmaster-General at the amount of labour rendered by the officials. What are called British Post Offices in Brazil and the River Plate are really appendages of the Consulates, carried on in the same buildings. I described the scene at Monte Video the previous Sunday. Last night, up to 8 p.m., was the latest to receive letters here for England, the box being closed (in technical language) at 6 p.m. for letters to Portugal and other parts of the Continent. During the whole of Sunday letters keep pouring in, and, to relieve the pressure for prepaid letters, an office has been opened on the opposite side of the street to the Consulate. After 6 p.m. there is a late fee of 300 reis (about 7d.) for Continental letters, and after 8 p.m. the same for English letters, the office remaining open the whole of *Sunday night* to receive letters under the late fee until the bags are finally dispatched at 7 a.m. on Monday morning. We must bear in mind that these late fees are not for account of the officials

here, who undergo the toil of collecting them, but go to credit of the Postmaster-General; and I believe I am correct in saying that this kind of Sunday occupation occurs about 30 times during the year. As a matter of course the foreign community, probably with few exceptions, are engaged in writing their letters on the Sunday, so that a wholesale system of Sunday occupation becomes imperative. As I have before pointed out, the originator of this Sunday traffic is the Postmaster-General, who allows or rather requires the branches out here to be opened on Sunday, and what is more, does not provide his agents with stamps for late fees, but actually compels the officials to *receive money and keep the office open all night*, as the steamers generally leave for Europe early in the morning. The Postmaster-General has only to give orders that those branch offices shall not be opened at all on Sunday, and things would soon regulate themselves, without any inconvenience to the commercial body; but the present system is a standing disgrace to a christian country like England. It is to be hoped that some member of the House of Commons will bring this subject before the House, and that before long the nuisance of having British Post Offices in foreign countries will be got rid of by postal conventions.*
Some inconvenience might arise at first, but this

---

* A Postal Convention has since been entered into both with Brazil and the River Plate, which does away with the Consular Post Offices.

would soon be remedied, and the mercantile community would look after their own interests as to the prompt delivery of their letters. There would be no divided responsibility, and I believe both the Brazilian and Argentine Governments are prepared to give increased facilities, and promote increased efficiency in this department of their service. At all events it is time to do away with such excrescences to the Consular service and making a profit out of Sunday traffic. The increase of labour entailed on the Rio, Monte Video, and Buenos Ayres branch Post Offices by the new contract mails is something formidable, no less than sixteen steamers with them to and fro during the month in Rio.

I went to see the La Plata off this morning, when there was quite a gathering of official people to take leave of some deputies going to the Northern Provinces, amongst them His Excellency Senhor Diogo Velho, late Minister of Agriculture, appointed President of Pernambuco, and Senator Zacharias, formerly head of the Liberal Government. The departure of the Royal Mail steamer is always an event here; but on this occasion there were few passengers, owing to her arriving home so late in the season. The Valdivia, which arrived yesterday, brought nothing important as regards the progress of the war.

We have the luck of falling in with professional people. Signor and Signora Gase are staying at the Estrangeiros. She is the Prima Donna who has been singing at Buenos Ayres, and came here with an efficient company to perform a series of Mayerbeer's operas, amongst them the celebrated *Africaine*, which has peculiar charms for this place, founded as the opera is on the discovery of India by the great Vasco de Gama. There has been no regular operatic company here for the last four years, so that the opportunity is eagerly availed of by the music-loving people of Rio; and from the critiques of the press the performances are very creditable to the artistes engaged in them.

At last, I rejoice to say, the heavens are opened and the long wanted rain has come down on the thirsty earth, the sun having been scorchingly hot for some days. It has been a regular outpouring, the mountains and most surrounding objects shrouded in mist, and the population of Rio will now have an abundant supply of water—an invaluable blessing in this country, which has suffered the last few years from drought. Under ordinary circumstances the southern provinces have been free from the scourge which at times afflicts the northern ones, and as a rule mountainous districts do not suffer from want of rain; but the seasons both in Brazil and the River Plate have latterly felt the extremes of heat and cold, more resembling the United States in this respect.

November 5th, 1870.—The arrivals of steamers north and south this week have exceeded all precedent—as many as two or three a day—and they now form a large portion of the trade of the port. I allude to European steamers, nearly all of which now go on to the River Plate and return here, the Pacific line having two a month both ways. The Cordillera came in to her day, the 3rd instant, bringing, besides a large number of cabin passengers, between 500 and 600 Basques and Spaniards for the River Plate, embarked at a port in the Bay of Biscay. The French mail steamer Amazon came up from the River Plate to-day, and sails to-morrow for Bordeaux with a lot of French volunteers on board returning to France to assist in fighting their country's battles if an opportunity is afforded them; but the general impression here is that peace will be made on some terms, and the world be spared further details of slaughter, of which most people are becoming sick. The volunteers alluded to are dressed in a singular costume —blue tunics with coloured scarves and ornamental caps, well drilled, and a very fine set of young fellows. If, contrary to expectation, their spirit animates the French nation, Prussia may yet regret not having made peace when she had the opportunity. As the French line has been largely subsidized by the Government, and this is now cut off, it is supposed it will be stopped, thus affording an opportunity for the Southampton Royal Mail Company to establish a fortnightly line, if they are determined to compete for the traffic and have ships to do so. The Liverpool line continues its steady traffic, and the Falmouth line has been reorganized under a new ownership. One of their first vessels, the Bonita, commanded by Captain Peters, formerly of the City of Rio de Janeiro, having arrived here last week and proceeded to the River Plate.

November 6th, 1870.—The French Mail steamer Amazone sailed from here to-day for Bordeaux with a large number of passengers on board, amongst whom were Mr. Blow (American Minister) and family, on a visit to Europe before returning to the United States. He appears to be highly esteemed, both in diplomatic and local circles, which is more than can be said of all foreign representatives here, some of whom spend their time in abusing the country and everything belonging to it.

The excellency and superior management of the tramways here over all others I have seen, and the contrast they present to the scramble at Buenos Ayres, is too striking not to be noticed; at the same time allowance must be made for the difference in locality, Rio also being far a-head of Buenos Ayres in municipal government. The southern line to Bota Fogo is now being extended to the Botanical Gardens, a distance of about three miles, which will be an enormous advantage both to the locality and to the population of the city, who can thus extend their peregrinations most beneficially. The Rio de Janeiro Street Railway Company, which occupies the northern district, are also extending their lines farther to the suburbs, including the Rio Comprida, a very favourite and salubrious spot for private residences; in fact, the only limits of tramways will soon be the foot of the mountains, every other available space of level ground being intersected by rails; and what is equally marvellous is that the number of carriages and vehicles of all descriptions appears to increase and multiply, as if the taste for locomotion kept pace with facilities afforded for it. All this is a healthy sign, proving that the people are determined to move about instead of shutting themselves up as formerly, just as the citizens of old London used to do. As a matter of course new houses are built, and the borders of the city become enlarged, the latter in time merging almost exclusively into a place of business; and for this great internal improvement the Brazilians are indebted to a few enterprising gentlemen. I may mention that the rails of the tramways are kept constantly clear of stones or sand by means of small brushes, and that they are watered in dusty weather, and greased occasionally in order to avoid rust or friction; so there is positively little sound from the passing of carriages beyond the tinkling of bells attached to the harness of the mules. The only inconvenience felt is in the carriages being occasionally over-crowded.

November 9th.—We have had two or three days of calm since the departure of the French mail. The Poitou arrived from Marseilles with 450 emigrants for the River Plate, to which there is a continual stream of this class of people; and sooner or later it must exercise a political influence in the Republic—whether for good or for evil it is difficult to say; at all events it is not that kind of emigration they profess to be most desirous to have, and which it is their own fault if they do not get. A correspondent of the *Diario do Commercio* at Buenos Ayres alludes to this subject, and suggests that the Government should institute a propaganda in order to induce the Anglo-Saxon race to migrate to the shores of the La Plata, thereby evincing his ignorance of existing arrangements in Europe for this object; but so long as the Government decline to give "assisted passages" they may as well preach to the winds.

San Paulo, 16th November.—I left Rio for this place on the 11th instant, on board my old conveyance the Santa Maria steamer, in company with some friends who were going into the interior of the province. There was not much wind, but a very nasty rolling sea, which caused the Santa Maria to dance about much more than was agreeable to weak stomachs, and there was consequently a very shy muster at dinner. The night was fine, with a moon, and inside the island of San Sebastian, where we landed some passengers, we had smooth water. Early in the morning the lighthouse was in sight, with a beautiful view of the Serra, topped with clouds, the bright sunshine gilding everything far and near. We anchored close to the landing-stage, having all the inconvenience of small boats, with shoals of niggers importuning to carry luggage, which is a great nuisance. There is deep water alongside the wharf, to which the steamer afterwards hauls, but it suits the purpose of their boat agents to cause money to be spent in the place. There is a project on foot for enclosing the whole water frontage of Santos, providing wharves and warehouses, which must be a vast improvement. Gas and water is also to be supplied to the town at an early date, so the people of Santos will soon emerge from their still rather dreary position in spite of its growing commercial importance. After a decent breakfast at a not very cleanly-looking hotel, we drove to the railway station, and started at 11 a.m. for another visit to the great works of the San Paulo Railway, already fully described in my last book. Arrived at the foot of the Serra, where a station house has been built, a few of us mounted on the brake, enjoying the glorious scenery as we passed successively the four lifts to the summit, where the train was soon formed, and we proceeded on to San Paulo at a rapid rate, arriving there at 2.15, or at the rate of about thirty miles an hour. The line was in thorough good working order, very smooth, and much less motion than the average of railways. It was pleasant to revisit the old city and to be greeted by many friends and acquaintances formerly made here; nor did the "glissades of death," as Captain Burton describes the lifts up the mountain, impress us with a sense of danger, everything is so carefully and systematically worked. I was present at a recent meeting of the civil engineers in Great George Street, when a valuable paper was read from Mr. Fox, engineer of the line, accompanied by large diagrams, which fully explained the nature of the Serra works and the manner in which the lifts were worked. In the interesting discussion which followed, Mr. Hawkshaw made a few very pertinent remarks, showing the comparative safety of wire ropes, and that most of our great mining operations were carried on by this means; moreover, in the case of the railway lifts, there is the additional security of the brake van always connected with the carriages. Crossing the viaduct we found a plate inserted with the following inscription, which the magnitude of the work certainly deserves:

James Brunlees, Engineer-in-Chief.
Daniel M. Fox, Resident Engineer.
Robert Sharp and Sons, Contractors, 1865.

San Paulo is little altered since my last visit, with exception of a few scattered houses in the outskirts, but the city has a bright sunny look, contrasting to much advantage with others in

Brazil of similar size. The day following our arrival was very hot, with a northerly wind, the thermometer at 85°, but the wind suddenly changed to the south, and in two or three hours it was down to 70°, declining in the night to 60°. Monday opened cloudy, with rain and absolutely cold. Tuesday it remained about the same temperature or under, but last night it went down to 55°; to-day it is up to 80°. Such great and sudden atmospheric changes I have rarely met with in any country, and they must be very trying to delicate constitutions, although the province is considered a very healthy one. It was my intention to make an excursion with some friends to see the splendid coffee fazendas of Senhor José Verguero, some distance up the province, and who accompanied us from Rio de Janeiro; but circumstances prevented me devoting the needful time to what would have been a very interesting excursion, so I was obliged to content myself with a trip to Campinas, one of the principal towns of the province, situate about 27 miles from the railway terminus at Jundiahy. Mr. Fox (whose guests we are) kindly offered to accompany me, also Mr. Dundas, her Majesty's Consul at Santos. We left by the 6.30 train on Tuesday morning, breakfasted at Jundiahy, and thence on by what is called a trolley, being a Yankee invention, well adapted to the rough roads to be travelled over here, though at the expense of severe jolting and shaking. The vehicle is composed of longitudinal pieces of strong wood, lined with iron, the four wheels a considerable distance apart, and seats placed on the top of the low platform, the whole hung on strong springs. We started soon after 11 a.m. with four good mules, at a rapid pace, descending a very steep hill, with views of the new railway making to Campinas before us, passing numerous troops of mules and carts—both ways—the latter mostly drawn by oxen, laden with coffee and merchandize, which continued to Campinas; a strong indication of the traffic that awaits the opening of the new extension line from Jundiahy to Campinas. I may say of the road, that the whole distance is one continued up hill and down dale, occasionally amounting to positive precipices, and the road of the roughest possible description, so that it is frequently a case of holding on with both hands, if you do not wish to run the risk of being pitched out head foremost. The scenery is pretty, mostly through a woody country, but occasionally with an extensive view from some lofty eminence. At Rosario, two-thirds of the distance, we stopped to change mules—it is an elevated position, and a number of Germans have located themselves in the district. Here the coffee plantations commence, extending on all sides as far as the eye can reach, and they continue on for at least a hundred miles, or so far as cultivation has extended itself, within an attainable distance from the shipping port of Santos; but once railway facilities reach the intended point of Rio Claro (160 miles from Santos), coffee planting will be carried on much further, as the soil is rich and suitable, provided labour can be imported into the province, a matter of serious consideration, particularly with the prospect of changes in the servile element at present in operation. We reached Campinas about 2.30 p.m., or three and a-quarter hours (not bad travelling over such execrable roads), and put up at the Oriental Hotel—tolerably comfortable quarters. Campinas may be said to lie in a hole, not in a valley, as the elevation is considerable. It is a modern town, with about 8,000 inhabitants, a few good houses, belonging to fazendeiros, who come here for a change; the general aspect of the place not very inviting. After rambling about and making some calls, we dined and spent the evening at the house of an American missionary, Mr. Morton, who has settled here with his wife, a young and interesting lady; and a Mr. Lane also resides with them—both highly intelligent men. There are some three hundred Americans (all exiled Southerners) living in the district, which is visited in turn by these ministers of the gospel. Early the next morning (Wednesday) we went to look at a very pretty chacra, which they are about purchasing from Mr. Aubertin, late superintendent of the San Paulo Railway, intending to build themselves a house on one of the prettiest sites I have seen in this country, commanding an extensive view over Campinas and the surrounding district, whilst at the same time it is only a few minutes' walk from the town. Mr. Aubertin has spent a considerable sum in laying out the land (some twenty-four acres), and has planted a large number of English fruit trees, besides trees of the country. Should Mr. Morton and his friend carry out their intention of locating themselves on this spot, it bids fair to reward them amply for the outlay and care they will doubtless bestow upon it. After breakfast, and before starting on our return to Jundiahy, we went into a large unfinished church, called the Matriz, where I was astonished to find elaborate carved work on a most gigantic scale, done by Belgian, French, and Italian artists during a period of some seventy years. I have seen nothing like it in or out of Belgium or Italy; and it is indeed a pity to see such splendid specimens of carved wood (all cedar of the country) almost excluded from the light, and covered with dust. The cost must have been great—contributed, I believe, from time to time by rich landowners, at a period when their profits were much larger than at present. As before observed, time would not admit of our visiting any of the numerous fazendas (coffee estates) in the neighbourhood; so, on leaving the church, we mounted our trolley again, and after the same amount of break-neck galloping, the road not being quite so crowded as on the previous day, we reached Jundiahy at three p.m. (about the same time as occupied in the up-journey), had some refreshment at the Hotel Esperança, took the 4.13 train, and arrived at Mr. Fox's residence about seven, after a very delightful trip.

THE PROVINCE OF SAN PAULO AND RAILWAY COMMUNICATION.

A few observations on these most important topics will not be out of place here; and they are the more necessary in order to fully understand a question about which a good deal of ignorance prevails at home. First, as regards the railway. I pointed out during my last visit to San Paulo, in 1868, what I considered had been the original errors of its construction, showing at the same time its very advantageous position, and the future which awaited it, providing the work should prove solid and trustworthy—results now happily attained. The traffic returns speak for themselves; but unfortunately, whether owing to the want of a due appreciation of the subject, or to the caprice of directors, the cream of the traffic, which lies between Jundiahy and the Rio Claro, has been allowed to fall into the hands of a private company, the original one having given up the right under their concession to extend their line to Campinas.

Until now, I had not travelled over the old Campinas road, and could form no adequate idea of its enormous traffic, which I believe capable *per se* of covering the whole seven per cent. guarantee on the main lines between Santos and Jundiahy. The line from Santos to Jundiahy has been very costly; that from Jundiahy to Campinas will cost little more than one-third per mile of the former; so that a very favourable average would have been obtained in the cost of what would then have constituted a line of about 112 miles, the working expenses being reduced in proportion. Adding to this, and under equally favourable circumstances of construction, the extension from Campinas to Rio Clara, the company would then have had possession of a railway unequalled for traffic returns of over 160 miles, the whole calculated to yield at the most moderate computation a net dividend of ten per cent. How such a position could have escaped the notice of practical men at home is marvellous. It may be said that the shareholders in the original company were satisfied with their seven per cent. guarantee, and that the required capital for 80 miles of railway at a cost of £800,000, as against nearly £2,000,000 for the first 86 miles, would not have been forthcoming. I cannot believe that any body of shareholders, on a right view of the case being placed before them, would have declined so palpable an advantage; but even if they had done so, some fresh body of shareholders at home might have been found to take it up. What is the consequence? A local company has been formed here, the capital has been raised, and the line is let out to contractors on favourable terms; the latter finding plenty of sub-contractors, who are proceeding with the works very rapidly, of which I had ocular demonstration. How the running powers over the San Paulo line will be arranged I do not know; but all this involves disputes, such as generally exist under a double management, a divided interest, and a separate use of rolling stock. The Government will naturally lean towards their own countrymen, and the consequence may be endless trouble, unless the old line should be bought up by the National Government and merged into the Campinas and Rio Claro extensions—a not improbable event. That this province must have its through line of railways now admits of no doubt; and what an advantageous investment of English capital might have been made in furtherance of this object! The old company were masters of the position; and I must say I think they have most foolishly given it up, either through pique, or in consequence of their disputed accounts with the Government and contractors; but, to use a familiar expression, they have "killed the goose that laid the golden egg." It may not be too late to come to some terms with the holders of the Campinas extension; and I believe the company still possesses the power of going on from thence to Rio Claro, but whether or not they will be "wise in time" is another question. All I can say is that railway annals present no such an example of a brilliant future as would that of a company in possession of the entire line from Santos to Rio Claro.

A word as regards the making of railways in the province by capital raised on the spot. I believe the directors in London were under an impression this would not be forthcoming, but the event has proved they were wrong. The National Government could always raise loans in Europe wherewith to construct such railways as San Paulo; and I think it would be their wisest policy to do so, leaving the fazendeiros at liberty to employ their money on the spot, in extending their productions and otherwise improving their property. Money here is worth one and a-half to two per cent. per month on tolerably good security as managed by those who make this their business; but as a general rule there is not much *floating capital* in the Brazilian provinces, the bulk of it being centred in Rio de Janeiro. On these grounds English capital employed in making their railways is no doubt valuable to them; but if it will not come for such an object, they have shown their ability to raise it on the spot. That the value of produce in this province will be greatly augmented by railway communication there cannot be a shadow of a doubt.

San Paulo, November 22nd.—I believe, in my notice of the town of Campinas, I omitted their pretty little theatre, which is quite a credit to them, though little availed of in these dull times, when the landed interest, on which Campinas almost entirely depends, is so depressed, and the inhabitants are also suffering from a visitation of the small pox, which makes occasional ravages in these countries, where vaccination is not imperative and a strong prejudice exists against the use of it. Medical treatment, also, is rather of the antique kind in Brazil, but the presence of good foreign practitioners is effecting a change in this respect. Campinas has two large cemeteries close to each other, surrounded by high walls, apparently quite out of proportion to the size of the place. The new railway station is to be very close to them, and at a greater distance from the town than appears necessary.

On the 26th inst. there is to be a great gathering near Itu, another small town in the province, to celebrate the inauguration of a railway from Jundiahy to the aforesaid town of Itu, to be constructed cheaply, on a narrow, or three feet six inches gauge. The distance is fifty miles and it will open up quite a new district to the shipping port of Santos. The President of San Paulo and the leading men of the province will be there, showing the great interest felt in railway development by those who have the inclination as well as the means to support it. I was informed by the chief contractor of the Campinas line that there were about 1,200 men employed on the works, two-thirds of whom were native Brazilians, earning about 2$000, or 4s. per day, which shows the desire of this class of Brazilians to work when it is to be had.

Looking about the city and neighbourhood I perceive many improvements since I was last here, the city itself, together with the streets, being remarkably clean. Roads in the outskirts, which were formerly quagmires, have been bottomed with the excellent material they have for road making, and are now in very good order; in fact, there can be no doubt that San Paulo is destined to go-a-head, as the capital of the province and the central pivot of railway communication. Gas works are now in course of erection, to replace the existing oil lamps, and the Provincial Assembly has given powers to the Government to contract for a supply of water; so all modern conveniences will soon be found here. Opposite the public gardens, on the road to the Lux, is a very substantial public fountain, with the following inscriptions: " Baron de Ituana, 1869, President. A. J. Coimbra, Inspector of Works." Considerable improvements have been made about the railway station, which now presents a very cheerful aspect; the engineering workshops have been considerably enlarged, and everything placed on a comfortable footing for traffic arrangements, both as regards goods and passengers. All this and more will be required when the whole of the new railway traffic merges into this main trunk line, but unless the whole system is to be under one management it can never be worked in a satisfactory manner.

Sunday, November 27th.—Reminds me that I have to notice the observance of the Sabbath by the foreign community here, particularly the English portion of it. During my last visit to San Paulo divine service was performed in a room adjoining Mr. Fox's residence, Mr. Fox reading the prayers and one of the missionaries preaching. Since that time the English community has increased, and service is now performed in the evening instead of the morning in a part of the railway station capable of holding nearly 100 people. Mr. Fox reads the service, and generally an American missionary, Mr. Churchill, preaches. They have got up a tolerably good choir, who chant the Psalms and sing hymns from a special collection, the whole service being gone through in a very creditable manner. On the first Sunday evening we were present the attendance numbered about sixty—I believe about the usual average—besides which there is a special service for children connected with a school where some twenty children receive instruction. It is intended to enlarge the borders of this useful institution by building a church, with a school room attached, and getting out an English minister, towards which subscriptions are now being raised; and, I believe, the co-operation of the South American Missionary Society is promised. It is one of the reproaches against Englishmen resident in South America that they live generally as if they had never been brought up to value religious ordinances, nor is the example set them by those who officially represent a Christian country such as could be desired; quite the reverse, as I have had occasion to instance in the case of Rio de Janeiro. In San Paulo there are many English employés and mechanics connected with the railway, settled with their families, who, through the kindness of Mr. Fox, are thus supplied with religious instruction for themselves and their families, the consequence being that order and good conduct is the rule, and the English name is respected. There are also religious unions of Germans and Americans in San Paulo, the latter being a very zealous body, doing a great deal of good. It is not so much proselytism that is wanted in these countries as attention on the part of the foreign community to their own religious duties, setting an example to others; and, looking forward to the large increase of European immigration, which I am persuaded will soon take place in this splendid province, to supply the necessities of the soil, it is the more important that there should be formed the nucleus of religious instruction, which is calculated to render settlers more contented with their lot, and add materially to their happiness even in a worldly point of view. The religion of the country and of the people is, of course, Roman Catholic, but they have learnt to be tolerant to others who profess a different creed, and in this respect Brazil will ere long make further progress in the right direction.

Rio de Janeiro, December 2nd, 1870.—Civilization has its drawbacks in all countries, and laying down new gas and water mains in this city is attended with inconveniences, although the traffic is not so great, nor the disturbances so frequent, owing to the more durable nature of the material. This being the Emperor's birthday, it was ushered in with salutes from the different forts and vessels of war, the streets were hung with flags of all nations, and a most formidable display of bunting it was. About mid-day the Emperor with his suite drove to the City Palace, and what they call *o beija mao* (kissing of hands) commenced, which lasted some time. Of course there was a great display of uniforms and cocked hats, the consular and diplomatic corps also going to pay their respects to his Imperial Majesty, who is only 45 years of age. The day was very fine, with a cool breeze, and, as usual on a holiday, two steamers arrived, the Siberia, Pacific boat on her way home, and the Oneida, bringing telegraphic news from Lisbon to the 12th ult. that the war was still raging in France, the armistice having fallen through, as reported by the Poitou, which arrived from Gibraltar a few days back. Much sympathy is felt here for France; at the same time it is considered impossible, with such discordant elements in the governing body, that any protracted resistance can be carried on. From the south the only notable incident is the capture of Gualeguachu by the forces of Lopez Jordan, who seems to be almost as ubiquitous as his namesake of Paraguay. Another revolution on a small scale is reported at Jujuy, so that altogether the National Government appears to have its work cut out for some time. As regards the Banda Oriental, it is now a question of time as to which party can hold out longest, the Colorados, with possession of the harbour of Monte Video, having, of course, an uncontrolled supply of provisions and all other requirements to stand a siege. It remains to be seen what the armies outside will be able to accomplish, and they appear to be about equally matched, and these internal struggles are, of course, ruination to owners of property, and Entre Rios as well as the Banda Oriental must be completely devastated. The effects are seen in the withdrawal of a Monte Videan loan from the London market at a moment when its success was all but a reality. Such arguments are, however, lost on a people who only follow their brutal, selfish instincts by an appeal to arms, no matter who suffers, or the misery they entail on their own country.

A great deal of rain has fallen here lately, to the great relief of the water supply of the city, and doing much good to the country, which now teems with its luxuriant vegetation. The temperature has been mild and agreeable, and Rio looks its best just now. The new Ministry are working quietly, but an impression prevails it will not be of long duration. The Chambers being closed, there is still no political agitation, but party spirit runs high, and next year may bring about many changes. The city tramways are extending themselves to the suburbs, to the great advantage of property there; and I believe they are making money hand over hand—a wonderful contrast to the tramways in Buenos Ayres, which only appear to be in each other's way, though no doubt something like order will come out of the chaos which existed there on my departure.

December 4th.—There was a heavy storm of thunder and lightning here last night; for an hour the lightning flashed incessantly on the other side of the western range of mountains skirting the sea, sending out occasionally what might be compared to numerous fiery serpents. The panorama presented by the mountains during these vivid flashes was very beautiful; at last the storm came over the mountain, the peals of thunder became nearer and nearer, accompanied by rain. It was one of those wonderfully grand convulsions of the elements to which these countries are subject, but we do not hear of much damage done by the lightning. To-day it has blown half a gale of wind from the south-west, and looks very unsettled. The Oneida would have a rough time of it, but gales of wind are not frequently of long duration.

December 6th.—The French mail brings nothing decisive from the River beyond reports of successes by the national troops in Entre Rios; but, as usual, these want confirmation. Surprising the Cerro fort at Monte Video, which commands the city, is one of those events which, as Lord Dundreary says, "no fellah can understand." A sortie from the city, on the other side, seems to have been attended with some loss, but no compensating result.

December 12, 1870.—In noticing local improvements here tramways, of course, are the most modern, and the most important as a means of cheap, easy locomotion, of which the population avail themselves to an incredible extent, as few people believed Brazilians would to the extent they do. The line southward is now in course of construction to the Botanical Gardens, easy access to which will be an enormous advantage to the people of Rio de Janeiro, and materially increase the value of property in that direction. At the northern extremity of the city the company keep extending their rails so as to bring them within reach of the numerous residents in that direction, and ere long rails will be laid to the great central commercial thoroughfare traversed by the Rua Direita. It is simply a question of time, and overcoming some local prejudices, as well as the difficulty of traversing narrow streets. As if the tramways had stirred people up in other ways, you see improvements going on in various directions, some long projected, now beginning to show themselves, and ere long Rio de Janeiro will possess all modern facilities. The narrow streets in the heart of the city are difficult to manage, unless a fire should cause a gap that might be availed of as a better approach; but in this case the whole city might stand a chance of being destroyed—at least the business part of it. An abuse exists here as at home in the posting of advertising placards, and they generally select the corners of streets, the names of which are very much obliterated by this process. Advertising in the public papers is also carried on to a large extent, and the leading paper here, *The Jornal do Commercio*, is said to derive almost as large an income as *The Times* from this source. Speaking of foreign population, an impression prevails that it is large, but I believe it is less than generally supposed; at all events, as regards the English residents, I have pretty accurate information as follows: including the city, and for some miles round, the number is about 1,100, which comprises all Englishmen employed by the Brazilian Government, the steam companies, gas works, engineering establishments, &c.; contrast this with the 40,000 English and Irish in the City and Province of Buenos Ayres, and it will at once be seen how much greater scope there has been for the Anglo-Saxon race in the latter direction, to be accounted for by the prevalence of slavery in Brazil, and the more congenial pursuits for our countrymen in the River Plate, excluding from both comparisons what are simply commercial establishments. English commerce in Brazil has always held a leading position, from the large amount of manufactures imported here and at other ports; but the bulk of coffee exports is sent to the United States and the Continent of Europe, some English houses being large exporters of the article. The rise that has for some time been going on in exchange, though favourable to the importers of merchandize, has been against the exporter of produce, who has to draw chiefly on England for value of shipments, and in the present condition of France this must for some time be almost exclusively the case. If no new political complications arise in Europe, such as that shadowed forth by a re-opening of the Eastern question, the rate of exchange ought soon again to be at the par value of 27d. per milreis, making the English sovereign a legal tender at Rs. 8$883, whereas its current value is now about Rs. 10$400 against an exchange of 24d. per milreis. Of course there would then be more steadiness in trade, with no scope for speculating on the market price of gold, which has been subject to such violent fluctuations since the Paraguayan war, in proof of which I may remark that, when here in the early part of 1868, I got Rs. 18$000 paper for a sovereign that is now only worth Rs. 10$400.

A painful sensation has been created by the death, after a short illness, of Mr. Jordan Creuse, a director of the Bank of Brazil, and formerly manager of the London and Brazilian Bank here. Mr. Creuse was a very old resident of Rio, much respected, and leaves a widow with a large young family to lament this sudden bereavement.

I notice a very large increase in the receipts of the Dom Pedro II. Railway last month, being Rs. 604,869$230 as against Rs. 347,140$840 for November, 1869, of which sum Rs. 63,527$557 has to go to the 25 per cent. contribution towards the Petropolis Road Company, which is still kept in splendid order. It was a great act of folly on the part of the Government, as I had occasion to notice on my last visit, to neutralize the traffic of this admirable road by bringing the railway into competition with it at Entre Rios, instead of spending the money in extending the main line into the province of San Paulo, which they are now doing also, but of course at a large additional outlay. It has rendered the Mauá Railway and the splendid road up the mountain all but useless, and they have been obliged to subsidize the Mauá Railway in order to keep it open for passenger traffic. It is a singular fact, that of the total revenue of Rs. 604,869$230 earned by the Dom Pedro Segundo Railway during the month of November last, the Company Uniao é Industria contributed Rs. 237,986$050.

December 15th.—Another excitable day. The French mail came in early this morning, with recent war news and the further diplomatic negotiations with Russia, which are reported as in a more satisfactory state; but, judging by past events, it is difficult to see this. Owing to some mischance in the transit of mails to Bordeaux, very few English letters were received by this mail, but the telegrams to Lisbon post people up to the latest possible time, and soon after the steamer arrives the city is inundated with blacks selling the Lisbon papers; for which the demand is immense, these "sensational" journals quite superseding the ordinary English papers, which are delivered some hours after. The Pascal, mail steamer from Liverpool, which sailed on the 19th ult., is behind time; but the new postal contract steamer Olbers, which made such a splendid run out, is up from Monte Video in four days, with an extraordinary account of the rebel party (Blancos) having seized four steamers plying between Monte Video, Buenos Ayres, and the Uruguay, intending to convert them into war vessels and blockade the harbour of Monte Video. It is only a short time since they got possession of the strong "Cerro" fortress on which the lighthouse stands, and now this high-handed measure of seizing passenger steamers may call down upon them the displeasure of neutral powers, who have plenty of force ready, if required, to teach the belligerents better manners. What with this prolonged civil war in Uruguay, in Entre Rios, and outbreaks of one kind or other, the news will not be acceptable at home. A quarrel, too, had been got up between the Argentine Government and the Central Argentine Railway, arising out of our charging income tax on the dividend accruing to the Argentine Government and to Argentine shareholders, the President having in consequence issued a peremptory decree that the company should be domiciled in Buenos Ayres and the dividends to be made payable in hard dollars. This state of affairs must occasion a rather warm diplomatic controversy, and I must say that as regards shares held by the Argentine Government and Argentine citizens, in a railway the revenue of which is derived from their own country, it does seem an absurdity that they should have to pay income tax in England. This point will have to be conceded by our Government, but not that of removing the domicile as long as it remains an English registered company. The Argentine Government appears to have acted rather hastily in this matter, but no doubt it will be amicably adjusted. It however confirms the views of those who know best what the future policy of the Government is likely to be, namely, that of eventually absorbing all the railways under their own management by exercising their right of expropriation, but I believe this right does not exist in the case of the Central Argentine Railway.

The more favourable advices of coffee have imparted more animation here, and large shipments are being made at a higher rate of exchange.

On board the Royal Mail Steam Ship Oneida, December 26th, 1870.—Another Christmas Day passed on the ocean, and this year it also embraced Sunday, so we had a mustering of the crew and divine service performed in the cabin, which I think is always particularly impressive, reminding those present of the uncertainty of life, and how few who part on the ship, if she reaches her destination safely, may ever be spared to meet again in this world. It would be well if those who travel so much over the ocean, or take up their abodes in distant countries, could retain the memory of such simple Christian observances, instead of acting as if they had only this world to deal with or to be accountable to.

We left Rio on Saturday the 24th, soon after 8 a.m., steamed out of the harbour, and, as usual, soon found a ground swell which caused the ship to roll and sent many passengers to their berths.

The Tycho Brahe, from Liverpool, was at anchor inside, arriving to her day with later news, but we had no communication with her. Off Cape Negro we fell in with a boat, for which we stopped, and found she was from the steamer Donati, then in sight, disabled. The boat was going to Rio for assistance, but we were enabled to tell them a tug had already hold of her, having been sent out the night previous, when the Donati was telegraphed off Cape Frio. The Liverpool line of Lamport and Holt has lately been very unfortunate in breaking down, realizing the old saying that "misfortunes seldom come singly." It was almost a calm for some hours on leaving Rio, after which a light breeze sprung up dead in our teeth and has since continued with fine weather. We passed within a short distance of Cape Frio, which reminds one somewhat of Holyhead when you get in a certain position. The old lighthouse is a very conspicuous object, the new one being much better placed at a lower elevation. Before saying adieu to Rio de Janeiro, I may as well notice a short visit paid to Tijuca before leaving and after a lapse of twenty years. The Rio de Janeiro City Tramway Company conveys you to the foot of the mountain for a small charge, there being carriages waiting to ascend it. A splendid new road has been made at a heavy cost, which solves all difficulties, leaving you at liberty to admire both the varied and beautiful scenery presented by its windings and turnings until you reach Boa Vista, about 1,000 feet above the level of the sea, from which the view of Rio and the islands of the bay is magnificent. At Boa Vista commence the numerous villas for which Tijuca is now famous, many of them elaborately built, with ornamental gardens, through which flow mountain streams, affording a cool refreshing shade. Not only is the road up the mountain an excellent one, but it is continued on for some distance until it reaches what was formerly Bennett's Hotel, now kept by Mr. White, Mr. Bennett having built himself a good house higher up the mountain, near to the celebrated one of the late Mr. Ginty, who spent a fortune in making himself comfortable here. The house of Mr. Miller, where we were staying, is beautifully situated, overlooking the road going down to Mr. White's, and it possesses a mango tree that for size and utility is almost unrivalled.

We took a ride over to another fancy place belonging to Dr. Cochrane, which cost him upwards of £30,000, but he certainly got *value received* in a comfortable house, with gardens, grounds, wood, and water, all laid out with admirable taste amidst charming scenery; and what is of more importance, the whole is approached by admirable roads upon which the Government has spent large sums of money. One of the roads is called Cochrane's, and I believe he had the charge of its construction. After skirting his grounds the road continues on to the Botanical Gardens, so that a visitor can return to the city that way if disposed. The whole neighbourhood abounds with picturesque mountain scenery with occasional peeps at the sea. No doubt a sojourn at Tijuca during the hot season is beneficial, but to be obliged to visit the city daily is irksome, and there is the disadvantage of having the sun in your face going down, as well as returning, unless avoided by starting very early and only coming back at sunset. You sleep at all events in a cool atmosphere, which is no small advantage. Tijuca is of course much easier of access than Petropolis, where the court and diplomatic body spend a few months, when the place is gay and cheerful. I conclude the Emperor will soon be gone up to Petropolis, although he was still at San Christovao when I left, and I had the honour of an interview with his Imperial Majesty and the Empress, both of whom were looking well. Considerable improvements are going on in the approaches to the palace, and it is to be hoped the nuisance of public slaughter-houses will be removed from the neighbourhood of San Christovao to the Emperor's estate at Santa Cruz, in the way alluded to in my recital of a visit to the latter a few months back.

COMPARISON BETWEEN BRAZIL AND THE RIVER PLATE.

No one can visit these two countries, which form the largest portion of South America, without being struck by the remarkable contrast they present, whether physically or mentally, arising from the difference in thoughts, customs, and habits, such as constitutes the character of people. Brazil is a country of mountains, forests, and mighty rivers, with a large extent of table land, possessing great facilities for agricultural pursuits and a fine seaboard with numerous good harbours. The Argentine Republic is one vast plain until it approaches the Andine ranges, a portion only of this extensive land area being watered by the rivers Parana, Paraguay, and Uruguay, of which Buenos Ayres and Monte Video are the emporia, whilst at the south and approaching the Straits of Magellan there is a dreary waste in possession of Indian tribes. The one country has been peopled (so far as applies to the towns) by the Portuguese, whose descendants are quite a different, plodding race, inclined to take a practical view of things rather than adopt rash conclusions; and, with exception of a short period of anarchy in some of the provinces after the war of independence, the whole Empire has remained a consolidated Monarchy. The very scantiness of its own population prevented Portugal doing much towards the requirements of an immense country like Brazil, and the result was the introduction of the negro, which has to a large extent influenced the character of the people and destinies of the Empire. The River Plate was only one of the mighty possessions of the Spanish Crown, peopled by Spaniards and Indians, with a comparatively small admixture of negro blood. The nomadic life of the people of the River Plate was in the saddle: a wild, uncertain existence, which a temporary sojourn in towns and cities could not suppress; hence has resulted their roving, unsettled character even to the present day. To think or to weigh the course of events is too troublesome a process: a saddle and a knife are natural arbitrators. The character of the two peoples showed itself in a striking manner during the long Paraguayan war. The Argentines, full of "fire and fury," were for marching into Asuncion in three months, and on various occasions showed a despondency under defeat; whilst the Brazilians, less sanguine, but devoted to their work, returned steadily to the charge, and endured an enormous amount of bodily suffering, which in the end led to victory.

The question naturally arises, are two countries, governed by such different social and political elements, likely to agree or to have a common cause? I think so, decidedly. What the one is short of the other possesses, and it prevents a material rivalry such as might exist if both countries imbibed the same ideas or were running in the same groove. The River Plate has abundance of sheep, cattle, and horses, which Brazil is short of, and has long supplied the latter with jerked beef, which is the chief food of the blacks. On the other hand, Brazil sends her sugar, spirits, tobacco, and other productions to the River Plate, so a beneficial change of commercial intercourse is established. Events arising out of the Paraguayan war have brought the two peoples more in contact, and created a feeling of mutual respect such as did not exist before. It had long been the custom to decry Brazil, her people, and institutions; but times and circumstances have changed, nor do I see the slightest apprehension arising out of the settlement of the triple alliance, or the renewed mission of the Baron do Rio Branco (late Senhor Paranhos) to the River Plate.

A great advantage possessed by the River Plate has been its foreign population, which has gone on steadily increasing since its independence, and latterly has assumed large proportions from Italy and the south of France, but comparatively few from other European countries—if I except Irishmen and Englishmen, who settled in the province of Buenos Ayres at an early period and became the holders of large tracts of land. Colonies of Germans and Swiss have been established in various parts of the Argentine Republic with more or less success; but the unsettled state of the country, arising from various causes, is much against their increase at present, or until such time as the Government is fully alive to its urgent necessity, and promotes measures in accordance therewith. Brazil, on the other hand, with a territory much greater, has a still smaller relative population than her southern neighbours. Immigration has been on a very limited scale, chiefly owing to the existence of slavery; but a new era is springing up, calculated to result in great and beneficial changes, and to develope enormously the national wealth of the Empire. The capitals of the two countries differ materially, as all strangers find out who visit them. Buenos Ayres, with its large foreign population, social habits, clubs, and places of amusement, has advantages unknown in Rio. On the other hand, its miserably paved streets, with a prevalence of either dust or mud, is a drawback to comfort. Municipal improvements are slowly carried out, and the sanitary condition of the city and suburbs is wretched in the extreme. Rio possesses beautiful mountain scenery, is admirably paved and lighted, as well drained and sewered as money can make it, but is extremely deficient in social comforts, or those things which constitute the attractions of a large city. There are, in fact, few points in common between the two, whatever change in this respect the future may bring about.

December 29th, 1870.—Owing to a constant head wind we did not get into Bahia until 9 p.m. Sunday 27th, receiving pratique early the next morning, when most of the passengers went on shore for a few hours and had the advantage of seeing old friends. It was a very fine day, rather hot, but the sea breeze cool and refreshing. At 3 o'clock p.m. we again got under weigh, sailing along the coast, but still with the wind dead against us. A beautiful clear moonlight night and very cold on deck. After breakfast this morning we passed an old friend, the La Plata, with all her canvas set. She will be in Bahia early to-morrow, as we shall be at Pernambuco if all's well. In reply to our signal she gave "No news of importance," from which I infer there was not much change in the position of European affairs. With the fine weather we have had, sea-sick passengers are re-appearing at table, and we got a small addition at Bahia. A band of music, as on board the La Plata, enlivens us morning and evening, and the bugle-man with his summoning to meals, amongst them "Polly, put the kettle on," which will be more generally responded to as the weather gets cooler, helps to pass away time otherwise so monotonous at sea.

December 31st.—This is the last day of an eventful year, which has seen one of the greatest military powers of Europe stricken down and German armies marching rampant over prostrate France; nor is the end of the struggle far off, if we may judge from the accounts received in Pernambuco yesterday. We came to anchor in the roadstead about eight a.m., and after breakfast I went on shore with some of our fellow-passengers (amongst whom was Major Rickard, from the River Plate) to take a peep at old Pernambuco, where I commenced my career in life in the year 1821, and which I had not visited since 1853. Great improvements have taken place in the suburbs; what were formerly sandy roads being now well paved, and numerous fine buildings have been erected. A narrow gauge tramway extends some miles into the country, the carriages being drawn by locomotives along some of the main thoroughfares, which is not unattended with danger. We passed a train as we were driving out in a carriage to lunch with some friends, and returning to the city we had a look at the tramway station, with a bridge over the river. The whole concern had a very rough look, and the sheds were so small and narrow as to cause much danger to passengers, several accidents having already occurred. It is strange the Government should allow such a state of things to exist in what is otherwise a great public convenience; and the managers of the line would do well to devote some of their earnings to remedying what are glaring defects, even if they divide less dividends for a year or two. The comfortable accommodation provided both here and at Bahia, as a resort for the commercial body, is a standing reproach to Rio, and ought to lead to some change being made at the latter place, where the business transacted is on so much larger a scale. It was a hot tropical day, but there is something refreshing about Pernambuco, with its steady sea breezes and lightness of atmosphere. The sea happened to be very smooth, so we had no trouble in returning on board laden with fruit of various kinds, which abounds here, conspicuous amongst which are pine-apples of very choice quality. We found them very busy taking in cotton, no less than 1,000 bags of which had been engaged, cramming every hole and corner of the ship, a number of bales being stowed in the wings of the saloon, curtailing the accommodation of the passengers, and creating some discontent amongst the latter. We did not get under weigh until dark, after which the wind became more favourable, and we are now rolling along at a good pace with all fore and aft canvas set, a regular south-east trade, and beautiful sunny weather. The cotton has disappeared from the decks somewhere, and, with the exception of that stowed in the saloon, things have assumed their usual cheerful aspect. Amongst other events recorded in the English papers received at Pernambuco is the death of the well-known Mr. Buschentall, of Monte Video, who has long figured in River Plate politics and finances, and had lately gone to England on matters of business. He will be much missed out in the River; and the beautiful palace he had created at Monte Video, to which allusion has often been made by visitors, will no doubt soon fall into decay from the absence of its presiding deity. The news of his death will cause a sensation out in the River, where he was widely known and much respected; a man of much ability and enterprise, hospitable, and open-handed.

St. Vincent, January 7th, 1871.—We arrived here last night about 2 p.m., after a hard tug for three days against the strongest north-east trade I ever experienced, and which still continues; the wind came down in heavy squalls from the mountain, causing quite a sea in this little land-locked bay. Coming up the channel between the two islands was most severe work, and we were thankful to get safe into this harbour, though difficult to come to an anchor from the force of the wind acting upon the ship, and other ships lying in the way. It was a full moon, but to our surprise, soon after she rose, the moon became eclipsed, and we had a full view of it. Not having many new almanacks on board, the eclipse had escaped notice until it appeared. Our passage to the line was pleasant enough, and then we had two or three days of almost dead calm, followed by the strong north-easter, which seems to have prevailed here some time, so we must only hope it will become more moderate as we advance. Saw very few ships, but passed a large French steamer standing southward. We found here later dates from England, with papers of the 25th ult., and learnt that the steam-ship Beila, laying here some time with a broken shaft, had left here yesterday in tow of a powerful steam tug sent out from Liverpool, intending, if possible, to reach Madeira; but how this is to be accomplished in such weather as now prevails is another matter. St. Vincent is at all times an uninteresting spot, but the more so now, as there is no inducement to go on shore while it is blowing half a gale of wind. We are busy coaling, and expect to get away before dark, with the prospect of a rough night before us.

January 11th.—We had a foretaste at St. Vincent of what we might expect outside, and it was more than realized in having to face half a gale of wind with a heavy head sea, into which the ship plunged her head at times, and pitched the screw out of water in a manner anything but agreeable, although, take it all together, she is an excellent sea boat. The first sixteen hours we made 97 miles, the next twenty-four hours we made 150 miles, and the following day 155 miles, making with the 179 miles to-day, under more moderate weather, 576 in nearly four days—an unusually slow pace for a steamer of 500-horse power; but no one on board remembers having experienced so "hard-hearted" a north-east trade before. Now it is moderate and fine, but still a-head, barely enabling us to carry at times a little fore and aft canvas. Many conjectures were made as to what would become of the unfortunate Beila, which, as already noticed, left St. Vincent the day before us, as it would be utterly impossible for any tug to hold on to her in such weather, and her only chance would be in standing away to the westward under canvas, in the hope of fetching the Western Islands. Strange, we have not seen any vessels since we passed the French steamer on the 4th inst.: a most unusual occurrence in these latitudes. To-morrow evening we expect to see some of the Canary Islands or the Peak of Teneriffe; but unless the wind changes we shall be very late at Lisbon. It has been just the same kind of passage I had home last time in the summer, but with much stronger winds. With the exception of a fracas last night amongst two Spaniards, all has gone on comfortably; and a threat of locking them up if they attempted to commit another breach of the peace appears to have had the desired effect.

January 13th.—Our hard hearted "north-easter" (as we call the wind) still continues. We made the island of Ferro to the westward early yesterday. It came on to blow quite furiously in the morning, and carried away the fore stay sail almost out of the bolt-rope. It became moderate and fine towards afternoon, and we had a fine view of the Island of Palma, on which there is a town of some size, the hills being dotted with white cottages and trees—palm trees, I believe, with green, cultivated spots visible. After rounding the northernmost point towards evening, it came on to blow again in heavy gusts, and has continued so to the present time, allowing us only to make 174 miles since yesterday at noon. There is a good revolving light at this end of Palma, which we passed at a short distance, though for what object a light is placed there no one could say, as sailing ships outward bound generally keep outside the Canary Islands, and homeward-bound steamers try to pass to the eastward of Teneriffe, but the severe north-easter obliged us to take the western side. We are only due at Lisbon to-day by contract time, but if this wind continues we shall be three or four days after it. Rather uncomfortable work for sea-sick passengers; but it cannot be helped, nor could any ship be more easy, steaming head to wind for so long, than the Oneida. To-day the crew went through their fire-brigade evolutions, everything being in order and in its place; the men appeared ready for any emergency; the boats all well appointed; indeed, one great feature of the Royal

Mail service is the discipline and order maintained on board. Only a few centuries back the Canary Islands were the limit of Southern or Western exploration.

Sunday, January 15th.—Another anniversary of my birthday passed on the ocean, the second within the last three years; and in May next it will be exactly half-a-century since I first embarked for Brazil, a sanguine youth of fifteen. What changes and vicissitudes have taken place during that long period! This is what they call a working Sunday, as it is necessary to remove some cargo which has to be landed at Lisbon, and to replace it with the cotton from the saloon in case of passengers offering from thence to England. It is a bright sunny day, the wind having come round to the westward, blowing a nice steady breeze, the ship going faster than is required to bring us off the bar of Lisbon by daylight to-morrow. Yesterday it was comparatively calm; and happily so, for we had rather a startling incident on board. About three p.m., when many of the passengers were taking a "siesta," and I was writing quietly in the saloon, a cry arose of "A man overboard!" which soon brought every one on deck; and sure enough there was a poor fellow seen fast going astern in the wake of the ship, which was then steaming nine knots an hour. Fortunately the Quarter-Master had seen the accident and threw two life-buoys after him. In less time than I take to tell it, the ship was stopped, a boat lowered with six men and an officer, and all eyes were directed to the man, who was seen to have caught the life-buoy and therefore comparatively safe. After some minutes' suspense, but without the slightest confusion, the boat was seen to reach the man, the officer waving his hat to show that all was right, and they rowed back to the ship, which had been brought round to meet her. It was fortunate the sea was smooth, or it might have been a much more difficult task to save the man, who did not appear to be any the worse for his ducking, but to-day he is rather ill from its effects. He must have had considerable presence of mind, for he not only caught the first buoy thrown overboard, but swam to and secured the second one, observing that it was a pity it should be lost! The whole "sensation" lasted half-an-hour, and all rejoiced that the man was saved, although the accident appears to have arisen from his own carelessness, being over the side cleaning the ship without a rope made fast to his body, contrary to the rule in such cases. It was a great mercy he was not drawn into the vortex caused by the screw propeller.

January 19th.—We are driving through a north-west gale, which commenced before we left Lisbon on the 16th, and has continued ever since, with a very heavy sea, which prevents our making progress, as the engines have to be slowed, nor can we carry much sail—but we have got half-way through the Bay of Biscay, and hope to pass Ushant to-morrow. It is very uncomfortable work for all on board, but there is no help for it. Lisbon looked its best whilst we were there, as there was a bright sunshine for some hours, and the merry windmills were driving along under the influence of a strong westerly breeze. There was no English man-of-war in the Tagus, but two Yankees, and a Prussian which was reported to have had a brush with a Frenchman off the Azores, but no particulars were known. Our voyage has not been fortunate as regards weather. The Oneida is, however, a capital sea boat, if not a very fast one, and it would be difficult to drive any vessel through such a sea as there is now, so we must be content to arrive a day or two later at our destination. We passed the Cearense steamer from Para coming out of the Tagus, bound to Liverpool, and yesterday we passed a large steamer standing the same course as ourselves, so we were going faster than she, at all events. A good many passengers left us at Lisbon, who were replaced by about an equal number, going to Southampton, as the railway route through Madrid and France is not now practicable. Few of the new-comers have been able to appear at table.

January 21st.—We reached Southampton Docks at 10 a.m., with moderate weather up the Channel, thus completing our return

The Viscount do Rio Branco,
President of the Council of Ministers at the
time when the Law was passed for the
Emancipation of Slaves.

FROM 1870 TO 1876.

Up to the period when the foregoing Diary was written, in 1870, affairs in South America had gone on very prosperously, both in a commercial and in a financial sense. In Brazil, the continued high price of coffee had thrown a large amount of wealth into the country; and equally so with wool, tallow, and hides from the River Plate. All was quiet politically, with exception of the pending questions in reference to Paraguay—a danger looming in the distance between Brazil and the Argentine Republic, which at one time threatened serious consequences. Happily, the difficulty was settled by judicious diplomacy and the exercise of forbearance on both sides, Paraguay being now left perfectly free to follow out its own destinies under a programme of self-government. Both countries had been preparing for the possible contingency of war, and large sums of money were expended in ironclads, torpedos, and other accessories. This state of things did not, however, injuriously affect the credit of either country, and Brazil had negotiated two loans in London on the most favourable terms, one of £3,000,000 in 1871, and another of £5,000,000 in 1873. The Argentine Republic succeeded, in 1871, in raising a six-per-cent. loan for the prosecution of railways and other public works, at the favourable price of 88½, which was effected through the agency of Messrs. C. de Murietta & Co. Another Buenos Ayres City Loan of £2,140,800 was effected in 1873, by Messrs. Baring, Brothers, & Co., the credit of the Republic being then at its culminating point.

Whether stimulated by the successful launching of these loans, following the high prices of Argentine produce in European markets, or by inflated ideas of the growing prosperity of the Republic, a period of speculation set in at Buenos Ayres of the most extravagant nature, not only as regards imported articles of merchandize, but also in the purchase of lands and house property, carried on with facilities supplied by the Hypothecary and other banking establishments, to an unprecedented extent, driving up values in a fabulous manner. Individual expenditure, as a necessary consequence, followed, until the city of Buenos Ayres became one vast emporium of gambling operations and of personal extravagance, accompanied by a corresponding inflation of credit. Meanwhile events were occurring in Europe and the United States which were sure to affect the credit of South American States. Prices of wool, hides, and tallow were rapidly falling, and a general commercial and financial crisis prevailed both in Europe and the United States. The Paraguayan loan collapsed, as might have been anticipated, followed by that of Uruguay, and latterly by the heavy downfall of Peruvian financial credit. All this soon began to be felt in Buenos Ayres, where a steady decline commenced in the value of house property and land, purchased chiefly by the issue of paper engagements; commercial credit was shaken to its foundations; failures to an enormous extent followed, and for the last three years Buenos Ayres has passed through an ordeal to which few large commercial communities have been subjected. As a matter of course, the revenue of the State became affected; its multiplied engagements, arising out of civil wars and other local drains, began to tell heavily on the national resources, and indescribable confusion ensued, eagerly availed of by speculative newspapers in London to depreciate the market value of Argentine securities, which soon dropped 50 per cent., with many subsequently violent and wide fluctuations.

In the midst of this chaos, the Government and the Executive maintained their equanimity, although a succession of finance ministers took place, and various measures came before Congress to relieve the financial position, most of which were rejected, the result being a suspension of specie payments by the National and Provincial Banks, and the issue of what is there termed "curso forçado," or a forced paper currency. Fortunately means were found to meet the dividends and amortization on loans falling due, thus affording breathing time to the Government, which has throughout evinced its loyalty and determination to uphold national credit. I do not enter into details of these arrangements, which are of so recent a date; suffice it to say that the issue of £2,000,000 National notes, bearing interest at 4 per cent., with 5 per cent. annual redemption, solved the difficulty, and sent down the premium on gold from 33 per cent. almost to zero; it is an institution of *greenbacks* over again, and will prove equally successful, evincing the confidence in the Executive and in the resources of the country. The redeeming feature in the midst of all these drawbacks is that the internal resources of the country, its cattle, sheep, and horses remain intact and have gone on multiplying enormously. The proprietors of estancias, as a body, not having been mixed up with speculative transactions, only feel the diminished value of their produce. How the commercial and financial collapse at Buenos Ayres could have reached such wide proportions, leading to the closing of some 4,000 shops and dwelling houses, is one of those mysteries difficult to explain, as there was no doubt much accumulated wealth in the city, and the business carried on appeared to be legitimate enough. There must, however, have been something exceedingly wrong in the system, and a delusion existing somewhere, otherwise things would not have reached such a pass. The delusion has been rudely dispelled, after three years of intense suffering, and it is to be hoped a more healthy state, both of commercial and financial business, will henceforward be established throughout the Platine States, for which there is every possible scope and opportunity. Those who have bought houses and land at fabulous prices will have to submit to the disagreeable ordeal of seeing others possess them at a very reduced value, and the banks which made improvident advances may suffer accordingly; but posterity will gain by the folly of their predecessors.

Let us now turn to what Argentine resources really consist of, in order fully to estimate the capability to meet the National engagements at the present time, which, in the shape of internal and external indebtedness, amounts to some £14,000,000 sterling.

In the first place we must remember that the Argentine Confederation is only of recent growth, having been finally consolidated in 1861, after the battle of Pavon, when General Urquiza was defeated by the Buenos Ayrean army under command of General Mitre, afterwards unanimously elected President of the Argentine Republic; up to that period Buenos Ayres was a separate State, managed by its own local government, succeeding the long

Dictatorship of Rozas. The confederation then formed was on the model of that of the United States of America, each province having a governor exercising independent jurisdiction, with its own local revenue. The National revenue is derived chiefly from the Custom House and indirect taxation. The difficulty of bringing so many discordant elements into practical working need hardly be described, the distance of the provinces from the capital city of Buenos Ayres being at that time a great drawback; moreover, the largest and most influential province—that of Entre Rios—was really under the control of General Urquiza, who, on the outbreak of the Paraguayan war in 1865, withdrew his troops and refused to co-operate with the National Government. The assassination of Urquiza in 1870, and the subsequent rebellions under Lopez Jordan, are now matters of history, and I only allude to these circumstances as illustrative of the difficulties, both political and financial, which the National Government has had to contend with. As regards the distant provinces, they are so little known, and their products so undeveloped, that no calculation can yet be made of their future contribution to the national wealth, beyond the fact of their being very fertile, both as semi-tropical and temperate regions; and railways will soon bring them into play. Cattle breeding and sheep farming districts abound on the pampas, or plains of enormous extent, between the Atlantic and Pacific oceans, lying east and west of Buenos

Ayres, some portions bordering on Indian territory, from whence occasional marauding incursions take place, entailing the necessity of protecting the frontiers at a considerable outlay of money.

It will thus be seen that the national revenue has had many heavy drains upon it, not the least of which was caused by the unhappy revolution of General Mitre last year, who, with the majority of his party, were dissatisfied at the election of President Avellaneda. The decision and energy displayed by the latter quickly suppressed what at one time threatened most serious consequences to the cause of freedom and good government. Occurring, too, at a time when Buenos Ayres was suffering from a financial and commercial crisis, this fresh disturbance could not fail to augment it, by interfering with the usual course of business and creating a want of confidence in the stability of Argentine institutions. No wonder, therefore, that the credit of the country was shaken and the executive power weakened, requiring all the energy of the latter to bear up against the pressure thus put upon it. That the resources of the country are equal to the occasion has been abundantly proved, by a continuation of the payment of dividends and amortization of foreign loans, and by the great rise which has again taken place in the value of Argentine and Buenos Ayres stocks in this market. I shall now proceed to show what these resources really consist of.

I cannot do better than quote from the admirable

and truthful pamphlet published by Mr. C. Frederic Woodgate, in May this year. He commences by saying that "One of the most prosperous countries in the world, and well worthy of the attention of European capitalists, is the Argentine Confederation. Situated in the temperate zone of South America, between 22 and 52 degrees of south latitude, it is in the enjoyment of the very finest climate, the beauty of which is perhaps only thoroughly appreciated by Englishmen on their return to their own country after a long residence there." He then proceeds to describe its provinces, and what they produce, as shown in the official exports for 1874, wherein the value is given as £12,446,485 sterling, against an import of £10,184,031, exclusive of the value of materials for railways and public works, free of duty, amounting to £1,300,000.

The revenue of the National Government is given as follows (the greater part being derived from import duties):

	Dollars.	
1863	6,478,682	
1864	7,005,328	
1865	8,295,071	
1866	6,568,554	
1867	12,040,287	
1868	12,496,126	
1869	12,676,680	
1870	14,833,904	
1871	12,682,155	the yellow fever year.
1872	18,172,379	
1873	20,217,231	
1874	16,090,661	the monetary crisis.
1875	17,206,746	

"The budget for 1876 voted last year by Congress was twenty million dollars; but by recent decrees of the Government this amount has been reduced to eighteen millions, and the revenue promises to be twenty millions, the same as 1873, as the Custom House of Buenos Ayres *alone* had paid in to the National Treasury from 1st January to 31st March $3,687,275,15, against $3,245,618,98 at the same time last year. Twenty millions would be at the rate of $11.51 per head of the population, or £2 7s. 6d. sterling, and this is exclusive of the provincial and municipal taxation."

The national indebtedness at the same time (January, 1876), as taken from the Blue Book for the year 1875, shows the following figures:

Resume.	£	s.	d.
Internal debt 21,032,506,16 dols. Ex: 49½d ...	4,337,954	7	11
Foreign do.	7,821,100	0	0
Treasury Bill 3,860,000 dols. Ex: 49½d ...	804,450	6	8
Pending claims under examination	1,500,000	0	0
Total at the rate of £8 6s. 6d. per head ...	£14,463,504	14	7

Upon which Mr. Woodgate justly remarks: "This debt cannot be considered excessive, considering the revenue and the value of the railways, telegraphs, &c., which belong to the nation; and nevertheless English bondholders have only lately been assured that the country would never be able to pay the interest and sinking fund. The budget of 1877 will be presented to Congress this month, and on its arrival in England the determination of the Government to materially reduce expenses will be manifest. The late Sarmiento Government has been accused of lavishly spending the proceeds of the last Public Works Loan of 1871 in ironclads and armament. This is an unjust accusation. Of this loan of six millions only five million pounds have been issued, and the proceeds of this amount have all been expended in public works. It is true that about a million sterling has been spent in forming a small fleet of the most perfect heavily-armed vessels afloat for river warfare, and in providing the army with Remingtons instead of the old, useless muskets; but this was spent out of income, and considering that only two years ago any of her neighbours could have blockaded the port of Buenos Ayres and closed her trade—I will not say with an ironclad, but with a common gunboat—and that during the last revolution the whole of the rebel army under General Mitre was beaten by a battalion and a half of infantry armed with their new rifles, and obliged to capitulate, I think it must be admitted that Congress was justified in spending this money; and very little doubt can be entertained that the recent settlement of affairs with Brazil was rendered easier by the existence of this powerful little fleet."

These are the leading figures in the case, upon which the stability of Argentine National Securities rest; and I think they must be admitted as satisfactory, even by the most carping journalist; but behind this array of figures there are other subjects of great interest embodied in Mr. Woodgate's report. First I will take his notice of railways and telegraphs :

"*Railways.*—In the year 1857 the first railway was commenced; since then the following have been constructed, or will be finished before the end of this year, the country being admirably adapted for them—

	Works commenced.	Miles.	Proprietors.
Western	1857	150	Provincial Government of Buenos Ayres
Northern	1862	18	London Company.
Great Southern	1864	202	Do.
Boca and Ensenada	1863	37	Do.
Central Argentine	1863	245	Do.
Villa Maria & Rio Cuarto	1870	82	National Government.
Cordova and Tucuman	1873	336	Do.
Rio Cuarto and Mercedes	1873	76	National Government.
Eastern Argentine	1873	96	London Company.
Buenos Ayres & Campana	1873	42	London Company.
Total miles		1284	

of which 644 miles belong to the country."

"*Telegraphs.*—Not only is Buenos Ayres connected by cables with Europe, but within the last few years lines have been constructed to every one of the interior provinces, and even across the Andes to Chili."

Next comes a review of the Province of Buenos Ayres, with its multiplied wealth, the tramways of the city comprising :

P

	Miles	Men	Cars	Horses	Proprietors
City of Buenos Ayres	30	351	48	610	London Co.
Argentine	12	137	33	370	Ditto.
Belgrano	12	109	20	257	Native Co.
Lacroze	7	60	18	199	Ditto.
National	12	94	17	275	London Co.
Boca and Barracaos	10	100	30	300	Native Co.
	83·	851	166	2,011	

The case of the Provincial Bank is a remarkable illustration of the growth and prosperity of the country. Established in the year 1853, just after the expulsion of Rozas, with only a capital of 216,597 hard dollars, the latter had reached 1,793,683 hard dollars in 1863, the first decade; 15,465,231 hard dollars in 1873, the second decade; and 19,152,827 hard dollars (nearly four millions sterling) in 1875. On the figures given by Mr. Woodgate, he remarks:

"No writing, I think, could prove more forcibly the growing prosperity of the country; and if the country at large is getting so rich, the Government, unless overweighted with debt, which we have seen is not the case, cannot be in a very bad way.

"The first column shows us that the private deposits gaining to-day an interest of 6 per cent. per annum only, when the market rate is 10 to 12 per cent., has increased from £37,490 in 1854 to £4,905,203 at the end of last December; besides this amount, we have to add the deposits in all the country branches. I have not the last returns, but at the end of 1872 the deposits in the twelve branches then open amounted to £2,009,390.

"The second column shows that deposits gaining no interest have increased from £88,547 in 1853 to £997,315 last December.

"The third column shows that the amount employed by the bank in discounting has increased from £87,589 in 1853 to £8,050,785 last December, and that in December, 1873, it had reached the large amount of nine millions sterling.

"And, lastly, by the fourth column it will be seen that the capital of the bank has increased from £43,319 in 1853 to £3,830,565 last December, just half the capital of the Bank of France—a larger one than that of any English joint stock bank—and that it is increasing at the rate of £400,000 to £500,000 per annum. To what extent the Legislature will allow this capital to increase, events will show; but it is clear that the yearly profits of the bank are even now sufficient to pay one half the expenses of the provincial government; or if employed in public works, the drainage and water works, and even the port, could in a very few years be carried out without any other assistance."

Mr. Woodgate enters at some length into the important subject of the production of sheep and cattle, the following extract embracing the whole :

"Our tables show us that 4,500,000 poor sheep since 1852 have produced one hundred and fifty-six millions, and that the stock to-day cannot be less than fifty to sixty millions; and that although we have been killing about two million head of horned cattle every year for the last ten years, our stock is to-day perhaps greater than ever; these are simple facts."

This is supplemented by an official note in another place, as follows:

"This is fully confirmed by the previous tables, which show that the Custom House valuation (which may also be considered as the value in the country) of the total exports in 1874, which was not a good one, was silver dollars 39,413,265, of which 75.82 per cent. was produced by the Province of Buenos Ayres, say 29,883,137. The stock of sheep in 1874 as proved by the export of wool was 40,505,472, and at 35 dollars currency or 1.40 silver dollar each, the value was 56,707,660 silver dollars; and taking the stock of horned cattle as 10,000,000, their value at 135 dollars currency or 5.40 silver dollars each, would be 54,000,000, total 110,707,660, the return being 27 per cent."

The export tables attached to the pamphlet give the seasons production of wool, from 1852-53 to 1875-76, beginning with 20,514 bales, and ending in 215,000 bales, the quantity this year (1876) being estimated at 20,000 bales extra. Of sheep skins, the quantities are respectively 1,398 bales and 52,051 bales. These figures are eloquent of progress!

Mr. Woodgate concludes his remarkable statements with a word of advice to Argentine Bondholders, and which I can fully endorse from my own comparatively limited experience :

"When Argentine Bondholders find, as time rolls on, that their dividends and drawings are punctually paid, as they assuredly will be, notwithstanding all predictions to the contrary, public confidence will be restored, and this mode of investing English capital may possibly merit their attention. In the meantime, if these pages, written during the voyage home, should in any way contribute to strengthen their trust in the country in which I have resided for the last twenty-seven years, or tend to the development of its great resources, I shall consider that my object has been fully attained."

I will now proceed to notice other incidents which have taken place in the Argentine Republic, evincing the desire of the people to keep pace with the times; amongst them the establishment of cattle shows, and improvements in the breed of horses, cattle, and sheep, where much money has been spent by enterprising estanceiros, both natives and foreigners, to say nothing of horse races, now a national institution. There is a society in Buenos Ayres, called the "Sociedad Rural Argentina", which has published its ninth annual report, for 1875, consisting of a large folio volume headed "Review," dedicated to the defence of the rural interests of the country, and to the propagation of a knowledge of agriculture in all its branches. It is impossible for me to analyse the contents of this volume, or the numerous subjects treated of, beyond a cursory allusion to some topics with which we are more familiar, such as the breeding of animals, which swarm on the plains of the Pampas, particularly in the province of Buenos Ayres. There is a chapter dedicated to Arab horses, possessing peculiar interest at this time, when European countries are looking to South America for an augmentation of their supplies for mounting their cavalry, the wear and tear of which it is found difficult to provide for in these times of enormous military organization. As I have said, all nationalities are admitted to compete in the agricultural and pastoral race, and the honoured names of Sheridan, Latham, and Fair are amongst Englishmen best known in River Plate annals in this category. During the last half century many thousands of Englishmen and Irishmen have settled in the province of Buenos Ayres, successfully following pastoral pursuits. The volume alluded to gives a report of the agricultural show held in 1875, where the largest number of prizes appear to have been awarded to Mr. John Fair, owner of the Espartillar Estate under the able management of Mr. Patrick V. A. Reid, which again heads the list, having carried off the largest number of prizes at the Exhibition this year, and a pair of handsome Rambouillet ewes was ordered to be photographed by the society. The following animals were shown from the Espartillar Estate last year: six horses, of which one thoroughbred stallion, called "Lord Eskdale," took a first prize;

"Loch Fergus," a half-bred Clydesdale stallion, a second prize; five pure Lincoln sheep, a silver cup; five ewes, cross between Lincoln and Merino, silver cup; and five Rambouillet ewes, a silver medal.

A society of this kind must be essentially useful in a country where the area is so great, and the distances so widely asunder as to render meetings at some central points an absolute necessity, if the cause of agriculture is to be effectually promoted. The capacity of the country for agricultural and pastoral pursuits is almost unlimited; and the more these occupations are extended the greater will be the facilities for carrying them on, particularly as railways make their branches into parts of the country hitherto excluded by distance from participating in the more advanced provinces. Protection from Indian marauders is of course an absolute necessity, and with internal peace there is the greater chance of this being effected, as also the Guacho element being kept within proper restraint. Guachos are useful enough in their way, but they should not roam about wildly, alarming peaceful settlers and perpetrating crimes of the blackest dye.

RAILWAY DEVELOPMENT.

The best introduction to this most important subject is to take the official statement, published in the *Sociedad Rural Argentina*, showing the comparative statistics between the Western Railway and others in the province of Buenos Ayres:

ARGENTINE RAILWAYS.

DESIGNATION.	WESTERN.	GREAT SOUTHERN.	NORTHERN.	ENSENADA.
Length of line ...	kil. 254 50	kil. 324 65	kil. 29 871	kil. 58 546
Gross traffic	3321705 —	28154695 —	8319654 —	5212 897
Expenses	1827800 2 —	15917979 —	4723476 —	4843037 —
Net earnings ...	14843708 —	12236716 —	3596178 —	369860 —
Proportion between earnings & expenses	55184 —	56540 —	56771 —	92900 —
Gross traffic, per kilometre run	134915 30	86723 23	278519 43	89039 33
Expenses ditto ...	74452 15	49031 20	158129 16	82721 91
Net earnings, per kilometre run	60463 15	37692 03	120390 27	63141 42
Train, kilometres run ...	634685 —	538638 —	188650 —	209168 —
Ditto by carriages	,, 8742294 —	,, 8159380 —	—	703710 —
Ditto by locomotives	,, 20676 —	,, 19950 —	,, 20961 —	23200 —
Passengers ...	,, 961324 —	,, 524214 —	,, 495505 —	681867 —
Number of tons of equipages and cargo	6407 —	—	2736 —	1361 —
Mean product per ton ...	370 97	103822 —	·159 65	211 03
Number of tons of goods	219048 —	153 91	40809 —	29383 —
Mean produce per ton ...	74 27	23 21	45 69	49 28
Consumption of coal per train kil.	,, 18 76	,, 7 28	,, 22 12	17 74
Ditto grease and oil per 100 kils.	11 —	8 35	5 55	7 82
Traction expenses train kilometre	7 85	2 29	8 02	8 17
Ditto Personal ...	3 90		6 79	4 92

This statement does not include the Central Argentine Railway, which formed a prominent subject in the foregoing narrative. It is situated in the respective provinces of Santa Fé and Cordova, Rosario being the starting point and the city of Cordova the terminus—247 miles in length.

Upon the progressive traffic of this railway I would call to mind the fact that the Central Argentine Railway is the first railway constructed in the upper district of the River Plate; and I would therefore first endeavour to show, as fairly as can be, a comparison between the traffic originally estimated at the commencement and during the earlier stages of the undertaking, and the traffic as since developed, for which we have in our possession reliable data.

The original estimates of Mr. Campbell and Mr. Hutchinson of traffic between Rosario and Cordova taken, say for the years 1855, 1860, and 1862, were as follows: Goods, 1855, 17,686 tons; ditto, 1860, 13,371 tons; ditto, 1862 16,326 tons; whilst for the year 1855 Mr. Campbell estimated, or rather ascertained from reliable sources, that the full number of passengers might be taken not to exceed 1,500.

During the year 1866, whilst Mr. Robert Ogilvie was manager at Rosario for the late contractors, Messrs. Brassey, Wythes & Wheelwright, his attention was particularly directed to enquire into the various sources of traffic, and the rates at which it might be considered sound policy to commence the conveyance of goods and passengers, looking forward to the opening at an early period of the remainder of the line to Cordova, and bearing in mind the peculiar character of the competition, all goods being conveyed by cart or on the backs of mules. It may, therefore, now be of advantage to make reference to a communication which was made by that gentleman to the directors in January, 1867, and where the subject was fully entered into. We find that he estimated that a traffic in goods of 39,240 tons per annum might fairly be expected, and that this would produce, at 4d. per ton per mile, a revenue of about £153,000. With regard to passengers, even allowing for the period of ten years having elapsed since Mr. Campbell's report had been taken, it will be found that Mr. Robert Ogilvie, in 1866, did not consider that an annual number of more than 3,000 passengers could be calculated upon; which, with parcels, &c., might give an annual revenue of £14,000, or altogether a gross estimated revenue of £167,000. The railway was opened through to Cordova on the 17th May, 1870, and I would therefore recapitulate here the actual results, obtained from the directors' report to the shareholders at the 12th yearly general meeting, held on the 14th July, 1876:

Year ending May 17.	Passengers, including Soldiers. No.	Receipts for Passengers, Parcels, &c. £	Ordinary Goods Traffic.		Total Ordinary Receipts. £
			Tons.	£	
1870–71	37015	31161	36319	87514	118675
1871–72	59220	34846	48958	108664	143510
1872–73	72072	34111	51876	112280	146391
1873–74	71699	36218	57334	120473	156691
1874–75	84398	35888	61908	122757	158645
Five Years	324404	172224	256395	551688	723912
Average	64881	34445	51279	110337	144782

Year ending May 17	TOTAL.—ORDINARY TRAFFIC.			EXTRAORDINARY TRAFFIC				GROSS TRAFFIC.		
	Passengers. Number.	Goods. Tons.	£	Military £	Public Works. Tons.	Public Works. £		Passengers. No.	Goods Tons.	£
1870–71	37015	36319	118657	2333	—	—		37015	36319	121008
71–72	59220	48958	143510	2313	14914	23916		59220	63872	169739
72–73	72072	51876	146391	2338	7813	11991		72072	65689	160720
73–74	71699	57334	156691	5553	10964	22119		71699	68298	184363
74–75	84398	61908	158645	55991	25237	49801		84398	87145	254637
Five years	324404	256395	723912	58528	58928	107827		324404	321323	890267
Average.	64881	51279	144782	11705	11785	21565		64881	64265	178053

From the above statements it will be seen that the estimates of 1866 were very fairly confirmed during the first five years after the opening to Cordova. The ordinary traffic, showing an average of £144,782 per annum, and if the extraordinary traffic of military transport and material for new lines be included, an average has been obtained of £178,053 per annum. With regard to the military traffic, I do not think it quite correct that the revenue from this source should be excluded, because there is no doubt that during the periods of revolution the company was being deprived of a large portion of ordinary traffic. And with regard to the revenue from the transport of materials for new railways, I am of opinion that it ought not to be entirely excluded, if at all, as it is a fair and legitimate traffic, due to the development of the country, and was one of the original sources of revenue contemplated in the concession. The conclusion, therefore, which I come to in contemplation of the previous figures is that the railway has, for the period of five years from the opening to Cordova, fairly obtained a gross traffic and revenue greatly in excess of what was ever contemplated, and that we are justified in assuming that the means which have been adopted to obtain that result have been prudent; and it becomes very problematical, had lower fares for passengers or rates for cargo been adopted, whether a greater number of passengers or tons of goods would have been carried.

From the autumn of 1868 to May 1872 the general management of the traffic of the railway was under the superintendence of Mr. Cooper, a gentleman who had been previously, and has since, been connected with the Southern Railway of Buenos Ayres. His long residence in the country and knowledge of the language enabled him to form probably the most correct judgment with regard to the means of obtaining the largest amount of traffic and revenue at the least possible expense, and to inaugurate a policy which I believe has been in the main carried out by his successor, Mr. Fisher.

Examining, therefore, the following summary:

	Per Annum. Estimated Ordinary.		Average 5 years ordinary.		Average 5 years gross.	
	Quantities.	£	Quantities.	£	Quantities.	£
Passengers No.	3000	14000	64881	34445	64881	34445
Goods, Tons	39240	153000	51279	110337	63064	143607
		£167,000		£144,782		£178,052

Mr. Thomas Brassey, M.P., has lately been over this railway on his visit to South American countries in his beautiful steam yacht the "Sunbeam," and his report upon it will be received with much interest. The opening of the Tucuman railway renders the Central Argentine the main trunk line between Buenos Ayres and the northern provinces of the Confederation, which must greatly contribute to its general traffic. The break in the gauge (the Tucuman line being a narrow or metre gauge, and the latter 5 feet 6 inches, or Spanish one) is a drawback; but only in a secondary point of view, causing a change of trucks and carriages at Cordova. All South American railways are single, with double lines and sidings at the principal stations, where the trains pass each other; nor has this process yet been attended with any accident. The rate of speed is moderate, but rapid enough when contrasted with the former mode of travelling, as an instance of which I may mention that the first trip over the Tucuman line (336 miles) was accomplished in 20 hours, as against 15 days in the old style. Indeed, it is not easy to foresee the revolution which this new mode of locomotion must cause in traffic between the capital and its provinces.

The next railway I have to notice is my old friend the Great Southern of Buenos Ayres, with which I was formerly connected, and whose steady progress I have watched with great interest. The following extract is taken from my book published in 1868 when alluding to "railways in the River Plate." "Next in importance (after the Western Railway) comes the Great Southern, 71 miles in length, which was made by an English company, under a Government guarantee of 7 per cent. on £700,000, but the capital actually raised was

£750,000, the contractors taking £50,000 in unguaranteed stock on certain conditions as to their participation in dividends. The expenditure has been further increased to nearly £800,000, owing to additional disbursements for goods stations and for increased rolling stock. The line was opened throughout in December 1865, and the traffic has gone on steadily augmenting, with improved receipts, the result of the first year showing a net profit of nearly 3 per cent., the second year a fraction over 5 per cent., and the present year (1868) promises fair to reach 7 per cent., guaranteed by the Government, when it will be self-sustaining and free from all the drawbacks necessarily incident to a condition of State aid. This enterprize has a prosperous future before it. The great question which remains to be decided has relation to an extension further south, or in a south westerly direction, so as to intercept the large amount of traffic which still comes forward by the ordinary bullock carts." How far this prospect has been realized I leave the shareholders to judge. With a continued extension of the line to Dolores, as originally contemplated, and latterly to Las Flores and Azul, comprising a total distance of 270 miles, the traffic has gone on augmenting, so as to pay 8 and 10 per cent. dividend, nor will it stop there. As railways multiply, the land traversed by them becomes more valuable, population increases, and the beneficial ramifications are such as can only be fairly estimated by those who pay close attention to the subject.

I cannot better illustrate the subject of this railway than by inserting the following particulars just supplied me from an official source :

	Miles
Buenos Ayres to Chascomus, opened January, 1866	71
Altamirano to Las Flores (Salado section opened June, 1871 Las Flores section opened June, 1872)	75
Chascomus to Dolores, opened 1st January, 1875	56
Las Flores to Azul, opened 1st January, 1877	68
Total	270

The dates of opening are those on which the respective sections became part and parcel of the main line, and do not indicate the actual day of approval by the Government. Commencing in 1866 with a gross annual traffic of £63,500, the following have been the succeeding annual returns of this property, say—

Year 1867	....	....	£85,300
,, 1868	....	....	99,130
,, 1869	....	....	124,880
,, 1870	....	....	133,880
,, 1871	....	....	161,952
,, 1872	....	....	181,206
,, 1873	....	....	213,161
,, 1874	....	....	229,834
,, 1875	....	....	354,538

The returns for 1876 have not yet reached us, but we may assume that the figures will be some £10,000 or £15,000 less than those of 1875, consequent entirely upon the commercial crisis through which the country has passed. It must be clearly understood that no portion of the 1876 receipts belong to the Azul line.

The entire railway, less some thirty miles, is laid with steel rails of the best description and with the Livesey cast iron sleeper, and is without doubt one of the best and most substantial permanent ways in the world. The necessary materials are already in Buenos Ayres for renewing the remaining thirty miles with steel, and in a few months the entire 270 miles will be of steel. The company possesses 33 powerful engines, 117 passenger carriages, 812 goods waggons, and 32 brake vans.

The central station at the Plaza Constitution in Buenos Ayres has long ago proved too small for the immense traffic of the line, and the company have in the last few years acquired some 40 acres of land, at a little distance from the present terminus, and here they have erected large additional warehouses, workshops, &c., at a cost of over £200,000 sterling. All this has been brought about in ten years, and it is quite fair to assume that the facilities of transport now afforded by the railway will bring about an equal development in the next ten years, for the productive capacity of the district served is practically unlimited. This splendid property is owned by an English company, who maintain a local committee in Buenos Ayres. The present manager of the line is Mr. Edward Cooper, who is a man of great administrative ability and resource, and who has, by his management of this property, shewn what may be done by an industrial enterprise, which devotes itself solely to the development of the country it serves—thus conferring immense benefits, and receiving in return a high rate of interest upon the capital invested. No institution of the Republic has done more to strengthen and maintain the credit of the country than has the Great Southern Railway of Buenos Ayres.

Of the Western Railway less is known than any other, from the circumstance of its being entirely Government property. Its origin was a small suburban line made by Mr. Bragg, in 1853 (now a partner in the eminent firm of Sir John Brown and Co., of Sheffield), and at that time there was little money or inclination to embark in railway undertakings.

The success of the Great Southern acted as a stimulant to railway undertakings, and the Western was continued to Mercedes, then to Chivilcoy, and latterly it has been pushed on to Bragada, a total distance of about 140 miles, with a branch also from Mercedes to Lobos of $42\frac{1}{2}$ miles. This railway traverses a rich pastoral country, a portion being also agricultural. No regular traffic returns are published, but it is said to yield a net dividend of $8\frac{1}{2}$ per cent., which must render it a source of considerable revenue to the Provincial Government. It has been in contemplation to sell it to an English company, but the times are not very propitious for an operation of this kind. Under existing circumstances it might be good policy on the part of the Argentine Government to induce foreign capital to take up their railways, some of which would of course require to be accompanied with a substantial guarantee until such time as they become self supporting. The examples of the Western line, the Great Southern, the Central Argentine, and the Northern of Buenos Ayres are encouraging, as they prove conclusively that traffic grows as railways are extended, and once established they have seldom any retrogression, if only the conditions attached to them are favourable. It cannot be expected that every railway constructed in a new country is to be an immediate success, nor should railways be entered upon as a mere speculation, of which we have unfortunately too many examples; gradual development, with a due regard to pecuniary resources, is the only safe principle to act upon—a consideration that we doubt not will have its weight in future with the Argentine executive. If a warning was wanted in addition to these general observations, I might cite the case of Peru, where vaulting ambition to carry the iron road over the summit of the Andes has led to an expenditure quite beyond the resources of the country to bear, great as the latter have undoubtedly been,; and this, combined with the dishonesty of both Government and people, has entailed national bankruptcy.

THE ARGENTINE REPUBLIC AT THE PHILADELPHIA EXHIBITION.

If national exhibitions produced no other result they are wonderfully fecund in the way of writing; and in this case the Argentine Republic is represented by a closely-written folio volume of 463 pages, with innumerable statistics and various maps; the whole comprising a history of the Republic from the first settlement of the country by the Spaniards down to the present time : its natural and cultivated productions; its internal resources, both commercially and financially; in fact, there is everything to be found in the volume that could present itself to the minds of enquiring Yankees, satisfy curiosity, or supply information. This elaborate work is edited by Mr. Richard Napp and assistants, originally written in German, and translated into English. In the introduction to the work it is stated, after referring to the numerous advantages offered by the fertility of the soil, and the productiveness of the Pampas for animal life : " Doubtless Argentine flour will compete with that of the United States before long in the markets of Eastern South America, and it will help to provision Europe. Tobacco, oil, flax, etc., will soon figure amongst our articles of exportation; and the increase of the agricultural population will cause the cultivation of the vine, of cotton, of sugar cane, the raising of the silk worm, and the preparations of several dye-stuffs which abound in this country. A little later on, the immense forests which the Republic possesses will furnish precious wood for exportation. This assertion will astonish those who only know the Province of Buenos Ayres; but it is far from being the most favoured by nature, and it might be said that she has treated it as a step-mother, were its natural products to be compared to those of its sisters."

There is much truth in this conclusion, and it fully justifies what I have contended, that very little is yet known as to the resources of the Argentine Republic. It would be impossible for me to give anything like an analysis of this important work, so I must content myself with a corroboration of facts presented elsewhere. It is stated, as regards the breeding of animals in the Confederation, that the number of horned cattle is 13,493,000, representing a value in gold of $84,433,358; horses, 3,960,331, value $17,602,170; mules, 266,927, value $719,778; beef, 57,546,448, value $84,234,369; goats, 286,227, value $2,710,756; hogs, 257,368, value $617,868; besides poultry and numerous other domestic animals. The value of the above is thus summed up:

		Dollars.
Horned Cattle	value	84,443,354
Sheep	,,	84,234,369
Horses	,,	17,602,170
Mules	,,	719,778
Goats	,,	2,710,759
Hogs	,,	617,868
Representing		190,328,298
Or, in sterling value		£38,065,659

There is no exaggeration in this statement, as any one conversant with the subject can testify. Besides the above, which may be termed the staple capital of the country, there is the annual export of wool, hides, jerked beef, tallow, and other products resulting from them, constituting the floating or exchangeable capital, which goes to pay for goods and merchandize imported into the Republic, and I believe the balance of trade will soon be largely in favour of the latter. In addition to the foregoing enumeration, wheat and maize are now being largely cultivated, and becoming articles of export, instead of having to be paid for to Chili and other countries as formerly.

So much has lately been written in reference to Argentine finances, its revenue, comparative imports and exports. I can only add that the foregoing returns fully corroborate the statements set forth by Mr. Woodgate, and I leave the reader to draw his own conclusion, whether the resources of the Republic are not fully adequate to its responsibilities. It may require time and forbearance to work everything square, but this will be done; and the onward march of events must be in the right direction.

BRAZIL.

As I have before remarked in this review of occurrences since 1870, Brazil has suffered comparatively little during the financial and monetary crisis that has passed over the globe. Her great staple trade of coffee has continued good, and there has been no undue speculation in Rio de Janeiro. The rise that has lately taken place in the value of sugar will greatly relieve the Northern Provinces, and it is to be hoped lead to a revival of trade there. The chief events as regards Brazil have been the passing of a Slavery Emancipation Act in 1871, and a Reform Bill during the last session, under which a new parliament has been elected, supposed to be favourable to the Conservative party, but likely to contain more of the Ultramontane elements. I allude to this in a notice on the movements of the Vatican.

The Philadelphia Exhibition has afforded an opportunity for Brazil to bring her productions forward, and the visit of the Emperor has given additional zest to the programme, his Imperial Majesty having been most cordially received there, and welcomed throughout the United States. The publication of a large volume on the occasion will add materially to a knowledge of the resources of the Empire, and is calculated to inspire general confidence therein. His Majesty has since traversed a considerable portion of Europe, even reaching Constantinople, now the great scene of political contention, and wherever he goes he displays the same activity, combined with intelligent enquiry, which has rendered his name so famous. It was reported, on the authority of the *Athenæum*, that the Emperor was about to publish a book of his travels; but I cannot, so far, trace this information to any authentic source. The financial position of South American countries is now the great question of the day, and as regards Brazil I can give the following very satisfactory summary, lately published. The next budget will be promulgated at the meeting of the Chamber elected under the new Reform Act, and I believe it will be a full and frank one, calculated to confirm the favourable opinion entertained as to the financial position of the Empire.

BRAZILIAN DEBT AND FINANCES.

The Public debt amounts to (June, 1876) a sum of £72,013,434, made up as follows:

Foreign Debt	£19,815,400
Home Funded	29,000,000
Floating Debt	23.198,034
	£72,013,434

Brazil has seven loans (all at Rothschild's) in London, which amounted in January, 1876, to the following sums:

1852	4½ per cents.	£1,210,000	emitted at	95
1859	5 „	270,000	„	93
1860	4½ „	775,000	„	90
1863	4½ „	2,690,000	„	88
1865	5 „	6,184,200	„	94
1871	5 „	3,385,000	„	89
1875	5 „	5,301,200	„	98
		£19,815,400		

The original amount of the above seven loans reached £23,222,000, showing that £3,406,600 has been already redeemed.

The Home Debt of Brazil is made up as follows:

Government stocks, four, fives, and sixes	£26,000,000
Gold Bonds, 6 per cent.	3,000,000
Government notes and Treasury bills ...	20,000,000
Orphan Fund, &c.	3,200,000
	£52,200,000

The six per cents. are always above par, and these include almost the whole funded debt; five per cents. only amount to £220,000; and four per cents. to £12,000. About 84 per cent. of the Home Debt is held in Rio de Janeiro, 3 per cent. in Bahia, and 12 per cent. in foreign countries:

In Brazil	£25,200,000
In England	2,100,000
In other countries ...	1,700,000
	£29,000,000

The credit of Brazil on the London market ranks almost on a level with France, her 5 per cent. stock being usually near par. The home paper-money debt and Treasury bills do not include 4 millions sterling of bank notes not guaranteed by the State.

The Government paper-money of Brazil was only seven millions sterling before the Paraguayan war, but it rose to twenty-two millions sterling in 1869, and since then has been every year reduced; being now about nineteen millions sterling, including Treasury bills. Besides the Government paper-money three banks have right of emission, viz., Bank of Brazil £3,500,000, including £670,000 at the branches of Pernambuco, Bahia, San Paulo, Minas, Maranham, Para, and Rio Grande do Sul.

The Bank of Bahia emits £160,000, and that of Maranham £27,000; which, added to the sum for the Bank of Brazil, make up a total of £3,867,000 in bank emission.

The growth of Brazilian revenue in late years is shown by the following figures:

1864	£6,100,000
1868	7,830,000
1873	12,098,000
1874	11,240,000

The Budget for 1876 showed as follows:

RECEIPTS.

Import duties	£6,100,000
Export duties	2,000,000
Pedro II. RR	720,000
Stamps	2,200,000
New Loan Account	2,600,000
	£13,620,000

EXPENSES.

Interest London Debt	£1,040,000
Ditto Home Debt	1,860,000
Railways and Colonies	3,240,000
Army	1,680,000
Navy	1,240,000
Docks and Harbours	1,200,000
Custom House	2,800,000
Emperor, Parliament, &c.	320,000
Law Courts	600,000
Churches and Schools	520,000
Foreign affairs	100,000
	£14,600,000

It may be remarked that the sum of £2,600,000, derived from the London loan of last year for £5,000,000 sterling, has been entirely devoted to making new railways.

BRAZIL AND THE VATICAN.

Nowhere are the demands of the Vatican more exigeant than in Brazil. There the superior clergy, in faithful obedience to the mandates of Rome, unambiguously assert the supremacy of the ecclesiastical over the civil authority, which they have ignored, and even defied. The executive power, representing the national sovereignty, has not failed to resist the inadmissible claims of the church. A serious struggle is therefore now in progress in the empire, a struggle in which the priest party are making every effort to establish a dangerous *imperium in imperio*, and to subordinate the public interests to those of hierarchy.

The course adopted by the Vatican in Brazil is not exceptional. It is that pursued in every country whose population is devout in its adherence to the traditions and dogmas of the Romish church. I do not wish to assail that church, or to call in question the Articles of Belief peculiar to its communion; but I must frankly deplore that its rulers should formulate theories of predominance altogether opposed to the spirit of our times. Nevertheless, such is the fact. Far from abating its pretensions the church is raising them. We are, indeed, forced to the conclusion that, were its power equal to its will, kings, and princes, and peoples would be again reduced to that condition of servility to the spiritual authority which characterised the darkest periods of the mediæval ages. The Vatican has, in truth, challenged modern civilization—set itself in inexorable opposition to liberal thought. How the conflict will terminate may be safely predicted. The Vatican, we are free to admit, though happily shorn of its former terrors, is still a potent antagonist; but it is feeble in comparison with that overwhelming force with which it must contend—a force that has grown into power and greatness under the fostering influence of extended culture, political freedom, religious liberty, and scientific research.

The conflict between Church and State remains undecided in the only South American monarchy, as well as in many of the surrounding republics.

There, as elsewhere, I am convinced the national sovereignty will ultimately sustain its just rights against priestly usurpation. But at this moment there would appear to be some ground for discouragement. The election of members for the Representative Chamber of the Empire has just been consummated. The priest party (who have been most energetic in their canvas, bringing into active use, from the spiritual armoury at their disposal, the accustomed engines of clerical warfare) has, it is stated, succeeded in procuring the return of a very formidable contingent, pledged, without reference to political divisions of opinion, to vote in support of the objects of an arrogant episcopate. The English journal of Rio de Janeiro —*The Anglo-Brazilian Times*—in noticing this, remarks: "In the next Chamber of Deputies, therefore, although the Government will, as natural, have a large majority, it will be in the presence of two powerful sections, the one avowedly in opposition, the other ready to use either party to advance the aims which it holds pre-eminent over the highest principles of constitutional government." The Imperial Executive, with great firmness, though with politic temperance, has calmly vindicated the supremacy of the civil power; and it is to be hoped that it will continue to manifest the same determination to sustain the national sovereignty, notwithstanding the serious pressure brought to bear upon it by unscrupulous Ultramontanism. Much, however, must depend on the people themselves, and it cannot be denied that in Brazil the masses—being in a great measure uncultured, even in the most rudimentary sense—are greatly under the control of their spiritual teachers. Fortunately, not a few of the latter are aggrieved at the intrusion of foreign Jesuits, selected to fill the place of preferment to the exclusion of priests native born. The spirit of discontent has, too, been materially aggravated by the contempt of the Brazilian priesthood evinced by these Jesuit fathers. One consequence of this state of things, is that, in numerous instances, the humbler Brazilian clergy are somewhat disposed to sympathise with the assertion of national rights by the civil power in opposition to the inflated pretensions of an unpopular hierarchy.

Its hostility to freemasonry is the immediate cause of the contention with the church in Brazil. In that country certain fraternities have long existed, associated for charitable and friendly objects. Though quasi-religious in composition, they form no part of the corporate organization of the church to whose control they have never been other than incidentally amenable. It so happened that the members of these brotherhoods included some who were also freemasons; the latter, declining at the bidding of their bishops to abandon freemasonry, were excommunicated, and their expulsion from the "tainted" fraternity was insisted upon. Compliance with the episcopal order being refused, the Bishop of Olinda, in Pernambuco, launched the dread anathemas of the church, and pronounced an interdict depriving them of the comforts and privileges of religion, suspending its most solemn rites and offices. New fraternities, after the bishop's own heart, were formed, and civil rights were invaded by the proud prelate. These harsh proceedings which, as might be expected, were not regarded with indifference by the Imperial Government, naturally gave rise to an appeal by the sufferers for protection from illegal oppression. Thus invoked, the civil power, reluctantly enough, was compelled to interfere. Its action was at first limited to remonstrance, but all remonstrance was in vain. The Bishop of Olinda emulated the example of the Holy Father. His only answer to every representation was *non possumus*. He was a standard-bearer of the inerrable church; he could not lower the flag of an infallible Pope. It was impossible that he should concede that the episcopal power was subject to any other will than that proceeding from Rome. At last the Bishop of Olinda was arrested on a charge of treason. When brought to trial before the Supreme court he refused to plead, or to admit in any way the competency of a civil tribunal. His friends, however, availed of every technical or argumentative ground to avoid sentence, which was eventually pronounced, finding him guilty, and adjudging him to a short term of imprisonment. The imprisonment of the recalcitrant prelate was little more than nominal; it simply amounted to detention. He dined, or might have dined, sumptuously every day. Free access was given to his friends; his communications with the external world were uninterrupted. He could not make good any claim to martyrdom, which, had severer measures been adopted, might have been urged in his behalf. The civil power, in his formal imprisonment, intended solely to vindicate its supremacy.

The energy of the Imperial Government produced a corresponding influence on the Vatican, and a mission to the Pope resulted in a sort of armistice, which offered, we think, delusive prospects of future peace. Without relinquishing its pretensions, the church, as represented at Rome, seemed disposed to suspend their enforcement. This, at least, was believed to be the case in Rio de Janeiro, whereat there was much jubilation; and, subsequently, the Bishop of Olinda was released from durance by grace of the Emperor.

I regret to say that at this hour the relations between the civil and the ecclesiastical powers could hardly be less satisfactory. The Church is availing of all its resources to render itself dominant, and the Government has before it a very onerous conflict. As I have already stated, the policy of the State in making its defence has been of a very solicitous and patient character. How long this temper may last we cannot guess. Should the peril become imminent, it is probable that the civil power in Brazil would have recourse to more aggressive expedients. If so, the responsibility will be with those who shall have provoked reprisals.

Recent events in Venezuela have shown that, in South America, the rights of the civil power can be asserted with a resolution equal to that at any time exhibited by the nations of Europe. In that Republic the executive and legislature have concurred in meeting the usurpations of the Vatican with defiance as shown in a message addressed to the Congress, by General Guzman Blanco, in which he speaks as follows:—

"Citizen Senators and Citizen Deputies,— In my report of the administrative year, which closed on the 20th February last, I said, speaking of Archiepiscopal disputes, that the last term which I had been asked to grant, was in order that, in conformity with certain indications received from Rome, Señor Guevara should present to His Holiness his resignation of the Archbishopric, an act by which the usurping policy of the Holy See believes that Venezuela could alone be enabled to elect an Archbishop and the Pope authorised to grant him the faculty to act, all which is to ignore the sovereignty of the country (the whole source of power whence its prelates derive their jurisdiction in their Dioceses or Archbishoprics), and is moreover diametrically opposed to the express text of Articles 16 and 17 of the law of Patronage, in force since 1824, which literally is as follows:—

"'Art. 16. Those designated by the Congress for the Archbishopric and Bishoprics, before they present themselves to his Holiness through the Executive Government, must make before said Executive, or the person whom the Executive may delegate to this end, the oath to sustain and defend the constitution of the Republic, not to usurp her sovereignty, rights, and prerogatives, and to obey and fulfil the laws, orders, and dispositions of the Government. Two copies of this oath shall be drawn up, both to be signed by the nominees, one of which shall be passed to the Senate, and the other to the Chamber of Deputies, to be kept in their respective Archives.

"'Art. 17. As soon as the nominees have made the preceding oath they may enter into the exercise of their jurisdiction, the Executive summoning the ecclesiastical bodies to this effect, but they shall not enjoy the emoluments of their office until the Pope shall have confirmed their nomination.'

"The term granted terminated the 19th of April; but, as the Pope's Nuncio in Santa Domingo notified to me, on the 20th, that on the 21st he would proceed to Trinidad, in order to obtain the resignation of Señor Guevara, in conformity with the instructions he had just received, I judged it advisable that I should make a new and final effort, and await the result of the conference between Monsignor Roccabocetria and the Ex-Archbishop.

"Yesterday I received the official intimation that Señor Guevara refuses to resign, and I am also informed that the Nuncio has not the power to oblige him to resign nor to remove him.

"Such being the situation, all diplomatic means of settling the Archiepiscopal dispute are exhausted, and it must not be transmitted unsolved to the next Government without exposing it, as well as the national cause.

"Representing as I do that cause by virtue of the reiterated vote of the nation, as responsible before history for the consolidation of the work of April with which the people have charged me, and with the full conviction that our enemies, cloaked under the name of the religion of Christ, would change the splendid future which we are labouring for in our country's behalf for that dark past which fanaticism would render frightful in the future, I ask you with full conviction, and assuming the most welcome responsibility of all, that to fulfil my mission I have taken upon my name to pass a law which shall declare the church of Venezuela independent of the Roman Episcopate; and ask that you further order that parish priests shall be elected by the faithful, the bishops by the rectors of parishes, the archbishops by Congress, returning to the usage of the Primitive church founded by Jesus Christ and His Apostles.

"Such a law will not only resolve the clerical question, but it will be besides a grand example for the Christianism of Republican America hindered in her march towards liberty, order, and progress by the policy, always retrograde, of the Roman Church; and the civilized world will see in this act the most characteristic and palpable sign of advance in the regeneration of Venezuela."

"GUZMAN BLANCO.

"Caracas, 9th May, 1876."

The Congress responded to the President of the State in language even more emphatic. From its reply I extract as under:

"Illustrious American, President of the United States of Venezuela.

"The Legislative Chambers, assembled in Congress, have considered with patriotic interest the important message communicated to them through the Ministry, under date of the 9th instant, upon the Archiepiscopal question.

"Congress sees, with profound displeasure, that the Roman See refuses to satisfy the just desires of the people of Venezuela upon the grave question which we are engaged in debating, through the fault of a Prelate, false to his duties as a priest and a patriot, and who dares to insist upon the right to over-ride that national sovereignty, which we exercise, as an independent and free nation.

"The country knows, noble American, that with wisdom and prudence you have endeavoured to conciliate the interests of Venezuela with the capricious demands of the Roman See, as far as our national dignity, the majesty of our institutions, and the high duties which the revolution of April imposed upon you, have permitted; and thus the members of this Congress, founders of this glorious epoch of National Regeneration, convinced of the justice which assists Venezuela in this dispute, and inspired with the convictions of their constituents, which repel all foreign intervention, do not hesitate to associate themselves with Y. E. to fight in this last battle (all diplomatic efforts having failed) against the Roman See, in the name of modern civilization and our national sovereignty.

"Faithful to our duties, faithful to our convictions, and faithful to the Holy Dogmas of the religion of Jesus, of that great Being who consecrated the world's freedom with His blood, we do not hesitate to emancipate the Church of Venezuela from that Episcopacy which pretends, as an infallible and omnipotent power, to absorb from Rome the vitality of a free people, the beliefs of our consciences, and the noble aspirations and destinies which pertain to us as component parts of the great human family.

"Congress offers to Y. E. and will give you all

the aid you seek to preserve the honour and the rights of our nation, and announces now with patriotic pleasure that it has already commenced to elaborate the law which Y. E. asked it to frame.

"Rely upon our patriotism, and upon our loyalty to the great principles of our democratic Republic.

"Signed,—
"T. V. GUEVARD,
"President of Congress and of the Senate.
"EDUARDO CALCANO,
"President of the Chamber of Deputies.

"Together with the Vice-Presidents and Secretaries of both Chambers.

"Caracas, 16th May, 1876."

Truly these are "great words," but the rulers of Venezuela did not allow energetic deeds to wait tardily on doughty phrases. Without delay a decree was issued, in which the jurisdiction of the Roman episcopate was repudiated, and the church in Venezuela declared to be national and free. I will close this chapter by quoting the concluding paragraph of an article on this subject which appears in *The Brazil and River Plate Mail:* " What Henry VIII. did for England, Guzman Blanco, with higher motives, is doing for Venezuela. To cast off allegiance to the Pope, to repudiate the supremacy of the Vatican, and to create an independent national church, surely these are events of no mean importance, and we marvel to reflect that they should have apparently escaped the attention of the journals of this country, whose people must sympathise so greatly with the laudable effort this South American Republic is making for its disenthralment from the depressing influences of Papal control. We hail these occurrences as a palpable indication of the regeneration of Venezuela, and we are disposed to believe that a new era has been inaugurated for the South American continent. It is not to be supposed that the grand example of Venezuela will fail to find emulation in the sister Republics, where the burden of the clerical yoke is each day becoming more intolerable and oppressive."

BANKING INSTITUTIONS IN THE RIVER PLATE.

It has been shown in this narrative how successful banking operations in Buenos Ayres have been up to a very recent period, and it is difficult to conceive how in a few years the Provincial Bank, virtually established as such in 1853, with very slender means and no proprietary interest, should have accumulated a capital of nearly four millions sterling to December last year, as described by Mr. Woodgate. The explanation may be found in the fact that it is simply a huge savings bank, protected by fiscal privileges, and possessing almost a monopoly of the currency, charging whatever rate of interest the directors think proper, with perfect immunity from loss, enabling it to sweep away any assets of debtors before other creditors can come in at all. Naturally enough, in a country where the best securities were only discounted at 12 to 18 per cent. per annum, large profits were realized as trade and commerce increased, but at the expense, in a great measure, of the trading community. Private banking against such a monopoly was difficult to carry on; but individuals engaged in discounting bills were for a long period enabled to compete with the Provincial Bank, and to derive a share of the profits on such transactions—running a risk, of course, whenever they came in contact with that institution in the case of a defaulting debtor. Under such circumstances the encouragement for foreign capital to be employed in promoting and augmenting the commerce of Buenos Ayres was small; but in 1863 the London and River Plate Bank, with its domicile in London, made a successful start, and took a large share of business that had previously been carried on through private channels, such as the discounting of bills and making advances on produce. For several years large profits were made and good dividends paid to the shareholders; but when once a commercial and financial crisis arose the bank could no longer employ its funds either safely or profitably, owing to the fiscal privilege enjoyed by the Provincial Bank, and they consequently had to remain with more or less a dormant capital. It was only recently that the full effect of these drawbacks were fully realised, and no dividend was earned from the last half-year's working. Consequent on the success of the London and River Plate Bank others followed, such as the Argentine, the Italian, the Belgian, German, and the private bank of Wanklyn & Co., recently converted into the Mercantile Bank of the River Plate, with a London board; the oldest bank, that of Mana, being nearly contemporary with the Provincial. Finally, in 1873, the National Bank was formed by order of Congress, with a capital of twenty millions hard dollars, of which the Government subscribed for two millions, and the shares were run up to a high premium.

The competition naturally created by so many new banking establishments reduced materially the traditional rate of interest, and profits fell accordingly; but the great blow they received was from a long series of trade failures, dating as far back as 1873, resulting in a loss, as already shown, of some ten millions sterling. To the commercial body, the object of these observations is not so much a recapitulation of past events as to show the injurious tendency of the fiscal privilege enjoyed by the Provincial Bank, which places all other banking institutions at an unfair advantage with the favoured one, and must eventually drive foreign capital from the

Plate. Reverting to the London and River Plate Bank, its case has been strongly illustrated by proceedings of the Governor of Santa Fé, with which most people are familiar, it having received additional importance from the following letter of President Avellaneda addressed to the said governor.

"Tucuman, Nov. 9th, 1876.
"To Governor Rayo, Santa Fé.

" My Dear Governor,—I have received your favour of yesterday relative to our conversation about the petition of Rosario merchants, and I fully agree with you that it is the business of the Santa Fé Legislature to settle a question involving the trade interests of the principal markets of the Republic. We may also fairly hope that the Legislature will be as favourably disposed as your Excellency expresses yourself towards the petition for modifying those measures that have no longer any 'raison d'etre.'

" Fiscal privileges, as your Excellency truly observes, are not without precedent in our country; but they can never be accepted as a system of economy; nor are they admitted in any country worthy of imitation, on the scale here given to them. The greatest favour conceded to any special bank is the right of emission subject to certain stipulations with the Government.

"Outside the Argentine Republic we can nowhere find fiscal privileges such as the old Roman and Spanish codes supposed for one institution to recover its credits in preference to all others.

"Moreover, bear in mind that the province of Santa Fé, with its flourishing agricultural colonies and steady influx of settlers, is specially interested in encouraging an influx of capital from abroad and the protection of what is already here, if we would not nullify the good effects of the energy and intellect well directed of so many statesmen and private individuals. The maintenence of fiscal privileges will be fatal to all progress, because it is a constant menace to capital, preventing its profitable investment.

" Another consideration we should never lose sight of is this: experience shows that all sound policy and economical science is based on liberty, whose effects are alone lasting. Restriction and monopoly can only give some ephemeral advantage which quickly disappears, leaving an inheritance of painful deception.

"The principle of respect for authority, so essential in all civilized countries, is not weakened by the triumph of free institutions, but notably invigorated, because in a limited sphere of action it may be developed with the greater energy whenever the occasion requires.

"Again begging your Excellency to accept the assurance of my high esteem, "I remain,

"NICHOLAS AVELLANEDA."

It is obvious from the tenor of this letter that the views of the President of the Republic are in accordance with those of all enlightened nations, and that to bolster up a native bank by giving it fiscal privileges over all others is to deaden the sense of individual responsibility, and to render traders callous in the engagements they enter into; knowing that if anything goes wrong their assets are swept away by one bank, and the rest of their creditors left in the lurch. Such legislation is only worthy of worn out countries, like Spain, not applicable to a young and rising state, where all institutions should be on a perfect equality in the eye of the law, and the greatest possible facility afforded to the influx of capital in every shape and form. Until this change takes place foreign capital is placed at a disadvantage, and will in all probability be withdrawn. These remarks are applicable to both sides of the River, though at Monte Video it relates more to the right of issue than to fiscal privileges; nor is there any National Bank in the "Queen City," as it is called.

THE REPUBLIC OF URUGUAY,

COMMONLY CALLED

THE BANDA ORIENTAL.

The phases through which this little State has passed of late years are so many and so varied as to render any succinct account of it quite unintelligible. During my visits in 1868 and 1870 things were bad enough, as will be perceived by details then given, but they have been much worse since. In 1871 a six per cent. loan was obtained in London, through the agency of Messrs. J. Thomson, T. Bonar, & Co., for £3,360,000, at the favourable price of 72½; and it was confidently expected, from the position of Monte Video at that time, with the largely increasing Custom House receipts, that an era of political quietude and of commercial prosperity had set in. Unhappily the same spirit of insubordination and mania for revolution again broke out, and gradually all relapsed into anarchy. For a time the dividends on the loan were regularly paid, but at the commencement of last year they ceased altogether, nor has anything since been paid, though promises are held out that something in this way will soon be forthcoming. The dictatorship of Colonel Latorre has, at all events, been successful in the maintenence of peace, which is something to boast of; but it will take time to re-establish confidence. Monte Video has passed through the same commercial and financial crises as Buenos Ayres; but there is nothing to prevent it rising again, if only the people will abide by the law as established, no matter under what head or title. What is termed the dictatorship of Colonel Latorre is a firm, though a mild one, such as any loyal citizen may submit to; but whether it will suit the temper of the Orientals for any length of time remains to be seen. That Uruguay is a fruitful and productive country every one admits; its geographical position, too, being one of the finest in South America; yet, without peace and quietness, all these advantages are lost. A considerable amount of English capital has been embarked there, which at present is quite unproductive. I allude particularly to railways, of which several have been projected and partly carried out, but only one completed, called the Central of Uruguay, from Monte Video to Durazno, a distance of 135 miles. It was first established as a local company, having its domicile on the spot, but this has been found to work so badly that a change has been made, in the formation of a

London board, and the whole affair reconstructed. The lines are all guaranteed seven per cent. by the Government, which up to the present time is inoperative, as nothing is paid. The traffic on the Central Uruguay is not unpromising, and, with a return of commercial prosperity, it may be rendered self-supporting. At present great difficulties have to be overcome.

Monsieur Vaillant, a resident of Monte Video, has devoted much labour to show the favourable nature of Uruguayan resources and the productiveness of the country; but figures alone do not inspire confidence. They must be supported by facts showing the willingness of the people to submit to law and to maintain order. So far this desirable element of progress has not been visible, nor the desire manifested to stand well in the estimation of Europe. In many respects Uruguay has advantages over her opposite neighbour, from the circumstance of its constituting one compact State, without responsibilities beyond its own territory, which is bordered by Brazil, and many people think it would be an advantage for the Banda Oriental to be joined to Brazil, but national jealousies will never permit this to be carried out. The line of demarcation between the Spanish and Portuguese races is one too strongly drawn to admit of friendly union, nor would the exercise of force be desirable, even if of practical realization. The Platine States are as separated from the Brazilian monarchy as if the chain of the Andes interposed between them, and so it will probably continue for centuries, as it has done in the past. Monte Video holds in some measure the key to Platine States, and it is for the interest of all others concerned in them that she should exist as an independent one. Internal troubles are of their own creating, and have little to do with external political influences.

The last subject I have to notice is that of Paraguay, the unhappy victim of the lawless ambition of one man, who paid with his life the misery he brought on his country, leaving it almost a barren waste—so far as population is concerned. The attempt to resuscitate it by an infusion of English capital is too fresh in the minds of many sufferers to require illustration, nor is the true history of those transactions yet brought to light, in spite of enquiries before a committee of the British House of Commons. After the examples supplied by Honduras, Costa Rica, and other similar swindles, much cannot be said as regards the infatuation that existed in regard to Paraguay. With internal peace and industry the country may become self-supporting, but beyond that little can be looked for in this generation.

THE AMAZON VALLEY AND ITS COMMERCIAL FUTURE.

To the peoples of Europe, and to the vast majority of our own countrymen especially, the Amazon is little more than a geographical expression. If asked to mention the name of the largest river in the world, many might doubtless indicate the majestic Amazon, and the better instructed might even furnish some meagre particulars as to the course and volume of the great river; but very few indeed are possessed of real information as to the vast natural resources of the immense regions irrigated by its waters, and traversed by the numerous affluents that pay it tribute. Yet the day is not far distant when the Amazon basin will become a centre of active and important commerce, and when busy and influential populations will aggregate where now the solitudes

s

of the primeval forest are unbroken by those sounds familiar to civilization and human progress. The indications of material development, though not obtrusive, and hardly noticed by the daily records of our time, are nevertheless obvious to more careful observers, and too significant to be long ignored.

The Amazon takes its rise in the Andes, within 100 miles of the Pacific, and flows to the Atlantic Ocean, after a course of 3,950 miles. It passes through Peruvian territory for a distance of 1,800 miles, entering Brazil at the western limits of the Province of Amazonas. Having entered the territory of the Empire, with the proportions of a first-class stream, and navigable even for sailing vessels of considerable tonnage, the Amazon rolls on in fluvial grandeur for the remainder of its course to the sea, where it disembogues almost under the equator, previously dividing into two branches, of which the northern is by far the broadest. The rapidity of the stream varies, but it is usually about four miles an hour, at least, during the rainy season. In the dry season the flow is less impetuous. The influence upon the ocean of the entrance of so large a volume of water as that of the Amazon is very marked. When the tide begins to ebb—it is felt as high as the town of Obydos, 400 miles from the mouth of the river—and the retreat of the sea-water giving free way to the arrested current, the latter pours out with augmented force into the ocean. Near to the land it encounters the strong current which runs along the north-eastern coast of Brazil. Coming into contact with great violence, it is stated the waters rise to a height of 180 feet. The shock is so dreadful that the neighbouring islands tremble, and fishermen and navigators fly from it in the utmost terror and alarm.

The valley of the Amazon is level, and comprises one-third the entire extent of Brazil. The climate, though of course tropical, is nevertheless salubrious, and its virgin soil is extremely prolific when brought under cultivation. At present the commerce of the Amazon is almost exclusively confined to articles of spontaneous production.

The tributaries of the Amazon, many of them of greater size than any of the rivers of the Old World, form a net-work of fluvial communication of the most comprehensive character, and afford a natural highway for the commerce of the greater portion of the South American continent. The Rio Cassiquiari establishes a navigable connection between the Oronoco and the Rio Negro, one of the most important of the Amazonian affluents, and nearly all of the South American Republics, holding territory shedding its waters in the "great main of rivers," are deeply interested in every enterprise calculated to promote the development of the resources and capabilities of the mighty stream. But this is especially the case as regards

Brazil and Bolivia. As we have already noted, the Amazon basin comprehends two-thirds of the whole Empire, and Bolivia must continue to be isolated and commercially impotent until it can succeed in utilizing its riverine approaches to the Atlantic Ocean.

On the 7th of September, 1867, the Brazilian Government, casting aside the exclusive and narrow traditions inherited from the Portuguese, declared the Amazon open to the ships of all nations, and this enlightened and liberal policy has not been unproductive of beneficial results. The riverine traffic, stimulated by increased steam navigation, has attained more important proportions, and a powerful English company, owing its origin to the Viscount de Manà, with a large capital, carries on a growing business on the Amazonian waters. It has a good many steamers, and enjoys a subsidy from the Imperial and Provincial Governments. The full extent of the commerce of the river does not appear in the published statistics, but the figures accessible are full of promise, and the trade of this magnificent valley is capable of almost unlimited extension.

We are glad to observe that another step in the direction of mercantile progress has been taken in the formation of an Amazon Tug and Lighterage Company, which has despatched recently to Para two steamers and six lighters for the navigation of the river. One of the steamers—the Villa Bella—

is a magnificent paddle steamer, of more than 600 horse-power, constructed for the purpose of towing five of the lighters, fully laden, against the stream, at an average speed of seven knots an hour. This steamer, we learn, is also furnished with the most complete appointments for the conveyance of passengers, which is the more necessary, as owners are generally in the habit of accompanying their own produce. The contract for her construction was signed by Mr. E. J. Reed, late Chief Constructor of the British Navy. Referring to this subject, the *Anglo-Brazilian Times* remarks as follows:—" The success of the new system adopted by this company has been already proved by the efficient working of the company's steamer 'Theotonio' and two lighters, which commenced operations last year, and we hail this new and powerful addition to the company's fleet (which now consists of three steamers and eight schooner lighters, capable of carrying an aggregate of 2,500 tons) as the opening up of a new and more prosperous era to the vast provinces of Para and Amazonas, which have received no such addition to the navigation of their almost illimitable water highway since the Brazilian Government in 1867 declared the Amazon free to the flags of all nations."

The most considerable tributary of the Amazon is the Rio Madeira. It falls into the former at a point 900 miles from the Atlantic, and is over 2,000 miles in length. It receives the waters of the

Mamoré and the Beni, the first of which rises near the sources of the Paraguay, in the Chuquisacan Cordilleras, while the latter originates somewhere in the vicinity of Lake Titicaca. Both traverse the most inhabited and fertile regions of the Republic of Bolivia, for whose exports they would furnish a natural outlet, at once facile and inexpensive, were it not for the interruption of a series of cataracts or rapids, which prevent navigation, save by canoes. Even these descend and ascend with much difficulty, labour, and danger. At some points the canoes have to be taken out of the water and dragged along the margin for long distances. It is probable that the work of removing those rapids by canalization would be too costly to be undertaken at the present moment. The Government of Bolivia, principally concerned in securing a free navigation, is too impecunious to undertake such a task, and the prospects of return are not sufficiently prompt to induce capitalists to find the necessary money. But a line of railway has been projected to avoid the rapids—twenty in number— by connecting the navigation above and below; and although the realization of this enterprise has been delayed, in consequence of litigation in the English courts, there are now reasonable grounds that the works will be carried on to completion without further impediment. I, of course, refer to the Madeira and Mamoré Railway, the capital for which was raised in England in the form of a loan to the

Bolivian Government, whose policy in the inception of the scheme is certainly sufficiently intelligible; but it is not so easy to understand the grounds on which, later on, it appeared desirous to join with short-sighted bondholders in frustrating an enterprise so intimately identified with the vital interests of the Bolivian nation. Under existing circumstances, the commerce of Bolivia has to surmount the rugged summits of the Andes, merchandise being carried on the backs of mules or llamas, the only beasts of burden that can travel with safety the dangerous paths alone available for mercantile transit from the Bolivian interior to the Pacific; and even when the Pacific is reached, the stormy passage round Cape Horn has to be made before the markets of Europe are attained. Exchanges with the Old World, owing to the cost and toil necessarily entailed by this laborious and slow conveyance, are limited to articles of small bulk, but great value; none other would pay for the transit in and out of the country. When, however, the rapids are practically obviated by the construction of the proposed Madeira and Mamoré Railway—of which Colonel G. E. Church, an American citizen, has been the principal promoter —there can be no doubt that Bolivian commerce will almost exclusively flow towards its natural channel, and, in the words of a recent traveller in the Amazon Valley, " the virgin wealth of these comparatively unknown regions be poured into the lap of the Old World across the Atlantic, instead of over the Andes." The same writer observes: "The affluents of the Madeira are legion, some of them splendid rivers. All kinds of timber, most of the useful and precious metals, and several kinds of valuable stones are found on or near its banks; and although its course at present lies through the heart of savagedom, the mind involuntarily looks forward to the time when a teeming population will flourish upon its banks in civilized prosperity." Before passing from this topic, we cannot in justice abstain from commending the persistence and energy manifested by Colonel Church in connection with this important enterprise. He has contended against strenuous opposition, and encountered difficulties that must inevitably have broken the determination of a man cast in weaker mould. Those who should, with intelligent regard for their own interests, have been amongst his firmest friends, have offered him the most serious antagonism; but he has, we are happy to say, been successful in his efforts for the vindication and realization of a project worthy of the support of all who desire to help the march of commerce and civilization.

The chief tributaries of the Amazon are, on the right bank, the Javari, Purus, Madeira, Tapajos, and Tocantins; on the left bank, the Napo, Juapura, Rio Negro, Jamunda, and Orixamina. There are many others of lesser magnitude. The Indians on the banks of these great streams, which are covered with vast forests, are mostly in a state of nature, and in many cases dangerous of approach by white men. They live on the spoils of the chase, or upon products spontaneously yielded in regions where they inhabit. With the succulent tropical fruits, the great variety of game, and the salubrious climate, the Amazon valley is in truth a paradise for the indolent man; there he can maintain life almost without an effort. Many of the aborigines are, however, engaged in collecting india-rubber, cacao, sarsaparilla, castanha nuts, balsam copaiba, and aromatic gums.

Mr. J. W. Dowsing, in a communication addressed to the President of Pará, observes as follows:—

> To expatiate upon the beauty, capabilities, and resources of the numerous streams tributary to the great basin of the Amazon, the country margining these streams, the general characteristics of the inhabitants, &c., would invite and justify a voluminous report. I will content myself, however, with a few reflections upon the brilliant future that awaits this favoured country. My investigations disclose that the valley of the Amazon is one immense forest of valuable timber, woods of the finest grain, and susceptible of the highest polish; adapted to cabinet purposes. For building vessels there are no woods on the earth equal to those grown in the valley of the Amazon.
>
> This is the country for indiarubber, sarsaparilla, balsam copaiba, gum copal, animal and vegetable wax, cocoa, castanha nuts, sapucia nuts, tonka beans, ginger, black pepper, arrowroot, annetto, indigo, dyes of the gayest colours, and drugs of rarest medicinal virtues.

These immense forests are filled with game, and all the rivers and lakes are filled with fish and turtle.

The climate of this country is salubrious and the temperature most agreeable. The direct rays of the sun are tempered by a constant east wind, laden with moisture from the ocean, so that one never suffers from either heat or cold. I found the nights invariably cool enough to use blankets.

The Brazilian city of Pará is the principal emporium of the growing traffic of the Amazon. It is built on the eastern banks of a wide river, formed by the confluence of the Rio Tocantins with the Tagopurie, or southern arm of the Amazon. Opposite the town the latter is seven miles in width, and this extensive sheet of water contains numerous low and well-wooded islands. The navigable channel is winding, and generally of no considerable breadth, so that the approach of vessels is somewhat tedious. On the south side is the river Guama. The streets are laid out in blocks, and commonly run at right angles. The population is a motley mixture of Brazilians, Portuguese, aborigines, negroes, and cross-breeds of every description. The cathedral is the principal edifice and has a fine appearance. The other public buildings, with the exception of the college, are without architectural merit, though some of them are of large dimensions. It is lighted with gas by an English company. The exports are exceedingly diversified, and are brought from all parts of the Amazon Valley. It was founded in 1615.

The Rev. Stuart Clough, who, as the agent of

the South American Missionary Society, lately visited the Amazon Valley, on a mission of inquiry, gives an interesting picture of the social aspects of Pará as presented to a stranger. We quote as under:—

The Rua de Belem faces the river, the ground floors being mainly occupied by ship-chandlers, indiarubber and pirarucu stores, the latter exhaling anything but an agreeable odour, especially to a new arrival from the pure breezes of the ocean. Here is the Alfandega or Custom House, an undignified-looking building, with piles of small green cases outside, which I learned were full of gin, a spirit largely imported and sent up the river to the rubber plantations. The poor Indian is so fond of this beverage that the temptation to get drunk upon it when circumstances admit is too strong to be resisted. Just past the Custom House is one of the entrances to the market place, an open square surrounded by a collonade, and which in early morn presents a lively and interesting appearance, most of the female slaves, both black and mixed Indians, being there congregated to make purchases or indulge in household gossip, or audibly discuss the virtues and failings of their respective mistresses. A white, woolly-headed dame, with a chintz gown open to her waist, arms akimbo, and small basin on her crown, stands with pursed lips, while a youthful member of her own sex and colour, rejoicing in a spotless-white, neatly-embroidered petticoat, under a low black dress, opens her heart upon something of personal importance. Every moment she makes a coquettish arrangement of her triple necklace, or shifts the bracelets which almost reach her elbow. A row of dusky ladies sit with their backs to the wall, puffing away at carved, wooden-stemmed, red-bowled pipes, now and then condescending to sell their wares, which consist of a stock-in-trade a hat might hold. In the middle of the square are heaps of pineapples, guavas, bananas, and yellow cacaos, and many other tropical fruits with whose names and flavours, I suppose, I shall become acquainted ere long. Indian women do not possess the suppleness of figure and geniality of the negress; the latter generally having a merry face, twinkling eye, and good display of teeth, while the former wear a quiet, subdued, pensive look. Perhaps the very absence of thought may impart this expression, but I observe several have their eyes downcast, and though possessing a stately carriage, well developed frame, and their bare shoulders exhibiting a skin of the finest texture, they seem too absorbed to participate in the happiness enjoyed by everybody else around.

It is with difficulty that Pará resists the encroachments of the primeval forest, of which Mr. Clough furnishes the following impressive description :—

No tongue or pen can adequately describe the glories of a Brazilian forest. Vegetation is upon such a colossal scale that the eye scarcely knows where to linger most. Here teeming nature has grouped in picturesque confusion an endless variety of plants and trees, all struggling for light and life; and amid the bewildering chaos of splendour the mind wondering wanders on till lost in astonishment, admiration, and praise. Here stands a mighty monarch of the forest with a hundred buttresses to support his giant arms, and shooting upwards straight as an arrow, high above his compeers, he extends his stalwart arms around, while his majestic crown, dripping with morning dew, glistens with joy in the bright rays of the tropical sun. Nestling at his feet, as for protection, is the sensitive mimosa, and like a timorous, blushing maid she shrinks from the intrusive strangers' gaze by closing her eyelids and bowing her lovely head. There is the fantastic though exquisitely beautiful fan palm, with graceful fronds playing in the morning breeze. Beside yonder pool is a host of thirsty ferns of different forms, shades, and sizes, in the latter frequently resembling trees of sturdier genera.

The dark green deeply-degetated-leaved breadfruit and umbragious mango afford a grateful shade, and fruit such as angels might condescend to eat. In this vast wild of luxurious vegetation, undisturbed nature plays a thousand freaks. Two trees of equal growth are entwined round each other, resembling the spiral column of some Moorish Alcàzar, and each surmounted by an exactly similar head, stand just far enough apart to give scope, as it were, for mutual admiration. Soaring above the light green banana, with heavy clusters of luscious fruit pendant from its slender stem, are palms of various kinds, their feathery foliage standing clearly out against the azure sky. Date palms in the east more than derive their attraction from the fact of being the only trees of any size affording food and shade to man and beast amid wide sterile plains, but here their perfect development and graceful forms relieve the eye from after gazing upon an infinite variety of lesser productions. Perhaps nothing excites curious attention more than the multitude of creeping and parasitical plants. Some hang in looped festoons; others in lines side by side throw out their tendrils, embracing each other form a veil of living green. In one direction it is as though a thousand ropes were suspended, for they hang perpendicularly from a giddy height, and when shaken their tremulous undulations is precisely that of a quivering line. Some so completely cover the trunk of the trees as to render them scarcely distinguishable from parasites themselves. Some climb spirally, some in loops, while not a few run straight up from the ground to the branches. Occasionally as many as four or five climbers have attacked a tree simultaneously, and in the race for light and air have struggled with each other. Four have become gnarled and knotted like a hugh excrescence, while the fifth has steadily pursued its course ; but the four, apparently discovering the march stolen upon them, have agreed to fight it out elsewhere, and overtake their more fortunate kindred adventurer; but they are too late, unless they strangle him *en route*, which is not unfrequently done. Here are climbers resembling the fabled

Python in size and power, for in dimensions they actually rival the trees they attack. Often immense trees are completely hidden from sight by the myriads of parasites that cover them.

At different points of the Amazon and its tributaries are other communities, several of which are evidently destined to become important mercantile cities.

The Amazon forests are celebrated for the production of indiarubber, which valuable article forms an item of considerable export from Pará, as will be seen from the following official return:—

Average exports of indiarubber in 1830 to 1848, and 1869 to 1874

Quinquennium.	Average Quantities. Kilogrammes.	Value. Reis.
1830 to 1844	391,605 —	210,000$000
1869 to 1874	5,582,729 —	10,320,000$000
Increase in 35 years	5,191,196	10,110,000$000

The exports, as is seen, have increased considerably, at the mean annual rate of 38.98 per cent. as to quantity, and of 141.50 per cent. as to value; the latter, therefore, much in excess of the former.

I cannot close this chapter of the Amazon without making special allusion to the philanthropic and spiritual zeal of the South American Missionary Society, which has sent its peaceful agents to explore the mysteries of that great "waste of waters," and who have placed on record an account of their labours, than which it would be difficult to find anything more interesting in modern travel. With the feeble resources of the society, unaided by government or other assistance, its missionaries have traversed a large portion of the Amazon and its affluents, particularly the River Purus, where two or three are now residing amongst the Indian tribes, on its banks, pursuing their arduous work of endeavouring to christianize them. These details must be read in order to a thorough appreciation of the difficulties the missionaries have to contend with, greater in some respects than have been encountered in the centre of Africa, with the difference that the Indians are a free people, nor is the institution of slavery known amongst them. One of the earliest pioneers of the society, Dr. Lee, was unfortunately drowned, by the sinking of a small steamer, moored to the banks of the Purus, and on which he was sleeping, some of the crew being on shore. The event was a very melancholy and discouraging one, but it did not deter his fellow-workers, the Rev. Mr. Clough and Mr. Resyek, from following in his track, where they remained up to a recent period. Lately another missionary, the Rev. W. Thwaites Duke, has gone out to join his colleagues, and he has also sent home a very graphic account of his trip up the Amazon. Should these brave, worthy men succeed in their mission on the Amazon, or its affluents, it will be one of the greatest achievements of modern christianity, and may lead to much good, by improving the condition of the singular nomad races existing there in all the majesty of primeval solitude, amidst the dense forests which border the rivers. Some few attempts have been made by Roman Catholic missionaries to found missionary settlements in that direction, but hitherto with very little success. The efforts of the South American Missionary Society therefore deserve support at the hands of their countrymen, as well as of the Christian community throughout the world.

TELEGRAPHIC COMMUNICATIONS WITH BRAZIL AND THE RIVER PLATE.

At the time of my last visit to South America there was no ocean cable laid to Brazil or the River Plate, and the thrilling events of the Franco-Germanic war had, as it will be seen, to be transmitted by steamers from Lisbon, leaving a long interval before their arrival out, consequently creating much doubt and uncertainty in commercial circles as to the course which should be pursued by them. The expense of laying an ocean cable was then looked upon as a formidable thing to grapple with, at the same time its necessity became inevitable. Various attempts were made to raise the needful capital and to form a company, most of which collapsed, owing to the weak foundation on which they were based, and to an extensive system of intrigue, originating in high quarters in Europe; it was further believed that such a cable could hardly be made self-supporting,

T

and that a government subsidy would be required to carry the project to a successful issue. However, in the year 1872, owing to the energy of the then Baron, now Viscount de Mauá, an exclusive concession was obtained from the Brazilian Government, and an influential company formed in London, under his auspices, for the laying of a cable between Lisbon and Pernambuco, the nearest point on the Brazilian coast, first touching at Madeira, from thence on to the island of St. Vincent, and from St. Vincent to Pernambuco. It was a great undertaking, across seas where no attempt to lay a cable had ever been made, consequently it involved the necessity of much engineering skill and a cable of the best possible manufacture. The capital raised was £1,300,000, in 130,000 shares of £10 each, and the cable was confided to the well-known Telegraph Construction and Maintenance Company, who had been so successful on the United States and other routes. The progress of the work was watched with much interest, and the sections were completed in the following order. According to the prospectus the distances were as follows:

	Miles.
Lisbon to Madeira, June 17th, 1874	653
Madeira to St. Vincent, March 18th, 1874 ...	1,260
St. Vincent to Pernambuco, June 23rd, 1874	1,953
Total ...	3,866

The different sections being laid independent of each other.

Contemporaneously with this main line, concessions were granted to other companies for laying cables from Para to Santos, and from thence on to the River Plate—the first called the Western Brazilian, the other the Platino-Brazilieira, about which I shall have more to say further on—first remarking that it would have been much wiser on the part of the South American Governments, interested in these telegraphic cables, to have confided the whole of them to one company, thereby ensuring more unanimity of action, together with a great saving in working expenses; but individual patronage stood in the way of this desirable arrangement and the economical part of the system was lost sight of. The consequence has been that whilst the main line from Lisbon to Pernambuco has worked admirably the other cables have been subject to constant interruption from breakage and accidents of various kinds; still the great object of a through communication has been attained, of which the commercial community are now reaping the benefit.

Reverting to the Brazilian Submarine Company between Lisbon and Pernambuco, and the great experiment of laying it successfully, it may be instanced that more than one failure occurred in laying the cable between Lisbon and Madeira, the cable being picked up and spliced at a great depth, and in a remarkably scientific manner, almost without precedent, thereby creating a further amount of confidence in these wonderful undertakings, which had its origin in the feat performed by Sir James Anderson in picking up and splicing the old Atlantic cable, in September, 1866, a result that gave an impetus to cable enterprise, which has never since looked back. The fact that these cables can be recovered and utilized has made a lasting impression on the public, although on the other hand it has led to active competition, with reduced profits to shareholders. As regards the laying of the cables between Madeira and St. Vincent, and between St. Vincent and Pernambuco, there has been no drawback, and the lines continue to work steadily and successfully in their financial bearing. It is true that only a dividend of five per cent. is as yet paid by the Brazilian Submarine, with, however, a sum of £80,000, prudently carried to a surplus fund, together with over £20,000 value in spare cable, in order to meet casualties; still the shares are at a considerable discount. I may add that the revenue of the company is steadily increasing, the number of messages to and from South America being now nearly double what it was in 1874-5. I would add that this company has its representatives both in Portugal and Brazil, viz., Senhor Carlos F. do Santos Silva, at Lisbon, and Senhor Jose Castano de Andrade Pinto, in Rio de Janeiro.

The Western and Brazilian Telegraph Company has a much larger capital than the Brazilian Submarine, consisting of shares and debentures, together £1,648,200, and latterly a further sum of £200,000 has been proposed to be raised in debentures, for reasons difficult to define. The result of working has been very unfortunate, the company having only paid two dividends of $1\frac{1}{4}$ per cent. each during the year 1875, none in 1876. I have already alluded to the frequent interruptions which this cable has sustained by accidents and casualties of one kind or other, which may in some measure account for the unsatisfactory position of the company, at the same time there must be some inherent defect in connection with it not altogether understood by the public.

The Platino Brazileira cable lies between the Brazilian frontier and Monte Video, and is connected with the Western and Brazilian under traffic arrangements. It has been subject to breakages, nor is the company in a very flourishing position, if I may judge by the absence of published reports and the non-payment of dividends. It is regarded more as a local than an English enterprize, a considerable portion of the capital having been raised in Brazil and the Plate.

The advantages of telegraphy are so fully recognized over the world as to render it unnecessary to make any particular comment upon them, beyond the fact that since their establishment the fluctuations in the value of commodities have been much less violent, or subjected to the heavy losses and drawbacks which existed in the days of sailing ships and then of steamers. It may be that individual gains are reduced by the facility with which advices to and from foreign markets can be transmitted; but on the other hand general trade is exposed to less risks; a safer business can in fact be carried on, and prices be made to approximate more closely. As we have seen, however, in the recent rise of sugar, coffee, and some other articles, telegrams do not impede speculation where there is legitimate ground for it, and the movement originates in an absolute deficiency or scarcity in any particular article. Quick communications tell both ways as regards buyer and seller, besides the great advantage of being posted up as to political events, domestic occurrences, with the many changes of which life itself is composed. Monopolies of any particular article of commerce may be more difficult to establish, nor are the latter, as a rule, beneficial to mankind. As I have said before, the absence of ocean cables was much felt when I was last in South America, and their establishment has been hailed with general satisfaction; the families of the earth being thus brought in closer proximity to each other.

Coeval with, or prior to the advent of, an ocean cable, Brazil and the River Plate had the advantage both of a cable and land wires, the latter being on rather an extensive scale; a cable between Monte Video and Buenos Ayres having been successfully worked for some years. The Brazilian Government has steadily followed out its lines, as will be seen by a statement given in the supplement to this volume, collected from the same source of information as the report of its riverine development, and I have reason to know that the attention of the Brazilian Government is strongly directed to this important subject, both with the object of maintaining internal tranquility, and as a means of communication with the provinces of the empire. In the Argentine Republic during the Presidency of Dr. Sarmiento the system of telegraphs stretched its wires over the whole Republic, and now comprises some 8,000 kilometres in operation, and upwards of 3,000 kilometres in construction or projected. Buenos Ayres is, moreover, in direct communication with Valparaiso by wires across the Andes, extending now up the Pacific Coast by a cable laid along it, so that in a few years more nearly the whole of South America will be linked together by the wonderful power of electricity. That all this is calculated to develope the countries and to lessen the effect of anarchy or revolution, we had recently a striking proof, in the case with which the fanatic attempt of Lopez Jordan was suppressed in Entre Rios. The charge for messages in the Republic is a moderate, uniform one, and a considerable revenue is derived from this source.

Before quitting this subject I may notice the

recent issue, by Mr. William Abbott, stockbroker of the city, of a beautiful illustrated map, showing the ocean cables over the world, together with a report of established companies, their capital, names of directors, and dividends paid; with all other information that can be useful to the public. It is a very spirited undertaking, admirably executed, and reflects great credit on Mr. Abbott, who has made telegraph cables a special study.

Whilst fully admitting the advantage of the telegraph system as applied to South America, I must not lose sight of the fact that if through any unforeseen circumstances it is imperfectly administered, the attendant evils are very great, and certainly, with exception of the through cable between Lisbon and Pernambuco, there is not much reliance to be placed on other portions of the line; nor is the recent meeting of the Brazilian and Western Company calculated to inspire confidence in the future. A writer in the *Daily Telegraph*, who has evidently made himself thoroughly conversant with the subject, quite corroborates what I have just said. He says:

"To business men the frequent interruptions on the lines must have been extremely annoying, as well as pecuniarily prejudical; but that these breaks should occur, and that sometimes absurdly inaccurate transmissions over so many cables and landlines should happen, is not surprising to those acquainted with the complicated systems which make up the route from London to Callao. There are no less than 10 different companies and Government lines, worked by eight separate administrations, through which messages have to pass in traversing a distance rather over than under 10,000 miles. Of this distance the Western and Brazilian Company possesses about 3,700 miles, and, from its exclusive concessions on the coasts of Brazil and Uruguay, forms perhaps the most important connecting link in the system. It compares favourably with the other companies as possessing valuable local traffic, and being really the key to telegraphic intercourse between Europe, the United States, and the whole of South America. The business transactions between those countries must necessarily be large, and in this age of high-pressure intercourse telegraphy must play an important *rôle* in such transaction—*ergo*, a large traffic must exist, and, existing, should necessarily pass over the cables. But, unfortunately, facts have not hitherto borne out these conclusions. And why? This is the question I propose to answer. There are two principal reasons: 1st, the coast cables of the Western and Brazilian Company proper, from Pernambuco to Rio (and Para), are in parts faulty and unreliable. 2nd, the late administration and *personnel* as it existed in Brazil seems to have been even more faulty and incapable of serving the public than the cable. As a consequence, frequent interruptions took place, messages were sometimes delayed for days and weeks, until the public became disgusted and lost all confidence."

He goes on to describe the process of sending messages coastways, with which I will not trouble my readers, nor upon the faultiness of the cables on the Brazil coast, which was admitted at the meeting of the Western Brazilian Company; but his mode of applying a remedy to the existing state of things is worthy the notice of persons interested in the question. Of course the results he arrives at must be known to engineers connected with the companies, as well as to the public. The best thing that could possibly happen, under the circumstances, would probably be an amalgamation of the various companies into one grand institution; but I fear so desirable a result is not attainable, for the present, owing to the many conflicting interests, or until such time as bitter experience brings directors and shareholders together for one common object—the general salvation.

THE MINERAL RESOURCES OF BRAZIL AND THE RIVER PLATE.

No notice of Brazil and the River Plate would be complete that did not make at least passing reference to their immense and still undeveloped mineral resources.

In the empire, the most celebrated mineral region is that to which the name of Minas Geraes has been given, within whose limits is situated that most productive and profitable of gold mines, the St. John del Rey, whose fortunate proprietors only the other day had the satisfaction of receiving a dividend on their invested capital at the rate of 40 per cent. per annum. There are many other mining enterprises in which British money is employed with considerable benefit, though the most fortunate come far behind that we have just named. Gold has always been obtained in large quantities, and is found especially on both sides of the Serra dos Vertentes, from the Serra de Mantigueira to the north branch of the Serra dos Paricis, for a distance of about 200 miles. The alluvial deposits on the banks of many of the rivers have been discovered to contain the precious metal. Diamonds have also been found in certain districts, more particularly in that of Tejuco, where a great number have rewarded the diligence of the diamond seekers. The yellow topazes of Brazil are much esteemed. The more useful minerals exist in abundance; amongst these being iron and coal. As regards the latter substance, the Empire can boast the possession of vast carboniferous deposits of good coal for domestic and furnace purposes, and it is only a subject of astonishment that they are yet unworked. The Viscount de Barbacena, an intelligent and enterprising Brazilian nobleman, has secured a valuable concession, with a view to this development. Though this project has been submitted to the English public, the necessary capital for its realization was not subscribed; but we may hope that eventually the requisite funds will be forthcoming for their utilization. At present foreign coal is imported for nearly all purposes in Brazil, at great cost, and the Imperial industry and commerce would derive signal benefits by the use and consumption of native coal.

The Argentine Republic, in its Andine provinces, has an inexhaustible store of mineral treasure enclosed in the rocky entrails of the magnificent Cordilleras. The Government of the Confederation has lately manifested a strong desire to promote and stimulate mining enterprise, which, under the drawbacks of limited means and inadequate appliances, has, as yet, made little figure as a source of national wealth. Major Rickard, formerly Inspector-General of the Mines of the Republic, made an official inspection of the mines of the Republic, and his able report to the Minister of the Interior, conveys a very favourable impression of their capabilities when worked under more practical and satisfactory conditions. One important obstacle has been removed—the difficulty and cost of transit of the products to the coast. The locomotive now traverses the pampas, from Rosario to Tucuman, a distance of 584 miles, and the influence of the communication thereby established will give a great impulse to mining operations. The mineral products include the precious metals, iron, copper, tin, coal, and a great variety of useful and valuable mineral substances.

Particulars of the mining resources of both countries will be found in the supplement herewith, taken from the published authorities already referred to, which contain much valuable information and statistics illustrative of many subjects cursorily alluded to in this volume.

DIPLOMATIC AND CONSULAR RELATIONS

I extract from recent numbers of the *Brazil and River Plate Mail* the following satisfactory statement as to our diplomatic relations with Brazil and the River Plate:

"With no countries have our diplomatic relations been of a more friendly and cordial character than Brazil and the Argentine Republic. The former is represented here by his Excellency the Baron de Penedo, who has so long and ably filled his mission, and rendered valuable services to the Empire. Happily no questions of serious moment have recently arisen between England and Brazil. Some annoyance has been, however, caused in relation to emigrants, who have, we may assume, been induced to try their fortunes in Brazil under great disadvantages, but we think there is now an end of this element of difference, and Brazil will doubtless seek for emigrants in some more congenial spot, amongst a people better suited to the peculiarities, of her soil and climate. The hospitality of the

Baron de Penedo is well known, and his Excellency was honoured with the presence of the Prince and Princess of Wales at one of the entertainments during the last London season.

"The Argentine Republic had been long represented at the Court of St. James by the veteran diplomatist, his Excellency Don Mariano Balcarce, who for many years held the double post of Minister here and in France. But a year or two back, the Argentine Government, considering that the relations with this country required the presence of a Resident Minister, appointed Dr. Don. Diego de Alvear, leaving Senor Balcarce to look after the interests of the Republic in France and Spain. Recent financial difficulties, under which the Argentine Chambers decided to reduce their first-class missions, have led to the recall of Senor Alvear and the resumption by Senor Balcarce of his elevated diplomatic functions near the Court of St. James. Senor Alvear has returned to Buenos Ayres, after a brief but honourable sojourn amongst us. He has won golden opinions by his frank and cordial manners, and he was highly esteemed by our Secretary of State for Foreign Affairs, the Earl of Derby. His residence here was opportune from the confidence placed in his integrity and uprightness of character, and the assurances he was enabled to afford to Argentine bondholders that his Government would honourably fulfil its engagements to them, which have been carried out to the letter, thus restoring the credit of the Republic after the disgracful attempts made to injure it by some of the leading organs of our press.

"We cannot conclude this brief reference to our diplomatic relations with the Argentine Republic without paying a special tribute to the important services rendered to his country by Minister Balcarce. He has not, as is well known to all who have observed his useful and estimable career, limited his activity to a perfunctory discharge of official duties. His Excellency has, we believe, never allowed an opportunity to pass, when it enabled him to inform public opinion in Europe with respect to the resources of his country, and he has always vindicated its good name and honour with the ardour and intelligence of a pure and enlightened patriotism.

"It is satisfactory to find that his exertions are not ignored by his countrymen, and we had pleasure in giving in our columns an extract from a discussion which took place in the Argentine Senate. The speaker was Dr. Frias, and the words were provoked by some injurious and unmerited observations by a member of that Chamber.

"Our own Ministers at Rio de Janeiro and Buenos Ayres are Mr. Buckley Matthew and the Hon. Mr. Sackville West. The former has for many years resided at Rio, being greatly esteemed there, whilst Mr. Sackville West has interested himself warmly in the progress of the Argentine

Republic, visiting its numerous provinces, and in all respects proving himself an excellent representative of Great Britain. He was ably seconded by Mr. St. John, Chargé d'Affaires. Mr. Buckley Matthew had previously been Minister at Buenos Ayres, and during the serious contentions between the Republic and Brazil, which at one time existed, he rendered valuable services to both countries by his friendly mediation. Altogether, nothing could be more satisfactory than our existing diplomatic relations with both countries.

"With Uruguay we have no exchange of diplomatic relations, owing to differences which occurred some years back; but English interests are ably protected by Major St. John Munro, who has for upwards of 20 years been English Consul (now Consul-General) at Monte Video, amid all the troubles which have visited that unruly little Republic. Many attempts have been made to improve the pecuniary position of this old and faithful servant, but hitherto without success. He has, by his intelligent care of British interests in Uruguay especially merited the favourable consideration of our Foreign Office."

The particular application of these remarks, as regards the Argentine Confederation, is given in the following chapter, taken from the same source *(The Brazil and River Plate Mail)*, and to which I have great pleasure in giving further publicity in this volume.

U

ARGENTINE REPRESENTATION ABROAD.

The Argentine Government, in its Budget, provided for its representation abroad with a proper regard to the interests of the republic in Europe and America. For this purpose it proposed to retain the diplomatic services of five Legations of the first class, fixing the remuneration of the respective Ministers at a figure sufficiently modest, having in view the honourable position they are called upon to occupy in relation to the discharge of their official duties. The committee appointed by the Congress to consider the proposals of the Executive, in their report, recommended a reduction of the diplomatic service to four Legations, instead of five, and in the "Republica" of Buenos Ayres we find particulars of the discussion that ensued.

A principal feature of the debate was a speech by one of the deputies, Senor Cané, who urged the adoption of a policy which would have left the republic, as affects its diplomatic service, in a destitute condition. He was, of course, fully entitled to express, as well as to entertain the opinion that his country had no more need of representation abroad than any obscure municipality in the remotest corner of the world; but we regret that he should have availed of his privileges as a member of the National Congress to assail Argentine citizens who have merited—if patriotism and intelligence may be accepted as credentials— the grateful recogniti.n of their fellow-countrymen.

As might have been anticipated, this impeachment was not permitted to go without rejoinder. The Minister for Foreign affairs replied in dignified and befitting terms. Translating, we extract the following observations from the able address of his Excellency. He said:

"The honourable deputy deems it convenient to reduce the Legations of first class to two. I regret to say that I cannot participate in that opinion; and without entering into explanations, which, at this moment might be imprudent, I proceed to demonstrate to him that the two Legations he proposes would not suffice. It is evident that we require a Legation in Europe, inasmuch as we have there most important interests, which it is necessary to confide to the care and vigilance of some high public functionaries. The most reduced and economic scale that can be proposed must provide for, at least one Envoy Extraordinary and Minister Plenipotentiary to represent the republic in France, England, Spain, Italy, and in all the other European States, where we have interests to attend to. That Legation is indispensable, and I believe that it is requisite to give to it much more active functions than it has hitherto possessed; that it is necessary to give a different organization to the consular body, by making the consuls agents or auxiliaries of the Legations, which may intervene advantageously, not only in the diplomatic relations of the republic, but, if not in financial affairs, in matters having reference to immigration, a question of supreme consequence for the national prosperity. Then comes the Legation of the United States, where at present we have actually a very important question submitted to arbitration. There it is also indispensable that the republic should be represented by a Plenipotentiary. In Brazil a first-class Legation is needed, and at least another for all the Pacific States is demanded by the circumstances of our international relations."

His Excellency proceeded to observe :

"When, in former year, I had the honour to occupy a seat in the Chamber, I must frankly confess that I myself entertained opinions similar to those Senor Cané has just expressed. I also believed that the Legations were badly served, that it was useless to maintain them. But I am bound to declare that since I have had the honour of discharging the duties of the Ministry of Foreign Relations I have entirely altered my opinion on this point. The truth is, Mr. President, that the Ministers abroad faithfully and efficiently responded to the instructions they received, and if they have not done more, it is because they have not received orders. At this moment the whole responsibility of the activity or inactivity of the Legations in foreign parts rests upon the Ministry for Foreign Affairs, for I must declare emphatically that when these Ministers are instructed in anything particular, they perform their duty both with despatch and ability. It is impossible to tell the Chamber all that they do, what instructions they receive, and how they fulfil them. With respect to the Legation in France, to which the Honourable Deputy has referred in one part of his speech, I will say that it is precisely one of the Legations which responds most carefully and efficaciously to orders, and which has rendered most important services to the country. . . . . As to the Legation in England, it is one that has been very recently established, and to the instructions it has received it has given the greatest attention, having celebrated postal conventions and made other convenient arrangements."

The President of the Chamber, Senor Frias, who has grown grey in the diplomatic service of his country, vacated the chair in order to express his indignation at the attack which had been made upon the foreign Legations of the Republic. He remarked :

" My conscience does not permit me to allow the words which have been spoken by the honorable deputy of Buenos Ayres to pass unchallenged, containing, as they do, a direct attack upon two representative of the country abroad, in my opinion very deserving of its gratitude, and well suited to discharge the duties of the elevated position they occupy. Senor Balcarce has for many years directed the Argentine Legation in France. I was one of those who, in the Senate, warmly supported his appointment for that exalted office. It appeared to me, and this was one of the many reasons on which I founded my vote, that the son of an illustrious general, married to the daughter of General San Martin, the most illustrious, of Argentines, merited the consideration of his country ; but it is not on these grounds alone that he deserves to occupy this high place, but because he has always discharged its duties with great dignity and honour. Senor Belcarce holds an elevated position in France; he is in relations with eminent persons, and has always fulfilled, with laudable zeal and the most perfect devotion, the requirements of his position in the service of his country. I might have brought here an immense quantity of articles and publications of every kind, ;if I had collected all that Senor Balcarce has caused to appear, in his constant desire to show in Europe the progress of the Argentine Republic and to refute the errors with regard to us that have been circulated in the journals of Europe. In this respect his services have been most valuable. But he has not been satisfied with merely making known in Europe the truth, in order to stimulate the emigration of Europeans to populate our soil; he has left nothing worthy of being said with respect to the progress and resources of our Republic unpublished, so that the attention of the peoples of Europe might be always fixed upon the positive advantages possessed by our country. Finally, and this is a fact which ought to be mentioned in this Chamber, if the meritorious works of some distinguished Argentines are recognised in the Institute of France—where one of our countrymen occupies a seat—and if they have been brought under the notice of that learned body by an eminent man, formerly Foreign Minister of the Emperor Napoleon, it is altogether due to the constant zeal of Senor Balcarce in making the men and affairs of our country known in Europe. Further, I comply with a debt of gratitude, which is solely personal, in doing this justice to Senor Balcarce. It is unnecessary to state the nature of the mission with which I was lately entrusted in Chili—it is a delicate question—and I am bound to say that it was owing to the care and patriotism of Senor Balcarce that many documents reached our Legation of the greatest importance for the defence of our rights, and many others have since been received here. Even at this very moment a competent person is charged by him to remit new proofs of the justice of our contention, including many documents not to be found in the Spanish archives. I think, therefore, that the Chamber owes a tribute of gratitude for the services given by Senor Balcarce in France."

The eloquent and just remarks of Senor Frias evidently represented the feeling in the Chamber, having been received with every mark of approbation by the assembled deputies. Deputy Alcorta subsequently remarked :

"Since a personal question has been discussed in this Chamber, I cannot allow the opportunity to pass without manifesting my opinion, equally as a friend of Senor Balcarce and as an Argentine, as to what I have seen of the labours of that eminent servant of the Republic in Europe. For several years I resided in France, and I have always seen Senor Balcarce labouring for his country and defending it. But I have something more to add with respect to his services. Already, Mr. President, he in a measure discharged the functions which the Minister of Foreign Affairs proposes to attach to the Legation in Europe. He exercised a species of direction over our consuls, as well as over our immigration agents. He was constantly in communication with them, affording them information and statistics, and responding to the requests they made. These are services which are notorious, and which should not be ignored by honourable deputies. As to the Legation itself, it cannot be disputed that it has rendered great services. Through that Legation, which is creditable to some other nations, various important treaties have been realised, in particular that with Spain, which had been a cause of serious difficulties for this country. Senor Balcarce arranged this matter with much ability, annulling the treaty which Spain had made with the Government of Parana, and which, as I have stated, was productive of much annoyance and inconvenience to our Republic. I do not believe that Minister Balcarce has ever been lacking in application to the duties of his high post, and he has shown remarkable industry, not limiting his services to strictly diplomatic functions, but even acting as the commercial agent of the Argentine Republic. By his position in France, by his relations in Europe, he is able to treat questions in the most favourable sense for our country, and the first minister who might arrive in Paris could not enjoy the private connections and social position which Mr. Balcarce occupies as a private individual. In all questions he has manifested great tact, and I have been myself a witness of the prudence he displays in dealing with diplomatic discussions."

This ended the debate, and we are glad to be able to announce that the Chamber affirmed the proposal of the Commitee, to which the Government had assented. The Argentine Republic will, therefore, be represented abroad by four Legations of first class.

Before quitting this subject I wish to add a word in favour of the British consular body, who, both in South America as elsewhere, are the faithful and diligent representatives of British commercial interests. It has been the fashion to decry their usefulness, and to render them the butts of political economists; but the good sense of the country appreciates their value. As a rule, and considering the social position they are compelled to occupy in foreign commercial cities, their services are in many cases very inadequately rewarded, nor can they rise to high positions like other public servants. Once a consul always a consul, except in very rare cases, a retiring pension being all they have to look forward to.

SUPPLEMENT.

THE RIVERS OF BRAZIL AND INTERNAL COMMUNICATION.

HAVING in this volume given a special notice of the "Valley of the Amazon," I think it may be desirable to add, from *The Empire of Brazil at the Universal Exhibition of 1876, at Philadelphia*, an account of its entire fluvial system, as therein published, shewing what has been done in the way of exploration, and that the Government is fully alive to the necessity of facilitating communication by means of its internal rivers, where untold wealth may exist, besides the valuable links such rivers are calculated to form with the railways that are now being extended into the various provinces. It will be seen from the following details what an important bearing these numerous rivers have on the future development of the Empire.

Brazil has four great fluvial basins, besides others less important. The most remarkable is that of the Amazon; then, those of the Tocantins and Parana, and lastly, that of the S. Francisco.

The majestic Amazon has a cource of 3,828 kilometres through the territory of the Empire. The surface it occupies is estimated at 26,400 square kilometres, and during the floods it rises 16,4^m above the usual level. This river empties into the ocean with so prodigious a velocity that at a distance of 1,320^m from the coast, its current is still equal to 6 kil.^{m} 600^m an hour, and navigators after losing sight of land may yet drink of its waters. In its course it receives 18 first class tributaries, namely: The Xingu, the Tapajoz, the Madeira, the Purus, the Coary, the Teffe, the Jurua, the Jutahy, and the Javary, on the right bank; the Jary, the Paru, the Trombetas, the Nhamunda, the Uataman, the Urubu, the Negro, the Japura, and the Içá, on the left bank, some of which have a course of more than 3,300 kilometres.

Beyond the frontier of Brazil, the Amazon continues to be navigable by steamers for upwards of 1,980 kilometres in the territory of Peru, where it receives the important affluents, Napo, Morona, and Pastaza on the left bank, and the Ucayali and Uallaga on the right.

These rivers are freely navigable as far as the Andes, and offer easy means of communication with those portions of the Republics of Peru and Equador, which are situated to east of that range, and which are the most important.

The Amazon and its affluents are navigable by steamers for upwards of 43,250 kilometres, as shewn by the following table:

	Kilometres.
Amazon	3,828
Basins of its chief affluents	32,822
Lesser affluents and Lakes	6,600
	43,250

The Republics of Bolivia, Peru, Equador, Columbia, and Venezuela, communicate with the port of Para, and with the

Brazilian provinces of Maranhao, Goyaz, Matto-Grosso, and Amazonas, by the waters of the Amazon and its tributaries.

The basin of the Tocantins comprehends the vast territory between 1° and 19° S. Lat., from the mouth of the Pará to the sources of the Araguaya, its most powerful affluent on account of its length and of the volume of its waters; this basin embraces in its greatest breadth more than 8 degrees from east to west. The Tocantins has, besides the Araguaya, the following great affluents: on the right bank, the Somrro and the Paraná; and on the left bank the Tacanhumas and the Santa Thereza; the Maranhao is its confluent.

The Tocantins has a course of about 2,640 kilometres; that of the Araguaya extends over 2,627 kilometres.

Steam navigation, subsidized by Government, has been established on the 3,828 kilometres of the Brazilian Amazon, and on 1,320 kilometres of the Tocantins and other rivers.

In 1867 subsidies were granted to two other companies, which undertook to navigate by steam 1,584 kilometres of the Purús, 792 of the Negro, 1,228 of the Madeira, 330 of the Tapajoz, and 660 of the lower Tocantins; there are now, therefore, 9,742 kilometres navigated by steam in the basins of the Amazon and Tocantins.

The above-mentioned companies have lately amalgamated.

Above the falls the Madeira and its affluents have 6,000 kilometres of continuous navigation, which affords means of conveyance to the whole of the Republic of Bolivia and to the western part of the province of Mato Grosso.

In order to connect the navigation of the upper to that of the lower portion of this river, and to facilitate communications between the centre of South America and the port of Para, Government has subsidized a foreign company that undertook to build an important marginal railroad, as the only means of advantageously avoiding the said falls.

To connect in like manner the 1,518 kilometres of navigation of the Araguaya to the navigable part of the lower Tocantins, Government ordered a road 391 kilometres in length, to be built, by means of which the falls in that river will be avoided. This road will serve the provinces of Goyaz and Maranhao, and Para comprising an extension of 2,640 kilometres and, for the future, will be connected with the capital of the Empire by the D. Pedro II railway, and with the navigable portion of the river Paraguay by a road 264 kilometres in length.

The Parana, formed by the junction of the Rio Grande and the Paranahyba in 19.° 40' S. Lat., drains, to the east, the Brazilian provinces of S. Paulo and Parana and the Argentine provinces of Missoes and Corrientes, and to the west, Mato Grosso, in Brazil; the Republic of Paraguay, and that part of the Argentine territory which is situated beyond the confluence of the river Paraguay.

The river Parana has, besides the Rio Grande and the Paranahyba, numerous other affluents; some are noticable as being navigable, others for their length, and all for the fertility of their valleys.

Of all these affluents, the Paraguay is undoubtedly the most important; rising in the province of Mato Grosso, in 13.° 30' S. Lat., it traverses the territory of Brazil and that of the Republic whose name it bears. It is navigable by small vessels from 14.° 30' to 16.° S. Lat., and thence forward by steamers. It has several navigable tributaries, among which, in the Brazilian territory, are the Sipotuba, the Jauru, the Taquary, the Miranda or Mondego, and the Sao Lourenço, by which, and by the Cuyaba, steamers go up as far as the capital of Mato Grosso.

From this province the Parana receives the rivers Pardo, Ivinheima, Nhanduhy, and Iguatemy; and from the provinces of S. Paulo and Parana the Tiete, the Paranapanema, the Ivahy, the Piquiry, and the Iguassu, which are more or less navigable.

The navigation of the Parana offers no impediment from a short distance above the confluence of the Iguassu to the River Plate; but it is interrupted by the falls of Sete Quedas or Guayra cataract, from beyond which commences the navigable section of the Upper Parana, in Brazilian territory, for about 528 kilometres to the falls of Urubupungá.

When these obstructions shall have been overcome by the construction of marginal roads, the Parana will become most serviceable to future commercial relations between the provinces of Goyaz, Mato Grosso, Minas Geraes, S. Paulo, Parana, and Buenos Ayres and Monte Video.

Sete Quedas (seven falls), one of the most important falls known, and may be compared to Niagara, if not in height in the volume of its waters, which, having a breadth of 2,200 metres in the upper section, fall in an incline plane at an angle of 50 degrees from a height of 17 metres, after being compressed in a narrow channel 70 metres wide.

The mist produced by the fall of the waters on the banks of this granitic channel, and on the rocks which rise in the midst of the stream, says Azara, who visited it at the end of the last century, "forms columns of vapour, which are seen from a distance of many leagues, and in which the sun reflects numberless rainbows. The roar of the cataract is heard at a distance of 5 leagues,"—33 kilometres.

To give an idea of the magnitude of this natural marvel of Brazil, we also quote the words of M. Hunt, an engineer employed on the survey of the railway from Coritiba to Miranda; he says: "at a distance of 100 kilometres from the falls of Sete Quedas, the bed of the river is 1,500 metres wide, the depth of the water in the rainy season 12 metres, the velocity of the current being one metre; consequently the volume of water which falls in one second is equal to 18,000 cubic metres."

Besides this, there is also the famous cataract of Sipotuba, formed by the large river with the same name, a tributary of the Paraguay, whose waters fall perpendicularly from a height of 132 metres, according to Joao de Souza e Azevedo the first backwoodsman who, in 1746, crossed from the head waters of that river to those of Juruema; there are also the Augusto Falls, the Itapura, the Avanhandava, and the Itu, on the river Tiete, in the province of S. Paulo, and others also remarkable; not to speak of that of the river S. Francisco, which will be mentioned hereafter.

The course of the river S. Francisco is through the central part of Brazil, it waters the provinces of Minas Geraes, Bahia, Pernambuco, Alagoas, and Sergipe.

The most note-worthy of its affluents are the Para, the Paraopeba, the Rio das Velhas, Paracatu, the Corrente, the Carinhanha, the Rio Verde Grande, and the Rio Grande.

Beyond the grand and majestic falls of Paulo Affonso there is no obstruction to navigation in any season of the year along the 1,270 kilometres which separate the village of Guaicuhy, in Minas Graes, from the hamlet of Riacho da Casa Nova, in Bahia.

The cataract of Paulo Affonso has seven falls, three of which are in the middle of the river, and the other four between steep rocks on the bank belonging to the province of Sergipe. The height of the greatest fall is 80 metres; those of Angiquinho and Dous Amores are of admirable effect. Below the rapids is the Furna dos Morcegos (Vampires Grotto), the descent to which is very precipitous; the entrance is more than 6 metres high and 1,5 wide; the grotto is 48 metres long and 88 in height, and can shelter 2,000 persons.

Below the rapids 264 kilometres are navigated by steamers from Piranhas down to the mouth of the river, below the city of Penedo, in the province of Alagoas. There is sufficient water for vessels drawing 3,3 metres.

Besides the four largest rivers others, also important, empty into the sea, namely: the Gurupy, the Tury-Assú, the Mearim, the Itapicurú, the Parnahyba, the Vasa-barris, the Paraguassú, the Contas, the Jequitinhonha or Belmonte, the Pardo, the Mucury, the S. Matheus, the Doce, the Parahyba do Sul, the Itajahay, the Tubarao, and the Ribeira de Iguape.

Some of these are navigable by steamers for upwards of 660 kilometres.

Government being convinced of the great advantages which are to be derived from surveys of the more important rivers of Brazil, whereby to ascertain which parts of them are navigable, what obstacles impede the navigation as well as the means of removing these impediments, continue to devote serious attention to the subject.

The following surveys were made in the few years prior to 1867:

By Dr. Jose Vieira Couto de Magalhaes and by the engineer Ernesto Vallee, that of the rivers Tocantins and Araguaya, which resulted in the establishment of regular river navigation between the provinces of Goyaz and Para.

A report and plan of these studies were laid before Government.

By the engineer Joao Martins da Silva Coutinho, that of the rivers Purus and Ituxy, tributaries of the Amazon.

The result of this exploration is also consigned in a detailed report.

By the same engineer, of the rivers Japura and Madeira.

By the engineer M. Chandless, that of the river Aquiry, affluent of the Purus.

By the engineer Gustavo Dodt, that of the river Cearamirim in the province of Rio Grande do Norte, in which some works have been executed, in order to give free egress to the waters, which, during the floods, completely destroy the plantations, from near its mouth up to Pedregulho, a distance of nearly 59 kil.^{m} 400^m.

By the engineer Newton Burlamaque, that of the river Parnahyba, in the province of Piauhy.

By the engineer Ferdinand Halfeld, that of the river S. Francisco, from the falls of Pirapora to the ocean.

By Dr. Em. Liais, aided by the engineers Eduardo Jose de Moraes, and Dr. Ladislao Netto, that of the same river between those falls and its sources.

These explorers also surveyed the river das Velhas, in the province of Minas Geraes, an important tributary of the river S. Francisco.

The engineers José and Francisco Keller surveyed the river Parahyba do Sul from Pirahy, in the province of Rio de Janeiro, as far as Cachoeira, in that of S. Paulo, and the river Pomba, in the province of Minas Geraes, one of the tributaries of the Parahyba.

The same gentlemen, with the engineer Rumbelsperger, the river Ivahy, in the province of Parana.

The former also studied a portion of the river Paraná, between the Ivahy and the Paranapanema, and the rivers Ivinheima, Paranapanema, and Tibagy.

The engineer Eusebio Stevaux studied the means of cutting canals in the rivers Pomonga and Japaratuba, and the engineer Vignolles did the same for the rivers Poxim and Santa Maria, all in the province of Sergipe; these latter works have already been commenced. The engineer Charles Demoly made a survey for a canal between lake dos Patos and the port of Laguna, in the provinces of S. Pedro do Rio Grande do Sul and Santa Catharina.

The chart of the river Amazon was drawn up by Captain José da Costa Azevedo; and that of the whole of the river Paraguay and its affluents by Rear Admiral Baron, of Melgaco.

Professor Agassiz also explored the Amazonian region, and the lectures which he delivered on the subject were published in the newspapers of the capital of the Empire.

The Upper Uruguay and the Upper Parana have both been studied by several engineers and naval officers.

All these studies are highly interesting, not only to Brazil, but to the navigation and commerce of the whole world.

Since the year 1867 the following surveys were made:

The part of the river Madeira where the rapids exist, between a place named Santo Antonio and the hamlet of Exaltacion in Bolivia, some distance beyond the mouth of the Mamoré, was surveyed by the engineers José and Francisco Keller, who, by Government's order, drew up plans for improving this important land and fluvial way between the provinces of Para and Mato Grosso and the Republic of Bolivia.

With the view of improving the means of communication between the provinces of Mato Grosso and Para by way of the river Tapajoz and of a road, estimated at 61 kil^m 200^m in length, along the banks of this river, avoiding the falls of Salto Grande and others less dangerous, the president of the latter province commissioned the engineers Juliao Honorato Corrêa de Miranda and Antonio Manoel Gonçalves Tocantins to make the necessary surveys.

In order to practically verify if the river S. Francisco, and the Rio das Velhas, from the place called Sumidouro, are navigable by steamers, Government ordered an experimental voyage to be made by Francisco Manoel Alvares de Araujo, a first lieutenant in the navy, who took the vessel as far as the village of Boa Vista, in the province of Pernambuco.

Then for the first time were the waters of the Upper S. Francisco ploughed by a steamer.

A committee of engineers surveyed those sections of the rivers Araguaya and Tocantins where navigation is obstructed by falls and rapids, in order to enable them to propose adequate means of avoiding them, or, that being impossible, to plan a marginal road.

The river Iguassu, in the province of Parana, was explored by the engineer Eduardo Jose Moraes.

The surveys of the rivers Carinhanha, Grande, Preto, and Somno are well advanced; they will shew those sections navigable by steamers, which may be serviceable to the projected railway between the basin of the S. Francisco and that of the Tocantins. The studies of the rivers Ivahy, Parana, Ivinheima, Brilhante, and Mondego are concluded, and are to be availed of in the projected line of communications between Coritiba, in the province of Parana, and Miranda, in that of Mato Grosso.

In the chapter relative to railroads more will be said with reference to these important surveys.

Still we must mention here that the engineer William Lloyd ascertained the existence of a vast net of fluvial navigation for vessels drawing one metre, without any need of excavations, namely :

In the river Ivahy	250	kiloms.
,, Paraná	600	,,
,, Tieté	500	,,
,, Ivinheima	203	,,
,, Brilhante	231	,,
,, Paranapanema	300	,,
	2,084	,,

The river Parnahyba was again explored by the engineer Gustavo Dodt from its mouth to the sources, according to his report.

The naturalist Joao Barbosa Rodrigues studied the river Urubú, in the province of Amazonas, up to its sources, as well as the Uatuma up to the first rapids, and the Jatapú as far as the confluence of the Caremary and Uassahy.

The same naturalist also explored in the province of Para the following rivers: the Nhamunda up to the second rapids, the Trombetas as far as Mocambos, and the Capim, as far as Tembes.

With a view of promoting the aggrandizement of the Empire by offering greater facilities for international relations, for the encouragement of commerce and navigation on the river Amazon and its affluents, as well as on the Tocantins and S. Francisco, the following rivers were opened to merchant vessels of all nations on the 7th of September, 1867: the Amazon as far as the Brazilian frontier, the Tocantins up to Cameta, the Tapajoz up to Santarem, the Madeira up to Borba, the Negro up to Manaos, and the S. Francisco, up to the city of Penedo.

The navigation of those portions of the affluents of the Amazon, of which only one of the banks belong to Brazil, depends on boundary treaties and police and fiscal regulations, to be settled with the neighbouring States.

The promulgation of these measures, in no way altered the observance of the existing treaties of navigation and commerce with the Republics of Peru and Venezuela, in accordance with the regulations already published.

The engineer Fernando G. de Rocheville was lately commissioned to survey the rivers Andira, Jatapu, Urubu, Coary, Teffe, and Jutahy.

Augusto Jose do Souza Soares de Andrea, first lieutenant in the navy, was employed by the Amazon Steam Navigation Company, to explore the river Purus, partly surveyed before by the engineer Chandless, with the special object of ascertaining the existence of a communication, supposed to exist, between that river and the Madre de Deos.

If this undertaking be successful the rich and populous department of Cuzco, in Peru, will have easy issue to the Atlantic, to the advantage of those nations which navigate, and entertain commercial relations with, the Amazon.

Raphael Reyes, a Columbian, on his own account, and as a representative of the firm of Elias Reyes and Brother, of the city of Popayan, belonging to the United States of Columbia, explored the fluvial line between the city of Pasto and the capital of Para.

Descending the Iça or Putumayo, which has a course of 1,500 kilometres with 36 tributaries, some of which are navigable, he ascertained that this river is easily navigable by steamers from the new port of S. José dos Guamués, distant 900 kilometres from the frontier of the Empire, to the point where the steamers of the Amazon Company at present reach.

He also ascertained that, by opening a road 125 kilometres in length, the journey from the mouth of the Iça to the city of Pastos can be made in 14 days. This city, which already numbers 12,000 inhabitants, will then become an important commercial emporium for the department on that side of the Republic of Columbia, and for those of Equador, as far as Quito, besides a portion of Peru, by which means the production and the consumption of 500,000 inhabitants will be increased.

The Government of Brazil granted him permission to export and import goods in Brazilian sailing or steam vessels, during three years, between the ports of the Amazon and those of the interior of the Republic of Columbia, through the river Iça or

Putomayo, with the exemptions and clauses contained in the instructions then published.

Joaquim Thomaz da Silva Coelho, first lieutenant in the navy, explored the river Jaupery; after a six days' journey, having descended an important rapid, he arrived at Moura, and thence proceeded to lake Airao.

According to the explorer, this river runs N.E. by E., varying in breadth along 2,200 kilometres of its course, flooding extensive islands in the rainy season.

The Para nut tree, sarsaparilla, copahiba and other interesting plants, grow on its banks.

The same officer explored the river Amanau as far as the rapids of the same name, which he was unable to cross. He informs that this river runs N. N. E., with but little velocity, having an almost uniform breadth throughout its length.

This is one of the rivers most frequented by the aborigines, and lieutenant Silva Coelho verified that they do not use, as others do, a kind of canoe called *uba* to come down to the banks of the Rio Negro, but walk down in the dry season to the banks of the Cariau, crossing to the other side by the rapids.

Dr. Antonio Affonso de Aguiar Whitaker, judge of the district of Corumba, in 1874 during the dry season, descended from Anicuns, 79 kil.^{m}, 200^m distant from the capital of Goyaz down to the falls of S. Simao, and confirms that between those two places no important obstacle impedes steam navigation.

As the river Mogy-guassu, in the province of S. Paulo, has already steam navigation, and the obstructions at its mouth may be avoided by a road from the first rapids of the Rio Grande to the above-named falls, a line of communication between the two provinces may be thus established, and the journey from the capital of the Empire to that of the province may be reduced to 15 or 16 days *viâ* Santos; whereas at present the post takes 35 days, troops of mules, 60 to 70, and carts drawn by oxen three months.

MINING RESOURCES OF BRAZIL AND THE ARGENTINE REPUBLIC.

I cannot do better in noticing this important element in the wealth of nations than to quote from the two publications so frequently alluded to in this volume, compiled for the purposes of the Centenary Exhibition at Philadelphia. Comparatively little is yet known as to the extent of minerals existing in the Andine regions of the Argentine Republic; but as regards Brazil, a large exploration has already taken place, and both gold and diamond mines have been profitably worked, chiefly with the aid of English capital. How far the mining systems of both countries may be augmented by railway access cannot yet be known, but there is little doubt as to its facilitating the development of mines. Land carriage has always been the great difficulty, whether as regards the conveyance of machinery or bringing down ores to the seaboard, and this will now be materially lessened.

First.—As regards Brazil mining operations :

GOLD.—It may be said that every district of the provinces numbers this precious metal among its natural products.

As however, reference will only be made to those localities which are undoubtedly auriferous, and, as such, destined to be worked, a great portion of the province of Minas Geraes must be noticed, and, more particularly, all the eastern versants of the upper basin of the river S. Francisco, where some English companies and many private individuals extract gold.

The same may be said of the municipal districts of Caçapava, Rio Pardo, Santa Maria, and Cruz Alta, in the province of S. Pedro do Rio Grande do Sul.

A company was floated called the "Companhia das minas de ouro e cobre do sul do Brazil" (the South of Brazil gold and copper mine Company) to carry on mining operations in the first of these municipal districts, and has commenced work with a capital of 800:000$000.

Next is the district of Turyassu, in Marahao, and several places in Bahia, Piauhy, Goyaz, Matto-Grosso, Ceara, Parahyba, Pernambuco, and S. Paulo. Within the last few years Government has granted several privileges for the exploration of these mines.

In all these deposits gold is found in compact quartz or quartzite veins, embedded in primitive or micaceous iron rock; it is also found in great quantities in the alluvial soil of rivers.

The system hitherto employed for the extraction of this metal by the English companies, and by Brazilian companies, now being established, are those of washing and amalgamation; the last, however, on a smaller scale. Private individuals continue the old system of washing the sands from auriferous rocks, deposited in the beds of neighbouring rivers.

Mixed with the gold in these sands platinum, iridium, and, in many places, palladium appear.

In some mines tellurium is found, as well as bismuth and great quantities of arsenical pyrites.

The assays of palladium gold made at the Rio de Janeiro Mint gave the following per centage:

	I.	II.	III.
Gold	88,9	90,25	92,3
Palladium	11,1	9,75	7,7

This gold comes from various mines in the provinces of Minas Geraes and Mato-Groso, and is there called ouro preto (black gold).

This metal has for a long time been extracted in the Mint, without any special application for it.

The late Dr. Custodio Alves Serraõ made some important experiments on it, specially with regard to a property it possesses of contracting, on heating; and he obtained by this means a successive reduction in medals.

SILVER.—Is found in many of the galenas existing in all the provinces; but the proportion of this metal is always less than one per cent. of the lead.

It is however now ascertained that in some of the copper ores of the municipal district of Caçapava, in the province of S. Pedro do Rio Grande do Sul, silver exists in the proportion of 2,5 per cent.

Nearly two hundred years since, this metal was found mixed with the gold, which, until late years, was extracted and reduced at the Araçoiaba mountain, in the municipality of Sorocaba, province of S. Paulo.

At Itupava, near Sorocaba, there is a mine which was abandoned, probably because it did not pay.

Some of the galenas of Yporanga, on the river Iguape, are also argentiferous.

Historical tradition mentions the existence of rich mines in the province of Bahia. But the whereabouts of these deposits is unknown.

MERCURY.—On an estate called Capao d'Anta, in the province of Parana, this metal was discovered in circumstances that will permit competition with the mines of Europe and Peru.

It is also said that in the beginning of this century it was found in the province of Santa Catharina.

Mercury in its metallic state also exists in S. Paulo, principally in the alluvial deposits, but it has never been extracted.

COPPER.—This metal is found in the provinces of Mato-Grosso, Goyaz, Minas-Geraes, Bahia, Maranhao, Ceara, and Rio Grande do Sul, in the municipal district of Caçapava and others; but chiefly at the hamlet of Santo Antonio das Lavras, 6 kil.^{m}6 metres distant from the town of that name, whence it may easily be carried to the city Cachoeira, a distance of 85 kil.^{m}8 metres, the last post on the river Jacuhy, in the portion navigable by steam.

The ore of this district, which contains the richest cupriferous deposits of Brazil, yields as much as 60 per cent. of pure metal, according to the lode exploited.

In these mines malachite, lazulite and klaprothine are met with.

MANGANESE.—In the basin of Paranagua, in Minas-Geraes, at Ypanema, and in other provinces this metal is found; and in large quantities in Bahia, near the city of Nazareth, whence there are steamers to the capital of the province.

TIN.—So little of this metal has been discovered that it is far from being considered an industrial product of the country.

It is said to have been seen in the sands of the Paraopeba, in the province of Minas-Geraes, and in some granites of Rio de Janeiro.

ZINC.—Some specimens of sulphuret of zinc came with the galenas from the Ibiapaba range in the province of Ceara.

It is also said to have been found on a spur of the Araripe range in the same province.

LEAD.—There are great quantities of galenas, some of which are argentiferous.

The following places are well known to have deposits: Yporanga, in the province of S. Paulo, the province of S. Pedro do Rio Grande do Sul, the river Abaete, and near Sete Lagoas, both in Minas-Geraes; the provinces of Rio de Janeiro, Parahyba do Norte, Bahia, Santa Catharina, Ceara, Maranhao and

Piauhy; there are also deposits on the Ibiapaba range, in the province of Ceara.

Chromate of lead is abundant at Congonhas do Campo, in Minas-Geraes, but, as yet, it is of little profit. Its composition is oxide of lead 69 per cent., chromic acid 31 per cent.

Of all these lead mines, the most important is that of the river Abaete, from which silver was also extracted, when it was formerly worked for account of Government.

ANTIMONY.—In the National Museum there are specimens of sulphuret of antimony found in the province of Minas-Geraes, and it is said to exist in S. Paulo, and Parana. It is also found in Espirito Santo.

BISMUTH.—At S. Vicente, and Passagem, in the province of Minas-Geraes, ores of bismuth have been met with.

ARSENIC.—It is generally found with pyrites in auriferous formation, but also in the acid state combined with iron, forming scorodite, in the parish of Antonio Pereira, in Menas-Geraes.

IRON.—There are, in the Empire, some places where this metal is found under the most favourable conditions.

All the Itabira ridge, in the vicinity of Ouro Preto, on the Espinhaço range, near the Piedade spur, and in many other places of the province of Minas-Geraes, incalculable quantities of this metal exist; a large proportion of these mountains is composed of oligistic, magnetic, and micaceous iron; the oligistic undergoes decomposition on the surface, owing to the action of the atmosphere, and forms layers of limonite which overspread vast sandy expanses.

In the northern provinces, in the interior of Minas-Geraes, in those of S. Pedro do Rio Grande do Sul, and Parana, there are enormous quantities of iron, more or less decomposed, in the argillaceous deposits, which cover the plains and the slopes of hills.

The richest mines, which do not constitute an independent formation, are lodes of more or less bulk, such as those of S. Joao, d'Ypanema, and some in the provinces of Alagoas, Ceara, Rio Grande do Norte, and Parahyba.

W

In Brazil their are iron mines, which, owing to the complete absence of pyrites, are incontestibly superior to the most famous of Sweden.

The magnetic ore of Brazil contains 72,5 per cent. of iron; the oligistic, the martite, and the best micaceous 70 per cent.; falling in the inferior qualities to 25 and 20 per cent.

Iron, from its abundance and good quality, is, by itself, one of the most important elements of the wealth of the Empire; in general, the deposits may be easily and economically worked, being, for the most part, placed near extensive forests, which, being cut down, constantly reappear within from six to ten years, and which, therefore, form immense deposits of excellent fuel, near abundant streams and falls, which constitute immense water power for working the machinery.

In the province of Minas-Geraes there are private individuals who, taking advantage of these favourable circumstances, have obtained very profitable results from iron mining.

A great deal of the iron consumed in the province of Minas-Geraes is extracted from its mines and wrought on the spot; it is therefore to be supposed that this useful industry will, in a few more years, spread to many other places in the Empire.

The most important iron foundry of South America is on the banks of the small river Ypanema, one of the affluents of the Sorocaba, in the province of S. Paulo; it is 191 kilometres distant from the port of Santos, 125 from the capital of the province, and 25 from the base of the Araçoiaba mountain.

This establishment possesses important and very valuable resources: ore of excellent quality, carbonate of lime for fluxes, refactory clay for building furnaces, sufficient water power for the more important engines, and very good forests.

Having been created and maintained by the State, Government has paid particular attention to it since 1865, when it was reorganized.

The present director, who was commissioned to engage in Europe skilled labour for the works of the foundry, has returned, bringing thirteen operatives with their families.

These, though not numerous, will stimulate the aptitude, and the good taste of the native workmen, who number more than a hundred, and so contribute to the improvement of the *personnel* of the establishment, an effect which is already felt.

The same solicitude was displayed by the director in the purchase of the machinery in Europe. This has arrived and has been set up. It may therefore be fairly surmised that the success of the foundry is assured.

Government, wishing to realize the ends they had in view, with the reorganization of this establishment, have instructed the director to supply the war arsenal of the capital of the Empire with bar iron as required : a large quantity is already prepared, and shortly the supply will, in all probability, be regular.

The forests attached to the foundry cover an area of 6.651.5 hectares, which can afford a daily supply of 15 metrical tons of charcoal, a sufficient quantity to keep the furnaces and accessory workshops in constant activity.

With the extension of the " Sorocabana" railway as far as the foundry, a grand future will open for that establishment, not only with regard to military requirements, but to industry in general.

Several buildings are finished, and others are being rapidly constructed, and the fact that all the materials employed in these works have been prepared in the establishment is deserving of notice.

The workshops can already make any kind of machinery, and the rollers for making thin sheet iron and the machines for drawing wire, fit for telegraphic lines, is being put up.

Besides the quarries of excellent marble, which exist near the fabric, a coal mine was discovered at a distance of 33 kilometres in a direction W.N.W. ; a most important fact.

Second.—Argentine Mines :

The mountains of the Argentine Republic, and above all those of the Provinces of Cordova, San Luis, Mendoza, San Juan,

Rioja, and Catamarca, contain great wealth in metals, and long since produced a lively mining industry by the search for gold, silver, copper, lead, and nickel. However, this occupation has not yet become of that importance which in reality belongs to the richness of the metalliferous ores; but it will certainly gain much more as soon as the railways now in construction are finished, so that by the increase of immigration the necessary workmen can be procured, and transport be rendered easier and more secure.

The metals we mention are found in real veins, and the gold is also found in placers. The rock in which the veins appear differs much in the different mining districts, *i.e.*, in the "high lands of Capillitas" it is granite; in the "Sierra of Cordova" and of "the Huerta" it is gneiss; in the chain of Famatina (Rioja) it is schist; near Gualilan (San Juan) it is paleozoic limestone, trachytic tufa, sandstone, etc. We also find that its occurrence is very varied. So much the more interesting is the fact already mentioned in Chapter VI. on the Geology of the Argentine Republic that, notwithstanding the great variety of the rock in which the veins appear, the greater part of, or perhaps all, the metalliferous veins in this country are only found in those places where the granite gneiss, limestone, etc., are penetrated by igneous rocks, such as trachyte and andesite belonging to the tertiary epoch.

This circumstance, so characteristic of Argentine metalliferous veins, demonstrates that their birth took place in the tertiary period, and was occasioned by volcanic action at that time. For the rest, in the neighbourhood of a trachytic penetration a single vein is rarely found; but, on the contrary, several veins are ordinarily found in the same district.

I will now follow these general remarks by an enumeration of the principal mining districts of the country.

The gang of the auriferous veins is quartz or horn-stone, impregnated with native gold, pyrites, and brown iron ore. It is found in this form in the Province of San Luis, at the environs of Tomalasto, above all in the Canada-Honda, and at the Portezuelo of the Sierra of Ullapé, as also in the heretofore celebrated mines of Gualilán and Guachi, San Juan.

Gold placers are found in the Sierra of Famatina, Rioja, in the valley of Calchaquí, Salta, and in the Department of Puna, Jujuy. In the two last the exploration is made in a most primitive manner by the Indian population; those of the Province of San Luis are a little more advanced.

SILVER.—The richest silver district of all the Republic is the Cerro-Negro, near Chilesito, Rioja. A surprising quantity of veins are found here in the schist, which, besides brown spar, blende, and pyrites, contain native silver, ruby silver, horn silver, and argentite, sometimes in such abundance that it may rival the richest districts we are acquainted with.

Unfortunately all the mining industry of this district is at present in the hands of the small traders (almost every inhabitant of Chilesito has his little mines), who have neither the necessary intelligence nor the indispensable capital to enable them to work with energy. When, however, in the future a good mine shall be constructed under proper direction, the village of Chilesito will be one of the most important mining districts of the Republic, notwithstanding its altitude of from 3,500 to 4,000 metres.

In the Sierra of Cordova quartz veins are also found rich in horn and native silver, in which, as a mineralogical rarity, a little iodic silver is found. The exploration, which is almost totally inactive in this district at present, could be greatly developed.

ARGENTIFEROUS GALENA.—Veins, whose chief ore is argentiferous galena, are very numerous in all the mountains of the Republic, and soon these districts will begin to prosper on the construction of the railways already begun. At present the greater part of them are exclusively occupied in the extraction of silver, because the lead is not worth the long transport on mule-back; it therefore gives no value to the distant mines, notwithstanding its abundance. The principal districts which possess veins of argentiferous galena are those of Paramillo de

Uspallata, Mendoza; in the Sierra of Fontal de Castona, in the Sierra of Huerta, San Juan, and in the Sierra of Cordova, above all in the district of Ojo de Agua. In all these places a quantity of veins are found which are not worked, save superficially from time to time, on account of want of capital. Tunnels, machines for the raising of ores and water, machines for the separation and washing of the ores, as yet are completeley unknown to the greatest part of these mines, nor have they been dug to any great depth. These remarks are sufficient to prove that the mines will become developed as soon as the expense of freight has diminished.

NICKEL ORES.—At Jagué, in the Province of Rioja, veins are found of which the principal substance is massive nickolite, and which have been exploited with much profit for some 20 years past. Unfortunately the political disorders during the present year (1874-5) forced the European proprietors to abandon their business.

COPPER ORES.—Native copper, chalcocite, bornite, tetrahedrite, emargite, and chalco-pyrites are found in thick and rich veins, and generally their value is considerably increased by a small alloy of gold and silver. The most important district is that of the Sierra of Capillitas, Catamarca, in which great mines are worked in an excellent manner. Its ores are auriferous chalco-pyrites, tetra-hydrites, and bornites. The district of Mexicana is situated alongside, at the inhospitable height of 4,000 metres, but rich in veins of enargite. In the Sierra of Famatina, Rioja, there is also a district of great promise for the future. The mines of copper-pyrites situated in the Southern Sierra of Cordova are of less importance; but, quite remarkable, they are at present abandoned. The same may be said of those in the valley of Calchaci, in the Department of Rosario on the Frontiers, Salta. The old heaps of refuse in the latter localities lead to the belief in a large distribution of the veins of copper-pyrites and grey copper. Finally, I here mention the well-known fact that the Mountain of Rayen, in the south of the Province of Mendoza, is characterized by an extraordinary richness in native copper. Unfortunately this country is still within the Indian territory, so that at present, notwithstanding its wealth, an explotation is not possible.

IRON ORES.—It is often pretended that certain mountains contain a great abundance of iron ores, and although it may be probable we have as yet no exact data on the subject.

We insert here the passing remark that, according to a calculation of Major Ignatius Richard made in 1869, when 2687 men were occupied in the mining industry of the Argentine Republic, with a capital of about 1½ million of hard dollars placed in mines, they produced in 1868 the amount of 105 kilograms of gold, 1,200 kilograms of silver, 13,829 quintals of copper, and 20,000 quintals of lead.

Inasmuch as more exact statistics are wanting, I reproduce these figures without guarranteeing them.

The problem whether there are coal measures worth working in the Argentine Republic has been already studied several times, and yet awaits a final resolution. As it is superfluous to demonstrate the great value of fossil-coal—should it exist here—to Argentine industry, I will simply communicate all we as yet know about it.

Commencing with the general result of all my researches, I say at once that coal measures exist here, but it is a question whether they are worth exploiting. It is already mentioned in chap. VI. that the greater part of the mountainous ranges of the Pampa which consist of gneiss and crystalline schists are surrounded by sandstone, and we endeavoured to demonstrate that this sandstone formation, under the cover of the clay of the Pampa, probably fills all the basins which exist between the different mountains. Thus we showed that this sandstone appertains to formations of different character, and consequently a generalization of the following remarks is not admissible. On the contrary, they will be especially dedicated to the basin, more or less ten leagues broad, which is found in the Province of San Juan between the Sierra de la Huerta and Pie-palo, divided by the river Bermejo. On the eastern edge of this basin, that is to say on the S.W. slope of the Sierra de la Huerta, in the district where the Papagayos takes its source, several places are found of out-crops of coal beds over an extent of some 25 square leagues. On the slopes of the source of the Papagayos, half a league from the Sierra de la Huerta, and two leagues from the post house situated more to the south, red sandstones are found with imbedded layers of conglomerates, whose pebbles are exclusively of gneiss, mica-schist, and quartz. A course-grained sandstone is found underneath, and in this last a bed of from 0.9 to 1.2 m. thick, vertical to the horizon, and consisting of an alternation of coal and shale in such a manner that this peat or coal forms almost half of the entire thickness. By means of a shaft of small depth I found at 5 metres under the surface a second bed not so thick. The mica-schist which alternates with the coal is extraordinarily rich in fossil plants; and these last, as I have already said, cause this formation to be recognized as corresponding to the carboniferous system which European geologists indicate by the name of "Rhetic." Also on the opposite—or western—side of the basin, that is to say on the eastern slopes of the Sierra del Jachal and of Huaco, a thin bed of coals is found in the same sandstone formation; but here the strata are much disturbed, so that the beds show a dip of several degrees, consisting of repeated alternations of pitch coal and sandy shales. All these out-crops of coal have no great technical value as yet; nevertheless, they are of great importance, because they lead us to suppose that all this basin, 10 leagues broad, between the above-named mountains is probably filled up by a carboniferous formation of which only the superficial strata are now known. Moreover, the thickness of these strata in the centre of the basin is entirely unknown; but when it is remembered that the beds of coal are generally thicker and of better quality in the centre of the basins than at their borders (a fully proved fact in the carboniferous districts of almost all countries), it is reasonable to suppose that here we have an analogous case. However this may be, the observed facts demand that borings should be instantly undertaken in the middle of the basin, which should penetrate down to the old crystalline schists. Such an enterprise would demonstrate whether the beds of coal increase in the centre, and whether —as it may be hoped—they are of sufficient thickness to justify working them.

As the basin between the two mountains is a desert almost deprived of water and covered only with a miserable thicket (for the River Bermejo which divides it is for the greatest part of the year only a river *seco*—dry), great difficulties would have to be conquered in making the borings, as well as in a possible future exploration; yet, with enough energy and capital, success might be rendered certain. The borings for coal would be at the same time borings for water, and thus also contribute to the final solution of the most important problem for the deserts of the interior, viz., "whether the construction of artesian wells is possible here."

As for the district in question a favourable solution may be predicted in a geological point of view, because the waters of the Bermejo which enter the valley are lost under the surface, where they meet an impermeable stratum in the shales of the coal measures. Consequently a great subterranean reservoir of water ought to exist above this schist, and by virtue of the geological structure of the whole country these circumstances promise that openings made in the centre of the basin would also give a passage to the subterranean waters. On account of the large transport of cattle across this district bound to the provinces of Cuyo and Chile, were the waters of an artesian well—instead of coal—to be found, the expense of construction would be well remunerated.

No other districts where coal or lignite could probably be found are known at present; meantime, in the provinces of the Republic some bituminous shales have been found, the study of which may give results of great importance in the future. These shales exist in the province of Mendoza, in a series of banks of sandstone and conglomerate spread over a great extent of the slope of the Sierra de Mendoza, and are also found strongly developed in the inhospitable country of the Paramillo de Uspallata. A very bituminous schist, in which I have found some vegetable remains, a quantity of shells of a small species of Esteria, and sometimes also scales of fishes has been found in the sandstone near Challas, in the Cerro de Cachenta, some 70 leagues south of Mendoza, on the road to Planchon; and, finally, also at a depth of several meters in the environs of Uspallata. This bituminous schist in several places gives birth to springs of naptha, which have formed these depositions of asphaltum. They are known at the Cerro de Cachenta, and above all—in abundance—on the road to the Planchon. A more or less detailed study of these two localities has not yet been undertaken.

A similar formation appears to exist in a great part of the province of Salta. All the intelligence we have received from thence in reference to its geological formation mentions numerous springs of naptha or petroleum, generally arising from these strata. It is said that above all the district of the Tar lagune of St. Michael, to the west of the Sierra de Santa Barbara, is rich in these springs. We must wait for further information, at the same time wishing that these springs may soon become the object of a lucrative explotation.

ELECTRIC TELEGRAPHS.

The establishment of the electric telegraph in Brazil dates from 1852.

It was at first represented by short lines in the capital of the empire, specially destined for government service; in 1856 the electric telegraph reached Petropolis, the line comprising 20 kilometres of submarine cable.

The requirements of the defence of the bay of Rio de Janeiro called, in 1863, for the employment of this powerful means of communication between the Government and the fortresses at the entrance of the bay; and, once there, the telegraphic line was continued to the city of Cape Frio, on the coast of the province of Rio de Janeiro, that it might be of use to maritime navigation, till then served by the optical telegraph, established in 1808.

The war against the Government of Paraguay, in the year 1865, gave a fresh impulse to this service; a line with double wires being constructed from the capital to the south of the Empire, which, whilst it supplied the war requirements, served at the same time a great number of places on the coast of the provinces of Rio de Janeiro, S. Paulo, Paraná and Santa Catharina, and more particularly the important commercial port of Santos.

Great difficulties had to be overcome in constructing this line, which crosses 16 rivers and creeks; mountains covered with virgin forests, and places destitute of every resource, and where no roads existed, whereby to convey the personnel and materiel.

These causes, which still subsist, though in a less degree,

contribute to render difficult the maintenance and repairs of this telegraphic line; nevertheless, since 1860, it has been of great use to government, to the public in general, to commerce in particular.

At the stations in the more important cities, such as Paraty, Santos, Iguape, Paranagua, Desterro, Laguna, Porto Alegre, Pelotas, Jaguarao and Rio Grande do Sul, Morse's double apparatus is employed, and in the intermediate stations, Siemmen's electro-magnetic apparatus.

Having been constructed under pressing circumstances, and subject to great difficulties which appeared at every step, the line in a short time began to need important repairs. Some posts of inferior wood, and others of good quality, but green and cut at an improper time, rapidly decayed, and their substitution by iron posts became necessary; to many other advantages these posts join that of sheltering the lines from the thunder storms so frequent in the south of the Empire, at certain periods of the year.

At present these posts, and wires of five millimetres, are used in preference, as also insulators modified by the director of the telegraphs, in which the contact with the wires has been greatly diminished, by which means they are much less subject to the action of rapid changes in the temperature, than the insulators protected by an iron cap, the porcelain bell of which cracked very easily, besides which those can be much more easily replaced, when no longer serviceable.

The state telegraph department is now definitely organized, advantages having been taken of the experience of the most advanced nations.

The Government lines are 6,120 kilometres in length, with 8,523 kilometres of wire laid down, serving 87 stations.

They are divided into three sections:

The first is, strictly speaking, urban, and extends over 24 kilometres, it has 13 stations, and 1,200 metres of submarine cable, between the war arsenal and the fortress of Villegaignon, to serve the different public departments.

The second, to the north, already constructed between the central station and Linhares, in the province of Espirito Santo, 873 kilometres in length, with 2,200 kilometres of wire, and 22 stations, including the Cape Frio line; and that to the light house on the said Cape, in the province of Rio de Janeiro. This line is meant to connect the capital of the Empire with the northern provinces.

Another portion of this line, of 1,242 kilometres in extent, is open to traffic; it has 14 stations from Camamú to Recife, passing through the capitals of Bahia, Sergipe, Alagoas, and Pernambuco.

The portion of the line between Linhares, in the province of Espirito Santo, and that of Camamú, in that of Bahia, will shortly be concluded, and then the capital of the Empire will be in telegraphic communication with the intermediate cities as far as the province of Ceará. The only thing wanting in this line, of 730 kilometres, is extending the wire and putting up the apparatus.

The southern section extends over 2,866 kilometres, and has 4,461 kilometres of wire, 38 stations, and double lines in some portions.

This line, which commences in the capital of the Empire and terminates at Jaguarao, on the frontier of the Oriental Republic of Uruguay, comprises four branches; the first from Santos to S. Paulo, with stations in those two cities; the second from Paranagua to Coritiba, capital of the province of Parana, branching from Morretes to the city of Antonina; the third, from Porto Alegre, capital of the province of S. Pedro do Rio Grande do Sul, to the city of Uruguayana, with seven stations; the fourth with two stations, from the city of Pelotas, at the mouth of the Rio Grande, in the same province.

Great improvements have been carried out in this line; a cable of 8 kilometres has been substituted by a line of 40 kilometres. The land line from Iguape to Paranagua is nearly finished, in substitution of the present line, six cables being thus avoided; and in Santa Catharina, the line which crossed the island has been carried over to the continent, two cables being thus suppressed.

The line from Cachoeira to Cruz Alta and Passo Fundo, in the province of S. Pedro do Rio Grande do Sul, is being constructed and is finished as far as Santa Maria do Monte; its length is 106 kilometres; as the branch from Rosario, in the Uruguayan line, as far a Santa Anna do Livramento is also finished.

To the north the line has been extended from Recife to Parahyba and Ceará.

As it is almost impossible to keep the lines in repair without roads, these are being constructed by order of Government, by which means lands, until lately abandoned, are becoming available.

In consequence of improvements realized on the lines, such as the substitution of wooden by iron posts, greater facilities for repairs, owing to the opening of roads, more regularity in the service is to be expected, specially as self-acting apparatus of transmission are to be employed, which will increase the rapidity and the precision of telegraphic writing.

Besides the lines under the charge of the Director General of Telegraphs, there are others belonging to the different railway companies, which not only satisfy the requirements of their respective traffic, but also serve the public at moderate rates, which are approved by Government.

Brazil is in telegraphic communication with Europe through the cable which, starting thence and going to Pernambuco, follows the coast of Brazil as far as Pará, whence, by way of Saint Thomas, it meets the United States line.

The cable which joins the province of Pernambuco to that of Bahia and of Rio de Janeiro, and that which goes to Santos, Santa Catharina, Rio Grande do Sul and Barra do Chuy, where it meets the Montevidean line, is in active service.

All the coast of Brazil is therefore linked to Europe, to the United States, and to the Argentine, the Paraguayan, and the Chilian Republics.

The receipts of the Government lines have increased in proportion to their advancement.

In the financial year 1861-62, when the Petropolis line alone existed, the receipts were only 328·140, which increased to a little over 3:000·000 when the southern line was inaugurated. In the year 1866-67, this line being open, though working irregularly, the receipts rose to over 26:000·000.

Thence forward the ascending progression continued, and in the financial year 1873-74 the receipts amounted to 170.174·800

The average distance between the stations, which is not in proportion to the length of the lines, is 70 kilometres

Since the financial year 1866-67, when the southern line was finished between the capital of the Empire and Porto-Alegre, the receipts of the telegraphs, in relation to the expenses, have been as follows: 1866-67, 25 per cent of the expenses; 1867-68, 21 per cent; 1868-69, 26 per cent; 1869-70, 32 per cent; 1870-71, 39 per cent; 1871-72, 39 per cent; 1872-73, 42 per cent; 1873-74, 28 per cent.

If the expenses of the stations be added to those arising from repairs, the receipts show a considerable per-centage.

In the year 1866-67 the expenditure with the construction and maintenance of the line amounted to 221:685·803; in 1872-73 it increased to 1,228:014·464; and in 1873-74 to 1.193:488·093.

ADVERTISEMENT

THE BRAZILIAN
SUBMARINE TELEGRAPH COMPANY.
(LIMITED)

Under exclusive concessions for Twenty Years from their Majesties the Emperor of Brazil and the King of Portugal.

CAPITAL £1,300,000, in 130,000 Shares of £10 each

Directors
THE RIGHT HONOURABLE VISCOUNT MONCK, Chairman.
SIR JAMES ANDERSON, Vice-Chairman.
MATTHEW HUTTON CHAYTOR, Esq.   SIR THOMAS FAIRBAIRN, Bart.
WILLIAM HENRY CLARK, Esq.   HENRY DANIEL GOOCH, Esq.
FREDERICK YOULE, Esq.

Directors representing the Company abroad
JOZE CAETANO DE ANDRADE PINTO, Esq. *(Rio de Janeiro).*
CARLOS FERREIRA dos SANTOS SILVA, Esq. *(Lisbon).*

Managing Director
THOMAS FULLER, Esq.

Secretary
RICHARD COLLETT, Esq.

OFFICES—8, *Great Winchester Street, Old Broad Street, E.C.*

Brazilian Submarine Telegraph Company (Limited) in connection with The Eastern and The Western and Brazilian Telegraph Companies.

The following rates per word will be charged for Messages to MADEIRA, ST. VINCENT, and SOUTH AMERICA, from any Stations in Great Britain and Ireland:

			£	s.	d.
To MADEIRA			0	1	7
,, ST. VINCENT			0	4	0
,, BRAZIL—Pernambuco			0	9	0
,, ,, Bahia and Para			0	12	4
,, ,, Rio de Janeiro			0	13	7
,, ,, Santos, Santa Catarina, and Rio Grande			0	15	8
,, ,, All other Stations			0	16	1
,, URUGUAY—Monte Video			0	15	8
,, ,, All other Stations			0	16	1
,, ARGENTINE REPUBLIC—Buenos Ayres ...			0	16	4
,, ,, ,, All other Stations ...			0	16	9
,, CHILI—Valparaiso, and all other Stations ...			1	1	4
,, PERU—Iquique			0	19	0
,, ,, Arica and Tacna			1	0	6
,, ,, Mollendo, Islay, Puno, and Arequipa ...			1	2	0
,, ,, Lima and Callao			1	5	0

ADVERTISEMENT

Brazilian Submarine Telegraph Company
(LIMITED)

RULES AND REGULATIONS
FOR THE TRANSMISSION OF TELEGRAMS.

1. All telegrams should be legibly written.
2. No responsibility is accepted by the company for any delay or errors in the transmission of messages, or for the non-delivery of telegrams from whatever cause arising. Every care, however, will be taken to ensure both accuracy in transit and speed in delivery.

REGISTRATION
3. The Company registers free of charge the names and addresses of firms receiving messages, so that this information may be given in two words thus— "APOLLO, PERNAMBUCO." This registration can be effected only at the Station in the town where the firm is established, and not by letter from England to South America, or vice versa. The registration in England must be made with the Eastern Telegraph Company and the General Post Office. *The Western and Brazilian Company make a charge of £2 for registration at their stations in South America.*
The name of the sender of a message need not necessarily be transmitted; if not signalled it will be represented by the concluding word of the message. Every message form, however, must be signed by the sender or his representative.

TARIFF
4. Messages are taxed at so much per single word, the Sender paying only for the number of words sent.
5. The maximum length of a word is fixed at 10 letters, any additional letters being counted and charged for at the rate of 10 letters to the word.
6. The name of the office of origin, the date, and hour of departure will, until further notice, be inserted on the form delivered to the Receiver; the company, however, reserves the right at any time to refuse to furnish this information unless it be paid for and included in the text of the despatch.
7. Expressions joined by a hyphen are counted according to the number of words employed in their formation.
8. Proper names of towns and persons, names of places, streets, boulevards, titles, &c., are counted according to the number of words used to express them.
9. Illegitimate compound words, that is words combined in a manner contrary to the usage of the language in which the messages are written, are not accepted. Abbreviated and wrongly-spelt words are also inadmissible.
10. Each group of figures is counted as a word, provided it does not exceed five ciphers; if over five figures the excess up to 10 is charged as an additional word.
11. Every separate character, whether figure or letter, is counted as a word. The combinations "fob," "cfi," and "cif" are each accepted as a single word.
12. An underline, whether applied to one word or to a whole sentence, is counted as an extra word.
13. Signs of punctuation, &c., are not signalled or charged for.
14. Printed receipts are given for all messages sent from the company's Receiving Offices.
15. The Sender is responsible for any expense which may be incurred in the delivery of a message beyond the Receiving Station. He is also responsible for the consequences of giving an incomplete or incorrect address.
16. The following code abbreviations are accepted as one word :
    RP. (Reponse payée)—answer prepaid.
    TC. (Télégramme collationné)—repeated message.
    CR. (Accusé de reception)—acknowledgment of receipt.
    PP. (Poste payée)—postage prepaid.

ADVERTISEMENT

SECRET LETTER MESSAGES

17. Telegrams composed of secret letters (such as b x k l m) cannot be taken from the public. Government Despatches will, however, be accepted, written either in secret letters or ciphers.

REPETITIONS

18. To ensure greater accuracy in transmission, the Sender may have his message repeated on payment of half the usual rates additional.

19. The words "repetition paid," or the abbreviation "TC." must be inscribed immediately after the Receiver's address, and will be charged for.

20. The repetition of all Government secret letter or cipher messages and of all private messages to South America is obligatory.

21. The Receiver of a message suspecting an error in transmission, may, on application within twenty-four hours after its delivery, have the whole or any part repeated on payment of the cost of a message demanding the repetition and a reply containing as many words as are required to be repeated. The Sender can also have the whole or any portion of his message repeated if application be made within seventy-two hours after its despatch, on payment of the price of the telegram he forwards and of the reply if one be required.

22. These charges will only be returned if the repetition asked for relates to a prepaid repeated message which is proved by the repetition to have suffered mutilation. To obtain reimbursement it will be necessary to fill up a form of reclamation, to be had on application.

ACKNOWLEDGMENT OF RECEIPT

23. The date and hour at which a message has been delivered will be notified to the Sender by wire if he insert the words "acknowledgment paid" or the abbreviation "CR." immediately after the Receiver's address, paying the charge for 10 words.

PREPAID REPLIES

24. The reply to a message can be prepaid, the Sender determining its length, which must not exceed three times that of the original message. The words "reply prepaid" or "RP." will have to be inserted after the Receiver's address, and paid for, thus—"RP. 10 words;" this instruction counting as three words.

The sum prepaid for reply will be held at the disposition of the Receiver of the original message to cover the cost of his reply.

Should the reply contain more words than have been indicated as prepaid, the Sender of the reply must pay the excess charge.

If the orginal message cannot be delivered, or if the Receiver refuse to send a reply, the delivery or terminal station will notify the fact to the Sender by a telegram, which takes the place of the reply.

MULTIPLE MESSAGES

25. Telegrams addressed to several persons in the same town, or the same person at several addresses in the same town, with or without re-expedition by post, will be taxed as so many separate despatches.

MESSAGES BY WIRE AND POST

26. Telegrams for places beyond the limits of the Telegraph system must bear the indication "post," or "telegraph," in the following form—"Miller, Caledon, post Madeira, telegraph forward"—"Orton, Capetown, post Madeira."

REIMBURSEMENTS

27. When a message has suffered a delay of 144 hours from other causes than an interruption of the Telegraph lines, the charges will be returned after investigation, provided they be applied for on a reclamation form within six months after date.

The cost of a repeated or collationné message which has been mutilated in such a way as to alter its sense will also be returned, but no reimbursement will be made for errors in ordinary or unrepeated messages.

The Receiver of a message may present a claim for reimbursement on behalf of the Sender.

28. The Rules of the St. Petersburg Convention are applicable to correspondence exchanged with Madeira and St. Vincent.

January 1st, 1877.

THOMAS FULLER,
Managing Director.

ADVERTISEMENT

THE BUENOS AYRES
AND
ENSENADA PORT RAILWAY COMPANY.
(LIMITED).

Incorporated under "The Companies Acts of 1862 and 1867." Registered as a Sociedad Anonima in Buenos Ayres, under the Argentine Law.

The Railway commences at Buenos Ayres, and extends by way of Boca, Barracas, and Quilmes, to the Port of Ensenada. Length of line, 35 miles, the whole of which was opened for public traffic 1st January, 1873.

CAPITAL £700,000, IN 70,000 SHARES OF £10 EACH,
Viz.:

35,000 Ordinary Shares	£350,000
35,000 Seven per cent. First Preference Shares	£350,000

General Meeting held in London in April each year.

DIRECTORS.

LIGHTLY SIMPSON, *Chairman*.   CHARLES BUCHANAN KER.
CHARLES SEALE HAYNE,   JOHN WINTERBOTHAM BATTEN
Deputy-Chairman.

Representative in Buenos Ayres . . . DANIEL GOWLAND.

OFFICERS.

Secretary—J. WILSON THEOBALD.   *General Manager*—HENRY CRABTREE.
Solicitors—Messrs. BIRCHAM & CO.   *Auditor*—JOHN BALL.

London Offices: 8, Union Court, Old Broad Street, E.C.

ADVERTISEMENTS.

Central Argentine Railway Company
LIMITED.

INCORPORATED UNDER "THE COMPANIES ACT 1862."

£ 2,000,000 { CAPITAL £1,300,000 IN 65,000 SHARES OF £20 EACH
DEBENTURES AUTHORIZED £700,000.

The Concession from the Government of the Argentine Republic is in perpetuity without any right of pre-emption; and the Guarantee of Seven per cent. per annum, on an expenditure not exceeding £6,400 per mile, is for a period of forty years from 1866.

The Company's authorized line (246½ miles) commences at the PORT OF ROSARIO on the River Paraná, passes through the provinces of Santa Fe and Cordova, and joins the Government Railway at the CITY OF CORDOVA, which extends in a northerly direction to Tucuman 339¼ miles A junction has likewise been formed with the Government Railway at Villa Maria, which extends in a westerly direction to Mercedes about 158 miles.

The Company's Line—Rosario to Cordova	246½	miles.
The Government Line—Cordova to Tucuman	339¼	,,
,, ,, Villa Maria to Mercedes	158	,,
Total connected Mileage	743¾	miles.

GENERAL MEETING HELD IN LONDON, IN JANARY.

Directors.
Chairman—HENRY BROCKETT.

LAWRENCE HEYWORTH.	ALEXANDER OGILVIE.
GEORGE A. H. HOLT,	FRANK PARISH.
WALTER MORRISON.	RUSSELL SHAW.

SAMUEL WATERHOUSE, M.P.

Director's Qualification .. .. **£2,000 in Shares.**

Officers.
Secretary—GEORGE WOOLCOTT.
Auditors—R. P. HARDING and W. T. LINFORD.
General Manager at Rosario—HENRY FISHER.
Representative in the Republic—WILLIAM THOMPSON, Buenos Ayres.

CHIEF OFFICE—85, PALMERSTON BUILDINGS, BISHOPSGATE STREET, LONDON.

San Paulo (Brazilian) Railway Company
(LIMITED).

Formed under the decree of the Emperor of Brazil and laws of the Imperial and San Paulo Legislatures, and incorporated, with Limited Liability, under the Joint Stock Companies Acts, 1856 & 1857.

This Company was formed to construct and work a railway (about 86 miles) from Santos (the chief port of the province) to Jundiahy, in the province of San Paulo, in the Empire of Brazil. The line commences at Santos, passes through San Paulo, the metropolis of the province, and terminates at the town of Jundiahy, about 27 miles from Campinas, the local capital of the planters, and the depôt from which the surrounding country is supplied with merchandize.

Directors
ROBERT A. HEATH, Esq., *Chairman.*
His Excellency the Brazilian Envoy Extraordinary and Minister Plenipotentiary or other the Diplomatic representative of Brazil in London, *ex officio* Director.

WILLIAM BIRD, Esq. M. R. SMITH, Esq.
JNO. MORGAN, Esq. FRED. YOULE, Esq.

Auditors
ALDERMAN SIR THOMAS DAKIN AND E. H. GALSWORTHY, ESQ.

Executive Staff, &c.
Superintendent and Engineer in San Paulo—D. M. FOX.
Secretary—GEORGE A. HILLIER, ESQ.
Solicitors—MESSRS. BIRCHAM & CO.
London Bankers—MESSRS. N. M. ROTHSCHILD, & SONS.

London Offices ... ... **Gresham House**

Capital
The capital authorized and created by the Company consists of £2,750,000, of which £2,000 is in Shares of £20 each, fully paid up, and £750,000 in Debentures and Debenture Stock. Of this total £2,650,000 is Guaranteed, and £100,000 Unguaranteed.

ADVERTISEMENT.

THE BUENOS AYRES
GREAT SOUTHERN RAILWAY COMPANY
(LIMITED)

Incorporated under the Companies Act of 1862 for the purpose of constructing Railways in the City and Province of Buenos Ayres.

Capital £2,500,000, consisting of £1,660,000 in £10 Shares and £840,000 Debenture Stock.

THE concession is in perpetuity, and the various privileges and immunities accorded in such concession exist for a period of Forty Years from 1862.

Productive Mileage on the 1st of January, 1877, as under:

	Miles
Buenos Ayres to Altamirano	54.31
Altamirano to Dolores	72.13
Altamirano to Las Flores	75.06
Las Flores to Azul	68.09
Total	269.59

The gross receipts for the year 1875 (202 miles of line open) were £354,538; the Dividend upon the Shares being 10 per cent. per annum.

GENERAL MEETINGS HELD IN LONDON, IN MAY AND NOVEMBER.

DIRECTORS' QUALIFICATION, £4,000 IN SHARES.

DIRECTORS.

G. A. H. HOLT, *Chairman.* FRANK PARISH, *Deputy-Chairman.*
EDWARD ASHWORTH   JOHN FAIR
SPENCER HERAPATH GEORGE W. DRABBLE
P. G. HEYWORTH

OFFICERS.

Secretary—C. O. BARKER.   *General Manager*—GEORGE COOPER.
Auditors—W. CASH and MESSRS. QUILTER, BALL & CO.

London Offices—4, Great Winchester Street, E.C.

ADVERTISEMENT

THE
NORTHERN RAILWAY OF BUENOS AYRES
COMPANY (LIMITED).

Incorporated under the Companies Acts of 1856 and 1857, for the purpose of constructing Railways in the City and Province of Buenos Ayres.

CAPITAL	£450,000
REPRESENTED BY	
Loans	£200,000
Guaranteed 7 per cent. Preference Shares	136,170
Deferred ,, ,, ...	53,830
Ordinary Shares (issued)	45,000
Ditto do. (unissued)	15,000
	£450,000

Line open on the 1st of January, 1876, as under:

From Buenos Ayres to Tigre ... ... Length, 19 miles

By the Articles of Association it is provided that at the end of each year, and before declaring any Dividend, the Directors shall be at liberty, in their discretion, to reserve from time to time and carry to the credit of a Fund, to be called "The Reserve Fund," such proportion of the nett profit, not exceeding 10 per cent. thereof, as they may think fit, and that the surplus profits remaining after payment of dividends shall be divided into portions of £10 each, and so many Preference Shares of both classes as shall be equal in number to such portions shall be drawn by lots; and in respect of such Shares so drawn the holders shall receive one portion as a Bonus, until the whole surplus shall be distributed; and the Shares so drawn shall thenceforward cease to be Preference Shares, and shall thereafter rank as Ordinary Shares, and as such only shall participate in all subsequent profits

Gross Receipts for the Year 1875 were £61,587
Nett Receipts ,, ,, ... £27,226

The Dividend paid upon the Shares was 7 per cent. per annum.

AN ANNUAL GENERAL MEETING IS HELD IN LONDON IN MAY

DIRECTORS' QUALIFICATION, £250 IN SHARES.

DIRECTORS
C. SEALE HAYNE, *Chairman.*
H. D. BROWNE   G. N. STRAWBRIDGE
C. RIVAZ   E. WRIGHT

OFFICER
Secretary—EDMUND AYRES.
General Manager in Buenos Ayres—HENRY CRABTREE.
Auditors—J. H. HUTCHINSON AND J. HUTT.

London Offices: 40, Finsbury Circus, E.C.

ADVERTISEMENT

CENTRAL ARGENTINE LAND COMPANY
(LIMITED).
Incorporated under "The Companies Act, 1862."
CAPITAL ... ... **£130,000, in £1 Shares.**

THIS COMPANY was incorporated on the 28th of March, 1870, for the acquisition, by transfer from the Central Argentine Railway Company and Messrs. Brassey, Wythes, and Wheelwright, of the Lands conceded to that company by the Government of the Argentine Republic, consisting of about 900,000 acres immediately adjoining the line of railway.

Also the colonization and management of such lands, and the development of the resources thereof by division into convenient allotments, the construction of roads and other works, the erection of dwelling houses and other buildings, and the effectuation of such other improvements as may be conducive to the settlement and cultivation of the said lands.

The Directors may, with the prior sanction of a resolution of the Company in General Meeting, raise money for the use of the Company by mortgage of the said lands or any of them, and from time to time pay off such monies, and generally in doing all acts and things within the scope of the undertaking of this Company.

GENERAL MEETING HELD IN LONDON IN JUNE OR JULY.

Directors
Chairman—HENRY BROCKETT

HENRY A. BRASSEY, M.P.
LAWRENCE HEYWORTH
PAUL KRELL
WALTER MORRISON
ALEXANDER OGILVIE
SAMUEL WATERHOUSE, M.P.
GEORGE WYTHES

Officers
Secretary—GEORGE WOOLCOTT.
Solicitors—TRAVERS, SMITH, & BRAITHWAITE
Auditors—R. S. HARDING AND W. T. LINFORD.
General Manager at Rosario—JAMES LLOYD.
Agent at Rosario—HENRY FISHER.
Representative in the Republic—WILLIAM THOMPSON, Buenos Ayres.

Chief Office: 85, Palmerston Buildings, Bishopsgate Street, London.

ADVERTISEMENTS.

THE NEW LONDON & BRAZILIAN BANK
LIMITED.

Capital £1,000,000 in 50,000 Shares of £20 Each.

Subscribed Capital.........................£900,000.

Paid up....................................£450,000.

HEAD OFFICE—2, OLD BROAD STREET, LONDON, E.C.

Directors.

JOHN WHITE CATER, Esq., *Chairman.*
WILLIAM FREER SCHOLFIELD, Esq., *Deputy-Chairman.*

JAMES ALEXANDER, Esq. [Esq.	JOHN HOLLOCOMBE, Esq.
EDWARD LONSDALE BECKWITH,	CHARLES EDWARD JOHNSTON, Esq.
Hon. PASCOE CHARLES GLYN.	CHARLES DAY ROSE, Esq.

Bankers.

THE BANK OF ENGLAND.	Messrs. GLYN, MILLS, CURRIE & Co.

Branch Banks and Agencies.

BRAZIL—Rio de Janeiro, Pernambuco, Bahia, Rio Grande do Sul, Pará, Porto Alegre, Ceará, Maranham, San Paulo, Santos, Pelotas.

PORTUGAL—Lisbon, Oporto, Amarante, Braga, Coimbra, Faro, Figueira, Guimaraes, Lagos, Portimao, Setubal, Silves, Sines, Tavira, Vianna, Villa Real.

RIVER PLATE—Buenos Ayres, Monte Video.

THE Directors of this Bank grant Drafts on the Branches and negotiate or collect Bills payable at the above places on the most favourable terms.

They issue Circular Notes and Letters of Credit for the use of travellers to all parts of the world.

They undertake the Agency of parties connected with Brazil and Portugal, make Investments in the Public Funds, and other British and Foreign securities; and receive Dividends and Interest free of charge to constituents.

They also receive Money on Deposit at rates of Interest varying according to the length of time for which the Deposit is made.

Current Accounts opened at the Head Office and Branches.

For further particulars apply at the Bank, 2, Old Broad Street. Office hours, 10 to 4; Saturdays, 10 to 2.

JOHN BEATON,
Manager.

2, OLD BROAD STREET, E.C.

ADVERTISEMENT

ENGLISH BANK OF RIO DE JANEIRO
(LIMITED).

Subscribed Capital £1,000,000, in 50,000 Shares of £20 each.
WITH POWER TO INCREASE.

Paid-up Capital ... ... **£500,000.**

HEAD OFFICE:
13, St. Helen's Place, Bishopsgate Street, London, E.C.

DIRECTORS
WILLIAM BEVAN, Esq. GEORGE A. H. HOLT, Esq.
GEORGE T. BROOKING, Esq. DAVID HOWDEN, Esq.
RICHARD FOSTER, Esq. THOMAS SELLAR, Esq.
ARTHUR B. WHITE, Esq.

AUDITORS
CHARLES HENRY NOBLE, Esq. MORGAN YEATMAN, Esq.
JOHN YOUNG, Esq. (Messrs. Turquand, Youngs & Co.)

BANKERS
THE LONDON JOINT STOCK BANK.

MANAGER
CHARLES CARRINGTON, Esq.

SOLICITORS
MESSRS. JOHNSONS, UPTON, BUDD, AND ATKEY.

Branch at Rio de Janeiro—EDWARD ROSS DUFFIELD, ESQ., *Manager.*
Branch at Pernambuco—FRANCIS BRIDGE BLOXHAM, ESQ., *Manager.*
Branch at Santos—JOHN SKEETE HAMILTON, ESQ., *Manager.*

CORRESPONDENTS IN
**Antwerp, Bordeaux, Genoa, Hamburg, Havre, Lisbon, Madrid, Marseilles, Oporto, Paris,
Ceara, Para, Maranham, Bahia, Rio Grande do Sul, Monte Video,
Buenos Ayres, New York, and New Orleans.**

Drafts issued on Brazil. The purchase and sale of Funds undertaken, as also the receipt of Dividends, the collection of Bills of Exchange, and all other legitimate Banking business.

Deposits received at the Branches, either in Current Account, or for fixed periods at Interest.

13, ST. HELEN'S PLACE, BISHOPSGATE STREET,
LONDON, E.C., *November,* 1876.

ADVERTISEMENT

London & River Plate Bank
(LIMITED).
CAPITAL £1,500,000

Head Office: No. 52, Moorgate Street, E.C.

Board of Directors

GEORGE W. DRABBLE, Esq., *Chairman.*
GEORGE A. H. HOLT, Esq., *Deputy-Chairman.*

JOHN ELIN, Esq.	THOMAS S. RICHARDSON, Esq.
DAVID HOWDEN, Esq.	H. A. WYATT SMITH, Esq.
J. DE MANCHA, Esq.	EDWARD ZIMMERMANN, Esq.

Manager—ARTHUR EDWARD SMITHERS, Esq.

Secretary—GEORGE WARDEN, Esq.

Branches
BUENOS AYRES, MONTE VIDEO, ROSARIO, and CORDOVA.

Agents

LIVERPOOL	BREMEN	ROME	VIGO
IRELAND	BERLIN	TURIN	LISBON
SCOTLAND	HAMBURG	VENICE	CANARY ISLANDS
PARIS	AMSTERDAM	BARCELONA	NEW YORK
MARSEILLES	GENOA	SANTANDER	BALTIMORE
BORDEAUX	NAPLES	CORUNNA	BOSTON
BAYONNE	MILAN	BILBAO	PHILADELPHIA
HAVRE	LEGHORN	CADIZ	AUSTRALIA
ANTWERP	PALERMO	MADRID	NEW ZEALAND

And the various *Branches of the National Provincial Bank of England, and Provincial Bank of Ireland.*

Bankers—THE CITY BANK, THREADNEEDLE STREET, LONDON.

Deposits for fixed periods are received at interest, particulars of which may be obtained at the Bank.

Letters of Credit and Bills of Exchange issued on the Branches.

Bills payable at Buenos Ayres, Monte Video, Rosario, or Cordova sent out for collection.

Purchases and Sales of Stock, Shares, and other Securities effected on the usual charges.

ADVERTISEMENT.

1877.

THE JINMAN STEAM SHIPPING COMPANY
(LIMITED).

London to River Plate

Scindia	...	...	2203	Tons	...	1250	H.P. Effective
Bertha	...	...	2197	,,	...	1250	,,
St. George	...	...	1617	,,	...	750	,,
Amboto	...	...	1571	,,	...	750	,,
St. Andrew	...	...	1055	,,	...	500	,,
Rose	...	...	796	,,	...	400	,,

One of the above steamers will be despatched from the

SOUTH WEST INDIA DOCKS, ON THE 26TH OF EACH MONTH,
FOR

MONTE VIDEO & BUENOS AYRES

(Calling at Antwerp, Havre, or Bordeaux, as may be found necessary).

All goods are received subject to the conditions embodied in the special form of Bill of Lading, to be obtained only of Messrs. WATERLOW & SONS, 24, Birchin Lane.

The Owners will not hold themselves bound to receive all or any goods tendered to them unless specially agreed for.

It is necessary that each package be distinctly marked by the shippers, before shipment, with the name of the port of destination, without which the goods may not be taken in regular turn, and the Owners will not be responsible for irregularity and delay in delivery.

Freight payable on delivery of Bills of Lading.

Any person who may wilfully and surreptitiously ship or attempt to ship any *gunpowder, aquafortis, oil of vitriol, gun-cotton, dynamite, glonoin or blasting oil, or nitro-glycerine, prepared tannin, fog-signals, petroleum, naptha, paraffin oil, spirits of wine, ether, camphine, turpentine, tar, percussion caps, lucifer matches, or other article of explosive, inflammable, or otherwise dangerous nature,* on board one of these Steamers will be liable to prosecution under the Act 17 & 18 Victoria, c. 104, s. 329; or under the Act 29 and 30 Victoria c. 69.

For Particulars as to Freight, &c., apply to the Brokers,

ALEXR. HOWDEN & CO.,
19, BIRCHIN LANE, LONDON, E.C.

REEIFE & SAO FRANCISCO PERNAMBUCO
RAILWAY COMPANY
(LIMITED).

Length of line . . . . 77½ miles

Capital Stock of the Company, £1,200,000

TRANSFERABLE BY DEED IN SUMS OF £1 AND UPWARDS.

Authorized Issue of Debentures, £275,000.

The Annual Income of the Company Guaranteed by the Imperial Government of Brazil is £80,283, of which £24,283 is for 30 years from August 1870, the remainder for 90 years from 1852.

The Dividend paid upon the Capital Stock of the Company for the Year ended 30th June, 1876, was 5¾ per cent.

General Meetings are held in London in April and October

Directors.
THE VISCOUNT GORT, CHAIRMAN.
General G. B. TREMENHEERE.   W. H. BELLAMY, Esq.
W. B. GREENFIELD, Esq.
J. E. PEMBER, Esq.   G. O. MANN, Esq.

Bankers.
MESSRS. ROBARTS, LUBBOCK & Co.

Secretary.
U. P. HARRIS, Esq.

Offices.
15, OLD JEWRY CHAMBERS, LONDON, E.C.

FREEMAN BROS.

300, REGENT STREET, LONDON, W.

GENERAL AGENTS.

COMMISSION CHARGES:
    5 per cent. for amounts not exceeding £500
    2½ ,, ,, ,, above £500·
Exceptional terms arranged for large accounts.

The above include Purchase of Goods, Negociation of Bills of Exchange, and Shipping Agency Charges.

BANKERS:
THE BANK OF ENGLAND, who will kindly answer the usual business enquiries.

FRENCH GENERAL TRANSATLANTIC MAIL STEAM SHIP COMPANY.
West End Agency.

T. S. FREEMAN & SONS,

48, FENCHURCH, STREET, LONDON.

ARMY CLOTHIERS.

FREEMAN & ALLEN,

GENERAL PASSENGER, SHIPPING, & INSURANCE AGENTS,

48, FENCHURCH STREET, LONDON,
E.C.

Agents for the "Cunard" and "Allan" Lines of Mail Steamers to the United States and Canada.

F. ENDERS & CO.

300, REGENT STREET, AND

43, MARGARET STREET,

TAILORS, &c.   LONDON, W.

www.ingramcontent.com/pod-product-compliance
Lightning Source LLC
Chambersburg PA
CBHW020245240426
43672CB00006B/646